The Crowd in Contemporary Britain

The Crowd in Contemporary Britain

Edited by
George Gaskell and Robert Benewick

Foreword by
Lord Scarman

SAGE Publications

London · Newbury Park · Beverly Hills · New Delhi

SAGE Publications Ltd
28 Banner Street
London EC1Y 8QE

SAGE Publications Inc
275 South Beverly Drive
Beverly Hills, California 90212

SAGE Publications India Pvt Ltd
C-236 Defence Colony
New Delhi 110 024

SAGE Publications Inc
2111 West Hillcrest Street
Newbury Park, California 91320

British Library Cataloguing in Publication Data

The Crowd in Contemporary Britain.
1. Great Britain — Social conditions — 1945–
2. Crowds   3. Collective behaviour
I. Gaskell, George   II. Benewick, Robert
302.3'3   HN385.5

ISBN 0–8039–8074–4
ISBN 0–8039–8075–2 Pbk

Library of Congress catalog card number 87–050307

Printed in Great Britain by J.W. Arrowsmith Ltd, Bristol

Contents

Contributors

Robert Benewick	School of English and American Studies, University of Sussex
Sean Carey	Freelance researcher and writer
Michael Chatterton	Department of Social Administration, University of Manchester
Chas Critcher	Department of Communication Studies, Sheffield City Polytechnic
Eric Dunning	Department of Sociology, University of Leicester
John Edwards	Department of Social Policy and Social Science, Royal Holloway and Bedford New College, University of London
George Gaskell	Department of Social Psychology, London School of Economics
Robert Holton	Department of Sociology, Flinders University of South Australia
Karen Jones	Department of Communication Studies, Sheffield City Polytechnic
George Moyser	Department of Government, University of Manchester
Patrick Murphy	Department of Sociology, University of Leicester
Tim Newburn	Department of Sociology, University of Leicester
Robin Oakley	Centre for the Study of Community and Race Relations, Brunel University
Geraint Parry	Department of Government, University of Manchester
John Stevenson	Department of History, University of Sheffield
David Waddington	Department of Communication Studies, Sheffield City Polytechnic
Ivan Waddington	Department of Sociology, University of Leicester
Margaret Wagstaffe	Department of Government, University of Manchester

Preface

This book is the product of a research programme initiated by the Crowd Behaviour Panel of the Economic and Social Research Council. Members of the Panel were: Professor W.J.M. MacKenzie, Glasgow University; Dr G. Gaskell, London School of Economics; Dr R.J. Benewick, University of Sussex; Professor A. Cohen, School of Oriental and African Studies, University of London; Superintendent R. Custance, Sussex County Constabulary; B. Irvine, The Police Foundation and Dr J. Stevenson, University of Sheffield. On behalf of the contributors we wish to express our gratitude to the Economic and Social Research Council for funding and supporting the research. Our personal thanks to Liz Wake of the London School of Economics for invaluable administrative assistance.

We dedicate this volume to Professor W.J.M. 'Bill' MacKenzie, the first chairperson of the Crowd Behaviour Panel.

George Gaskell
Robert Benewick
London 1987

Foreword

Lord Scarman

It is high time that a properly researched and scientific study should be published of the crowd in contemporary Britain. George Gaskell, Robert Benewick and their collaborators have met the need by producing and securing the publication of this work. The crowd is nothing new in human society. As David Attenborough commented in his splendid series *Life on Earth*, humans are 'compulsive communicators'. Indeed, their gregariousness has been the key to survival in a world in which individually stronger and better protected animals have gone to the wall. More specifically, democracy is a refinement of crowd power. The crowd is a manifestation of people's ever present need to associate together. For they cannot live, or even survive, alone.

We must, therefore, as the authors of this work demonstrate, approach the problem of crowd activity in a civilized community scientifically, abandoning any moral prejudices which we may have unconsciously absorbed from recent incidents of public disorder. Such an approach will enable us, perhaps at a later stage of our research, legitimately to enquire what has gone wrong when we come face-to-face with the crowd in a violent mood, threatening or activating public disorder.

There is so much of interest in the contributions to this study that it is invidious to single out any special mention. I was particularly interested in those concerned with the crowd in situations of violent disorder and with the study of the policing problem. But there is another very significant aspect of crowd behaviour, i.e. the crowd in a state of ecstasy as illustrated notably by the behaviour of the millions who turned out to see and hear the Pope. This is well analysed by Benewick and Holton in Chapter 6.

The temptation to generalize must, I know, be resisted. But 'the compulsive communicator' finds in crowding together a relieving factor when tensions get intolerably high, an opportunity of demonstrating deeply felt emotion when moved by inspiration, as well as the support of fellow human beings when danger is sensed. It is, therefore, no accident that the early essays in democracy were populist, i.e. government of the people by *all* the people, or that in today's society a perception (false or true) that representative democracy is not sufficiently responsive leads people to turn away from their political institutions and to assemble on the streets in protest, prepared even to exercise the crowd's formidable physical power to achieve their ends, if necessary by violent means.

Society's first line of protection against disorder is, of course, the police in the street. What is needed is a vigilant and highly trained police force on 'the front line' when the danger signals of discontent and hostility are flying in the streets of our cities. The crowd has, therefore, a further very real value: it gives warning which, heeded in time, may enable organized society to act to remedy grievances before disaster ensues.

Not everyone will agree with the conclusions tentatively reached by the authors of the studies contained in this book. The work is essentially a work of science — analysing evidence, formulating hypotheses, accepting some, rejecting others. And those that our authors accept may themselves have to be modified or rejected as our knowledge of the subject deepens and develops. That is what this work sets out to do: by scientific study to deepen and develop our knowledge of people's exercise of the wondrous power of communication when under stress.

1 December 1986

1

The crowd in context

George Gaskell and Robert Benewick

Theories of the crowd

Crowd violence in Britain has become a major preoccupation of the 1980s. Politicians, commentators and the public at large have been outraged by episodes of serious rioting in the inner cities, by the continued criminal activities of some football supporters and by the prevalence of street gangs. Are we entering, some ask, a new era of social upheaval in which crowd violence will feature more prominently on the streets of Britain?

This book seeks to provide a scientific and long-term perspective on the nature of crowd activities and the public and political responses to it. This is done both by raising questions fundamental to the study of the nature of the crowd and by analysing crowd phenomena from a variety of social scientific disciplines. In this chapter we present a brief overview of the academic literature on the crowd and provide a context for the contributions in this volume.

'The study of crowd behaviour has been very much neglected, especially given the increasing social and political ferment of recent years' so reported The Joint Sports Council/Social Science Research Council Panel on Public Disorder and Sporting Events (1978: 50).

This might seem a rather surprising conclusion given the pervasiveness of crowds in public life and a long history of relatively frequent episodes of collective disorder, albeit often small in scale, in Britain and other countries. It is also surprising given the long established tradition of writings about crowd phenomena starting with some of the founders of the social sciences, for example, Tarde (1910), Le Bon (1895), McDougal (1927) and Freud (1922), culminating in recent times in a massive research effort following the urban riots in America during the 1960s (Kerner, 1968).

Admittedly the earlier writing may be of limited relevance today since there has been a considerable change in perspective away from the approach initiated by the popular writer Gustave Le Bon who saw the crowd as irrational, degenerate and pathological. Le Bon explained the apparent coordination and cooperation in the crowd as a product of the group mind which emerged through a process of contagion affecting those made susceptible by the submergence of individual personalities into the libidinous mob. In his famous or infamous book, *The Crowd*, first published in 1895, Le Bon (1960: 32–3) set the scene for the development of the study of crowd behaviour:

> by the mere fact that he forms part of an organised crowd a man descends several rungs in the ladder of civilisation. Isolated he may be a cultivated individual, in a crowd he is a barbarian — that is a creature acting by instinct. He possesses the spontaneity, the violence, the ferocity and also the enthusiasm and heroism of primitive beings, whom he further tends to resemble by the facility with which he allows himself to be impressed by words and images.

Allport (1924), developed the theme of contagion by proposing a circular chain reaction of emotional facilitation. Individuals respond to and stimulate others generating an ascending spiral of crowd emotionality. Recent work on social facilitation (Zajonc, 1965) has been cited to support this hypothesis. The theory of deindividuation (Zimbardo, 1969) is a variation on the same general theme. Here the mechanisms underlying aggressive and uninhibited behaviours in crowds are anonymity, arousal, similarity of dress, unstructured situations and the very involvement in an aggressive act. A large, densely packed and noisy crowd leads to heightened arousal of the individual enhancing the slide from autonomy and restraint to deindividuation, a state of diminished self-awareness and self-control. Such individualistic theories appear to explain the homogeneity of the crowd but do so at the cost of predicting bedlam in every crowd, at Ascot and the lynch mob alike.

Historians, notably Rudé (1964) and Hobsbawn (1959), and sociologists, particularly Smelser (1962), argued against this individualistic and psychopathological orientation which necessarily implied a connection between crowds and deviant behaviour. They gave prominence to the rational and legitimate grievances which lay behind protest and fuelled conflict. Rudé documented that the crowds in popular disturbances had a social purpose and established an influential method, at least applicable to pre-industrial societies, which set criteria for establishing key aspects of crowd composition and activities. Smelser (1962) sees all collective manifestations as a response to underlying social strains, tensions and grievances and developed a 'value added' structural model to explain crowd behaviour.

In their analysis of the Captain Swing riots following the introduction of threshing machines, cheap Irish labour and the poor harvest of 1830, Hobsbawn and Rudé (1970), while charting the spread of threatening letters, arson and machine breaking in the South East of

England, note the orderliness and ceremony that accompanied the crowd disturbances. The age of Captain Swing was not one of mayhem but rather a labourers' revolt against distress and poverty in which machinery was the main target.

While highly influential in historical studies of European crowds, Rudé's emergent class model was less relevant to the American situation in which race and ethnic issues played an important role. However, social scientists used Rudé's approach as support for the findings that the American riots in the 1960s were purposeful rather than mindless, the rioters not seduced by self-styled radicals, selective in their choice of targets and not drawn from the alienated or criminal elements of society (Kerner, 1968; Caplan and Paige, 1968).

Ample evidence has been gathered showing that crowds far from being hypnotized by charismatic leaders are often incited by unremarkable characters: Reicher (1984: 9) describing the St Paul's riots in Bristol reports 'an old man walked up to a parked panda and kicked in its lights. There was a loud cheer and missiles were flying at the police. These were exposed on all sides and after a while were so fiercely pressed that they were forced to fall back'. The witnesses and participants saw the instigators as anonymous but typical local people:

All it needed was the catalyst of one person throwing a brick and all hell let loose (a white woman, aged 35)

A few kids would run out to throw stones, followed by a surge . . . (a white man, aged 30)

Equally it is not the case that any action sets off a copy cat response: crowds are cognizant of the 'appropriateness' of what they do. In the Brixton riot of 1981 when a black threatened another with a knife the crowd moved in to stop them: 'We shouldn't fight among ourselves' said an Asian. 'There's a principle involved. They shot a woman and that's why we're here'. (Murji, 1985).

In relation to riot participants Horowitz (1983: 193) concludes that 'theories of marginality are now well discredited'. Sears and McConahay (1973) and Feagin and Hahn (1973) found that rioters were more likely to be born in the Northern States and to be long-term residents of their cities. Level of education was not related to rates of participation in the violence in Los Angeles while in Detroit and Newark the rioters may have been slightly better educated. In the Toxteth riot of 1981 Cooper (1985) reports that those arrested came from a cross-section of the community and included significant numbers of persons who do not normally come into contact with the police. Rioters are also concerned to legitimate their participation and justify their actions: blacks in the United States spoke of 'protest' and 'rebellion' not 'rioting' (Sears, 1969). In America most of the riots in the 1960s were characterized as commodity riots aimed at property not people. In Britain too:

> Birmingham blacks have destroyed houses in which they live, shops on which they depend for provisions, environments in which they live. (Cashmore, 1985: 376)

Some have used the evidence of 'representativeness', the 'post-hoc' labelling of behaviour in terms of protest, and of flashpoints involving the police as justifications of riotous behaviour. This is as misleading as the opposing tendency to dismiss the rioters as 'riff-raff', 'deviant' or 'criminal', and their actions as a mindless response to 'outside agitators'. Theoretical work attempting to understand the crowd in terms of a multi-disciplinary social scientific perspective may develop a deeper understanding.

In explaining riots sociologists and social psychologists have turned to the concept of relative deprivation developed originally by Stouffer et al. (1949), extended by Runciman (1966), and applied to collective behaviour by Davies (1962) and Gurr (1970) among others. The central idea is that the root cause of rebellions lie in people's feelings of frustration, discontent and despair. This development is an acceptance of the fact that a satisfactory explanation must include a psychological dimension — economic accounts were insufficient. What mattered was how people perceived their objective circumstances, who constituted their reference group and whether a tolerable or intolerable gap existed between what people wanted and what they had. In relation to the American riots three main variants of relative deprivation were developed (Caplan and Paige, 1968; Abeles, 1976): increases in relative deprivation between blacks and whites; blocked opportunities, arising from their continued and unjust exclusion from economic prosperity — the result of racism; and rising expectations — the economic and social improvements brought about by the 1950s civil rights movement creating greater expectations than the system was able or willing to deliver — the so called J-Curve of rising expectations (Davies, 1974). However, as reviewed by McPhail (1971), while relative deprivation theory had some explanatory power it was hardly a sufficient explanation. Amongst other issues the theory could not embrace the political dimensions: the influence of black culture and of politicians and other influential people in creating and sustaining the myths that may either promote collective confrontation or quiescence.

These issues were addressed by Edelman (1971) in a detailed and persuasive symbolic interactionist analysis of politicization among the urban ghetto dwellers and the poor. He suggests that in inner city areas the key aspects for the poor and the blacks are the ambivalence and ambiguity about their social status and uncertainty about their objective circumstances. When future welfare, status and survival are felt to be at risk, authoritative cues are sought. Sometimes public policies are seen as evidence that people's legitimate interests are being protected but governmental actions or language may create distrust of official policy. Edelman shows how the myths and metaphors permeating the language of politics promote illusions and ambiguity, which can have far reaching and undesirable consequences.

> People anticipate the cognitive and behavioural impact upon those around them of past incidents, police harassment and brutality, police assistance to ghetto residents, arrests, new and old deprivations, news that conditions people to expect violence, real and symbolic concessions and indulgences, relatively stable feelings of deprivation in particular ghetto groups and in groups outside the ghetto, beliefs about future developments, and so on. Our explanations of mass political response have radically undervalued the ability of the human mind, through role taking and sensitization by exploratory emotions, to take a complex set of cues into account, evolve a mutually acceptable form of response among a group of significant others, and thereby devise a form of action that will be perceived by others as politically feasible. (Edelman, 1971: 133)

Sullivan (1977) argues for a process approach which conceptualizes riots as a product of communication and social interaction at the scene of the disturbance. Stark et al. (1974) adopted a similar position and quote Cohen (1965: 9) on the dominant bias in American sociology 'toward formulating theory in terms of variables that describe initial states on the one hand and outcomes on the other, rather than in terms of processes whereby acts and complex structures of action are built, elaborated and transformed'. Stark et al., (1974: 866) conclude that such an approach has been helpful in dispelling the deviant view of riots, 'however, to the extent that it has blinded social scientists to the need to examine what happens between apparent initial states preceding outbursts of collective violence and the 'resting states' which follow, we feel research efforts should be redirected'. One new direction is taken by Firestone (1972) who develops a transactional approach emphasizing the role of the evolving interaction between dominant group members and the dissidents. The key-noting activities of the dominant group, the role of the media in labelling riot situations, may contribute to polarization within the community and promote aggressive responses by the authorities. For their part rioters may respond with both consummatory violence — the non-rational, cathartic release of aggression — and instrumental violence — protest to redress grievances. Thus the ebb and flow of a riot is the result of a complex interaction between them. Toch (1985) extends the transactional approach in a discussion of different types of interpersonal encounters that may result in violence. He describes how police–citizen encounters may move from hostility to violence as each defines each other's behaviour as increasingly offensive and provocative. This approach draws attention to the mechanisms by which the police may become targets of crowd violence.

In fact Hobsbawn and Rudé (1970: 34) almost anticipated many of the shortcomings of theories explaining riots solely in terms of underlying conditions in their writings on Captain Swing.

> We have seen plenty of causes of labourers unrest and it is difficult to see how they could not have revolted. But causes are not the same as acts. Human beings do not react to the goad of hunger and oppression by some automatic and standard response of revolt. What they do, or fail to do, depends on their situation among other human beings, on their environment, culture, tradition and experience.

So we return to the conclusion of the Joint Panel. It is still the case that the nature of the crowd is far from understood even indeed to the extent of agreeing how to define 'the crowd'. As Holton (1978) notes, many have simply evaded the problem but he discerns two main approaches. The first restricts the crowd to spontaneous and temporary gatherings and as such contrasts crowds with assemblies and social movements of a permanent or organized nature (Blumer, 1965). This approach focuses on the excitable, emotional, and disruptive. Analyses of crowd action are more akin to a description of the people rather than the event itself; thus the mob, a contraction of the Latin *mobile vulgus* is often used as a synonymous term for the crowd.

The second approach is much broader treating all direct face-to-face groups (Rudé, 1964) or public collective behaviour (Holton, 1978) under the umbrella of the crowd.

According to Holton (1978), the problem with the former definition is that it assumes that there is a type of collective behaviour that is unorganized and different in character from social organization as a whole. In a sense it prejudges the issue and since studies have shown the existence of organization in apparently spontaneous collective behaviour it seems more profitable to define crowds in the all-embracing manner and see them as a part of social organization and social movements rather than external to them.

One reason for the definitional emphasis on the spontaneous and excitable crowd is that crowds tend to become a matter of public concern when they are perceived as a threat to the state or disruptive of public order. For Le Bon it was the crisis of democracy in the Third Republic (see Nye, 1975), for America it was the burning of the inner cities and for Britain it was the unsporting-like behaviour of predominantly young men on the football terraces. As such there has been a focus on the deviant and unruly crowd rather than collective behaviour in general and this in part contributed to the setting up of the Crowd Behaviour Panel by the then SSRC to formulate a strategy for research into the field.

While the Panel was determining the priorities for research, the urban riots of 1981 occurred not five miles from the seat of British government and the inquiry by Lord Scarman was set up by the Home Secretary. Since this inquiry was directed towards the more pressing policy issues the Panel formulated a proposal for studying the crowd in contemporary Britain with two main objectives. First, to frame questions of a basic or fundamental nature focusing on broad conceptual issues rather than addressing the more immediate problems and policy concerns and second, that given the complexity of the issues and the plethora of interesting questions the research should be multi-disciplinary covering historical, sociological, psychological, anthropological, political and public order aspects of crowds.

The Panel invited applications from which five major projects were funded as well as a pilot study of peaceful crowds and a crowd studies archive. Given the relatively small scale of this research programme and the breadth of the topic our generalizations must remain tentative. Yet taken together, the research described in this book represents a contribution to the informed public debate as well as providing a longer-term perspective for understanding historical, social and political aspects of crowds in Britain.

A review of the contributions
Crowds are a very complex phenomena. In recognition of this, key aspects have been selected for analysis from the vantage point of different social scientific disciplines. We now briefly review the findings and approaches of the contributors. In Chapter 2 by Dunning et al. a historical analysis is presented of reports of collective disturbances in the *Leicester Mercury* complemented by selective readings of *The Times* and oral histories which provides a unique picture of the pattern and change in crowd disorders this century. It is, so to speak, a sequel to Stevenson's account of popular disturbances in England from 1700–1870 (Stevenson, 1979). In contrast to the popular image in the period 1900–75 there has been a marked and generally downward trend in the number of violent disorders from a high point in the first two decades of the century. However, this downward trend has not been smooth. There have been short-term fluctuations in levels

of violence, and there is a notable exception: that of sports-related crowd violence. Dunning et al. categorize violence into four arenas: industry, politics, community and sports/leisure and investigate each in turn.

In industry the level of collective violence has declined from a high point around the time of the First World War. Since then industrial conflict has been increasingly institutionalized with the development of an orderly system of industrial relations, prevailing until the late 1960s. During this century the press changed the style of reporting from a rather matter of fact and even handed tone to far more sensational images of confrontation and conflict typical of recent years.

Political violence has also decreased sharply from the early years of the century. They argue that this is associated with the decline of the more traditional and highly expressive forms of disorder which were seen as normal and acceptable aspects of an election involving working and middle class alike. However, they note in parallel a growing number of smaller disorders characterized by the use of instrumental violence, for example the suffragettes. While expressive disorders were attributed to boisterousness those of an instrumental kind came to be viewed as subversive and as such justified a harsher reaction.

In the community arena the widespread instrumental gang violence of the 1920s declined sharply but the street remained a major focus for working-class entertainment and amusement until the Second World War and the subsequent dispersal of the inner city working class through slum clearance. Until the 1930s street fighting, even when the police were involved, was regarded as a legitimate form of entertainment.

The pattern of violence in the sports/leisure arena is the exception to the rule for here they find an upward trend with a marked increase in the last two decades associated with the rise of football hooliganism. It is important to note that violence in and around sports and leisure facilities is not an invention of the post-war generation but has occurred in various forms throughout the century at sporting events, in cinemas and dance halls.

Their analysis of soccer hooliganism has been detailed elsewhere (Dunning et al., 1987). It is perhaps worthwhile, given its current relevance, to review their thesis. They regard soccer hooliganism as a predominantly working-class phenomenon and point to the decline in the street as a centre of entertainment and to a shift in violence away from the street to organized sports and leisure facilities. They relate it to the intrinsic nature of the game of football itself with its emphasis on confrontation, strength, stamina, courage and group loyalty, to the aggressive masculine culture of the lower working classes and to the limited opportunities for excitement in the dull and routinized lives of youth in industrial towns. The mass media are also identified as a contributory factor in shaping the contemporary form of hooliganism by making matches more attractive to a section of society that had not attended before, who brought with them different standards of behaviour.

With the exception of sport their findings match the civilizing process as described by Elias (1978). In general, levels of interpersonal violence show a longer-term decline, while in parallel, public sensitivity to such violence as reflected by the reaction of the authorities and the reportage of the press increases. It is just not true to say that we are living in a violent age. At least in terms of collective disorders Britain, up to 1975, is more tranquil than in the earlier years of the century. But clearly, and this is a question for further research, why is it that many commentators believe we live in a violent society and, as Hough and Mayhew (1983) show in the British Crime Survey, we live more in fear. Why has our tolerance of violence changed?

According to McPhail (1971: 1070) a necessary condition for civil disorder is a large number of people with unscheduled and uncommitted time at their disposal. This he argued provides the platform for the launching of collective action. He goes on to pose a 'fundamental' question, 'what settings, at what points in time yield large numbers of available persons in general proximity to one another'.

In the context of Britain an answer was provided by Lord Scarman (1982) in his report on the Brixton disorders. He describes young black people as 'a people of the street', 'they live their lives on the street, they make their protest there and some of them live off crime'.

Although Dunning et al. find a general movement away from the street as a venue for working-class entertainment, street life is popularly characterized as relatively large numbers of young people predominantly male and black, hanging around on street corners, idling their time away in more-or-less purposeless pursuits, and as such has come to be seen as a problem. This view of street life arises because it is commonly associated with alienation, youth unemployment and aggressive lifestyles, because it exposes participants to criminal activity, and because it is seen to play a potentially significant part in the causation of social unrest. Crowds of youths on street corners constitute a threatening phenomenon.

In Chapter 3, Edwards et al. examine the phenomenon of street life. They find no evidence other than in perhaps three or four 'front-line' areas to support the popular view of street life. Patterns of street life, street use and street culture do not conform to the tidy caricature of popular beliefs. There are no crowds of youth — of any ethnic origin — idling their time away on street corners.

The daily round of their respondents — whether in school or truanting, in or out of employment — indeed varied with ethnicity as well as gender, age, local characteristics and the weather. It did include the use of the street but only as one among a variety of activities in pubs and clubs, pool rooms and their own, and their friend's homes. Street use was spasmodic, short term and mobile — within well-defined 'home territory'. It was less common and even more localized among Asian groups than among whites and those of Afro-Caribbean origin.

However, the street was seen as the place where there was likely to be more excitement and action. Usually alternative provisions such as youth clubs and other activities supervised by adults could not compete with the excitement of street events. When this is combined with the almost universal and strong dislike of the police that their respondents exhibited, it is highly likely that street events involving the police will rapidly draw crowds of spectators and potential participants. It is of note that youths' hostility to the police is focused on police performance rather than the role of the police. Like Gaskell and Smith (1985), Edwards et al. find that youth recognize the need for policing but object strongly to what they see as the oppressive and unreasonable behaviour of police officers. The assumption that the provision of more surrogate work and more youth facilities will minimize the danger of social and crowd unrest is rejected.

It is not, they conclude, the mere physical presence on the street that is significant, it is a set of attitudes, beliefs and lifestyles and they doubt that these will be susceptible to alteration by social policy, at least in the short term.

Given the importance of the police in matters of public order and street life, Chapter 4 by Chatterton is of particular interest. Policing is an intensely political and problematic area for social scientific investigation. In keeping with the research programme's objective to avoid short-term policy issues but rather to look at the more fundamental questions, Chatterton steps back from the more immediate issues addressed by both Lord Scarman (1982) and Smith and his colleagues in their study of the Metropolitan police (see Smith, 1983). He investigates the role played by sergeants in monitoring and controlling police behaviour in the 'front-line'. The 'front-line' is broadly defined as all encounters between police officers and the public because, it is argued, the quality of both the service and of the interaction that occurs has an important effect upon police–public relations. The professionalism of the police in handling routine and 'normal' incidents on the street is as important as their professionalism in dealing with collective disorders. The insensitive and unskilled handling of routine beat incidents can contribute part of the 'fuel' as well as the 'fuse' for flashpoints and collective disturbances. Thus for example 50 per cent of the riots examined by the Kerner Commission involved 'allegedly abusive or discriminatory police actions'.

Although the Report of the Royal Commission on Criminal Procedure (1981) and the Scarman Report (1982) place emphasis on the supervision of police work and the need to equip front-line supervisors for this role, Chatterton finds that sergeants do little street supervision. While training on the job is the model for constables, little attention is given to developing their basic skills. One constraint to effective personal supervision of constables is the amount of required work the sergeants have to do at the station.

Yet there is another, perhaps more important cause of discrepancy between the conventional image of the sergeant as a street supervisor and of the reality of the role as it is enacted. This discrepancy reflects a tension in the role of patrol sergeants created by attending incidents for a constable-oriented as opposed to an incident-oriented reason. When the sergeant has a role to play in directing, controlling and managing incidents, there is no tension. The suggestion that a sergeant should directly supervise constables and monitor their activities at routine, normal incidents cuts across 'the ground rules' of the occupational culture, undercuts both the official view that the beat constable's status should be elevated and the unofficial and unwritten rule that one should not criticize or interfere with the style of another officer.

This research is about a basic and key issue in policing, one that is central to the success or failure of any new policies, particularly public order issues. The sergeants determine what happens on the ground — what Chatterton calls the front-line. At times of high recruitment it will be the case that significant numbers of beat officers are probationers with limited experience of policing, and in areas of high ethnic concentration little familiarity with those areas or with the cultural backgrounds of the residents. Without adequate instruction and supervision and against a background of hostility from young people it is hardly surprising that conflicts occur between youth and the police, some becoming flashpoints which may escalate into serious collective disturbances. This is not to propose that police cause riots but rather to suggest that in the dynamics of collective disorder the police are key actors whose behaviour may have a decisive influence. If that influence is to be benign and constructive then it will be the result of the supervisors developing in their constables the necessary skills and sensitivities. The present structures may need to be changed to achieve this.

A number of concepts were widely and popularly employed to explain the 1981 urban riots. These included the 'copycat riot', a conspiracy theory based on 'outside agitators' and 'mob' or crowd psychology. Most prominent, however, was the 'flashpoint'. Drawing upon the experience of the urban riots in the United States during the 1960s, the media and other popular accounts focused upon an incident which triggered disorder in a context of economic and social deprivation, political powerlessness, racial tension and police confrontation. The Scarman Report provided a gloss of authority and acceptability for the trivial as the threshold. Yet good common sense left description and explanation, cause and effect, the rational and irrational muddled.

In Chapter 5, Waddington et al. examine the demonstrations that greeted the visit of the Prime Minister, Margaret Thatcher, to Sheffield in 1983 and two rallies by members of the National Union of Mineworkers (NUM) in April 1984. Sheffield as the locale for research proved to be not just a matter of convenience but suitable precisely because it did not experience serious rioting in 1981. Of the three demonstrations studied, two were peaceful and one was disorderly. In the case of the two NUM rallies, violence occurred after the rallies. What their evidence suggests is that fundamental conflicts are a necessary but not a sufficient condition for serious disorder. More immediate conditions include whether the issue involved is regarded as legitimate and how the participants are portrayed in the prevailing ideological/political climate, particularly if one group is perceived as a threat; the nature or the culture of the groups involved, what is at stake for them and the extent to which this is shared or disputed; whether or not there are opportunities for liaison and negotiation with the police which is dependent upon past history, experience, rumour or media treatment; a congenial or hostile physical environment; and finally while the preceding considerations may prove conducive to an escalation of a flashpoint or promote its containment, it is conditional on the expressive behaviour of a crowd in response to the handling of the incidents at the time in question. Self-policing deserves special mention and needs to be considered in the light of Chatterton's work on police supervision. While accepting that self-policing is not always possible, Waddington et al. recognize that most orderly crowds are those that are allowed to regulate themselves or choose their own means of regulation. The latter is an encouragement to cooperation rather than confrontation with the police. A discussion of self-policing is also an important reminder that most crowds are orderly and that crowds need to be differentiated with attention paid to their particular attributes. These themes are taken up in Chapter 6 by Benewick and Holton in a study of the Pope's visit to Britain in 1982.

Here social analysis is applied to peaceful crowds in the tradition of

Durkheim's work on the collective conscience and patterns of social solidarity. While conceived as a pilot study and focusing on the Wembley Mass, it is nevertheless suggestive in regard to its substantive conclusions and the methodological issues raised. The dominant rationale of crowd research has been an interest in social disorder, protest or pathology. From this viewpoint crowd behaviour provides both an index of breakdown in social relationships and institutions and a challenge to society to restore or create suitable conditions for social order. The policy implications follow on. An alternative approach is that crowds neither pose challenges to the preservation of public order nor threats to prevailing conceptions of social order within the community. Most crowds, like those during the Pope's visit, even where elaborate planning and management are involved, are peaceable, indicating that there is nothing inherent in crowding together that provokes aggression or psychopathology. This may explain the relative neglect of peaceful crowds as suitable subjects for study.

Yet, drawing upon Durkheim, there is the strong possibility that peaceful crowds mobilized for some mass public ritual may express and strengthen processes of social solidarity and social cohesion. Furthermore, research into such crowds may help to elucidate why protest and disorder are not endemic. Thus peaceful crowds offer one potential index of the nature, extent and limitations of contemporary social cohesions — an index to put against the extensive literature on crisis and breakdown.

In regard to policy, a better understanding of the conditions under which crowds remain peaceful and orderly may encourage decision-makers to protect and nurture civil liberties, thereby avoiding costly processes of mass policing and litigation.

The multi-dimensional aspects of crowds and the need to study them from the perspective of different social science disciplines is further highlighted in Chapter 7 by Parry et al. Their research was prompted by two questions: are crowd disturbances an expression of frustration against a sense of exclusion from the political process; and if crowds are a form of political action how effective is it? Locale is deemed critical to formulating answers to these questions as it is for research on flashpoints. The authors argue that issues such as local political circumstances, the viability of community institutions and confidence in processes of representation must be understood in addition to more general, national considerations. They stress that in Britain the idea that central and local government has important responsibilities for creating economic conditions and solving problems means that the perceived quality of community institutions and participation may provide an important clue to why disturbances occur in some areas but not others. This suggests that possible answers may not lie simply in the local crowd itself but amongst local elites.

The research was based primarily in Moss Side, Manchester, the scene of major crowd disturbances in 1981 and to a lesser extent in similar inner city areas, Burngreave in Sheffield and Glodwich in Oldham which had not experienced major disorders. Deprivation, especially unemployment, was greater in Moss Side than in Burngreave and Glodwich but it was not certain that it was of a totally different order of magnitude from other severely affected areas. The political dimension is more revealing. The authors recognize the difficulty of establishing causal links between community and crowd but note that the destruction of internal solidarities and loyalties contributed to the conditions for the crowd is a widely held view among people associated with Moss Side. Interviews in Moss Side indicated greater disenchantment with political processes than in Sheffield and Oldham. There were more complaints in Moss Side about the futility of participation and the breakdown in communication with the Council than elsewhere. At the same time, political leaders were concerned that although Moss Side had been privileged in regard to resources, dissatisfaction remained unabated. Charges of aggressive and insensitive policing were also very widespread in Moss Side compared to Sheffield and especially Oldham.

For policy implications it is helpful to look beyond crowds for although they may reflect community discontent they do so in complex ways. The lack of consensus in the interpretations placed on crowd actions by local elites, national leaders, the media and social scientists as well as by crowd participants suggests that it is an inefficient form of communication. Yet the need for effective forms of communication is apparent. The authors note that over and above economic deprivation it seems that a sense of political deprivation compounds problems in some inner city areas. They found that the political alienation in Moss Side dated back to the massive urban clearance programmes which undermined community identity and were undertaken without local support or consultation. This confirms Lord Scarman's views on the failure of the 'top down' approach to urban regeneration.

Finally, in an appendix, Stevenson discusses the problems of sources for research into crowd behaviour and describes an attempt to establish an archive of British materials for the years of 1980–3.

Discussion and implications

What, then, has this programme of research achieved? In the first instance it contributes towards placing the crowd in Britain in a broader context through the description and analysis of some of the important issues for example, longer-term trends in collective violence in different areas of social life, the incidence of street life and its role in youth culture, the supervision of day-to-day policing, political participation and deprivation, the dynamic of the escalation or containment of flashpoints and the implicit rules of order among people in crowds. In so doing the research contributes to the public debate and informs decision-makers by critically examining aspects of the current conventional wisdom. At minimum the research disabuses us of some popular concepts and ideas and helps to clarify issues on which policy initiatives and further research might be focused.

If, for example, it is generally believed that Britain is experiencing a period of increased crowd violence, that the street behaviour of youth is pervasive and threatening and that almost every crowd is teetering on the brink of emotionality and disorder then calls for greater social control and tougher policing will go unchallenged. What reasonable person could reject such solutions when the British way of life is perceived to be so clearly threatened? But this research is an antidote to such stereotypical views. Britain, while more sensitive and offended by violence is in general a more tranquil society than in the past; there is little evidence for gangs of youths roaming the streets in the pursuit of confrontations with authority and in both celebratory and protest crowds people carry strong controls against participating in the breakdown of social order. Yet at the same time, these studies document the tensions arising from the social deprivations of unemployment, feelings of political alienation and a widespread hostility to the police among young people. In so far that we are able to generalize from this evidence, it is remarkable that social unrest and public disorder is not more widespread.

It would be misleading, however, to ignore the problems some crowds pose for public order: they always will in a democratic polity. Moreover, the styles and techniques of crowd format change as evidenced by pre-ceremonial entertainment at the Wembley Mass, the unwelcoming ceremony for the Prime Minister in Sheffield and the shift from expressive to instrumental forms of disorder. These in turn may call for changes in the styles and techniques of crowd management and policing. What we must be on guard against is an interaction between crowd behaviour and police behaviour that becomes counter-productive by escalating tension on the one hand and on the other leads to public order policies which may have unintended consequences (Benewick, 1972).

A theme that runs through the research and one that parallels work in the United States is the definitions put forward by powerful groups with explicit or implicit political interests which view collective action as an issue for law and order measures rather than for civil liberties, crowd management and conflict resolution. At the political level this approach leads to moral indignation, a convenient forgetfulness or even the rewriting of history and calls for suitable action to restore a golden age. On the street it may lead to what Toch (1985) describes as a 'violence situation' definition of police–citizen encounters.

A dilemma for the authorities is that the public expects them to take visible and effective action against unruly crowds. This further promotes the law and order solution which paradoxically may be the solution which exacerbates the tension and ignores the fundamental causes such as economic deprivation, political alienation and suspicion and distrust of the police. Such responses may also undermine the role of self-policing and of citizens' collective attachment to norms of social order. Another view, while not ignoring law and order issues, acknowledges that often protest and conflicts may arise out of legitimate grievances that call for political recognition, problem solving, negotiation and constructive social action and policy.

Secondly, this research represents a step towards a better understanding of the conceptual and theoretical aspects of crowd behaviour. This has been achieved through an approach that is largely multi-disciplinary. It is clear that there is no all embracing conceptual analysis for understanding and relating the many facets of crowd phenomena. There is still a great deal of descriptive work required on elements of what might generically be called crowd antecedents and format. This would include the socio-cultural context of crowds, objectives and legitimations as perceived by crowd members and other groups, composition, physical properties and interaction with agencies of social control. Interest in the crowd must go beyond an exclusive focus on protest for as we have seen research into peaceful gatherings can also be revealing. This is not to suggest that research in this field does not have practical applications but if the social sciences have a contribution to make it is to the wider perspectives. So, for example, it is outside the scope of the social sciences to make recommendations about how police on the front-line should be supervised but we can point to inadequacies in the existing structure and discrepancies between official pronouncements and realities that will need action by others. The social sciences are not a substitute for political judgements but can inform the ground upon which political judgements are made.

References

Abeles, R.P. (1976) 'Relative Deprivation, Rising Expectations and Black Militancy', *Journal of Social Issues*, 32, 2: 119–37.
Allport, F.H. (1924) *Social Psychology*, Boston: Houghton Mifflin.

Benewick, R. (1972) 'The Threshold of Violence', in R. Benewick and T.A. Smith *Direct Action and Democratic Politics*. London: Allen & Unwin.

Blumer, H. (1965) 'The Justice of the Crowd', *Transaction*, 2, 6: 43–4.

Caplan, N.S. and Paige, J.M. (1968) 'A Study of Ghetto Rioters', *Scientific American*, 219: 15–21.

Cashmore, E.E. (1985) 'What Lay Behind the Birmingham Riots', *New Society*, 73, 1185: 374–6.

Cohen, A.K. (1965) 'The Sociology of the Deviant', *American Sociological Review*, 30: 5–14.

Cooper, P. (1985) 'Competing Explanations of the Merseyside Riots of 1981', *British Journal of Criminology*, 25, 1: 60–9.

Davies, J.C. (1962) 'Toward a Theory of Revolution', *American Sociological Review*, 27: 5–19.

Davies, J.C. (1974) 'The J-Curve and Power Struggle Theories of Collective Violence', *American Sociological Review*, 39: 607–12.

Dunning, E.G., Murphy, P.J. and Williams, J. (1987) *The Social Roots of Football Hooliganism*. London: Routledge & Kegan Paul.

Edelman, M. (1971) *Politics as Symbolic Action: Mass Arousal and Quiescence*. Chicago: Markham.

Elias, N. (1978) *The Civilizing Process: The History of Manners*. Oxford: Basil Blackwell.

Feagin, J.R. and Hahn, H. (1973) *Ghetto Revolts: The Politics of Violence in American Cities*. New York: MacMillan.

Firestone, J. (1972) 'Theory of the Riot Process', *American Behavioural Scientist*: 15, 6: 859–83.

Freud, S. (1922) *Group Psychology and the Analysis of the Ego*. London: Hogarth Press.

Gaskell, G. and Smith, P. (1985) 'Young Black's Hostility to the Police: An Investigation into its Causes', *New Community*, XII: 66–74.

Gurr, T. (1970) *Why Men Rebel*. Princeton, N.J.: Princeton University Press.

Hobsbawn, E.J. (1959) *Primitive Rebels*. Manchester: Manchester University Press.

Hobsbawn, E.J. and Rudé, G. (1970) *Captain Swing*. Harmondsworth: Penguin.

Holton, R.J. (1978) 'The Crown in History : Some Problems of Theory and Method', *Social History*, 3, 2: 219–33.

Horowitz, D.L. (1983) 'Racial Violence in the United States', in N. Glazer & K. Young (eds) *Ethnic Pluralism and Public Policy*. London: Heinemann.

Hough, M. and Mayhew, P. (1983) *The British Crime Survey*. London: HMSO.

Kerner, O. (1968) *Report of the National Advisory Commission on Civil Disorder*. New York, Bantam.

Le Bon, G. (1960) *The Crowd: A Study of the Popular Mind*. New York: Viking Press. (First published 1895.)

McDougall, W. (1927) *The Group Mind*. (2nd Ed.) Cambridge: Cambridge University Press.

McPhail, C. (1971) 'Civil Disorder Participation: A Critical Examination of Recent Research', *American Sociological Review*, 36: 1058–73.

Murji, K. (1985) 'Observing the Brixton Riot', *New Society*, 74, 1188: 6–8.

Nye, R.A. (1975) *The Origins of Crowd Psychology*. London and Beverly Hills: Sage.

Reicher, S.S. (1984) 'The St Paul's Riot: An Explanation of the Limits of Crowd Action in Terms of a Social Identity Model', *European Journal of Social Psychology*, 14: 1–21.

Rudé, G. (1964) *The Crowd in History*. New York: John Wiley.

Runciman, W.G. (1966) *Relative Deprivation and Social Justice*. Berkeley, C.A.: University of California Press.

Scarman (1982) *The Brixton Disorders: 10–12 April 1981*. Harmondsworth: Penguin.

Sears, D.O. (1969) 'Black Attitudes Toward the Political System in the Aftermath of the Watts Insurrection', *Mid West Journal of Political Science*, 13: 517.

Sears, D.O. and McConahay, J.B. (1973) *The Politics of Violence: The New Urban Blacks and the Watts Riot*. Boston: Houghton Mifflin.

Smelser, N.J. (1962) *Theory of Collective Behaviour*. New York: The Free Press.

Smith, D. (1983) *Police and People in London*. London: Policy Studies Institute.

Sports Council/Social Science Research Council (1978) *Public Disorder and Sporting Events*.

Stark, M., Rance, W., Burbeck, S. and Davidson, K. (1974) 'Some Empirical Patterns in a Riot Process', *American Sociological Review*, 39: 865–76.

Stevenson, J. (1979) *Popular Disturbances in England, 1700–1870*. London: Longman.

Stouffer, S.A., Suchman, E.A., De Vinney, L.C., Starr, S.A. and Williams, R.M. (1949) *The American Soldier: Adjustment during Army Life (Vol. 1)*. Princeton, N.J.: Princeton University Press.

Sullivan, T. (1977) 'The "Critical Mass" in Crowd Behaviour: Crowd Size, Contagion and the Evolution of Riots', *Humboldt Journal of Social Relations*, 4, 2: 6–59.

Tarde, G. (1910) *L'opinion et la foule*. Paris: Alcan.

Toch, H. (1985) 'The Catalytic Situation in the Violence Equation', *Journal of Applied Social Psychology*, 15, 2: 105–23.

Zajonc, R. (1965) 'Social facilitation', *Science*, 149: 269–74.

Zimbardo, P.G. (1969) 'The Human Choice: Individuation, Reason and Order Versus Deindividuation, Impulse and Chaos', in W.J. Arnold & D. Levine (eds): *Nebraska Symposium on Motivation 17*. Lincoln: University of Nebraska Press.

Violent disorders in twentieth-century Britain

Eric Dunning, Patrick Murphy, Tim Newburn and Ivan Waddington

Introduction

> Society today is more violent and criminal and corrupt than it was . . . The trigger of today's outburst of crime and violence . . . lies in the era and attitudes of post-war funk which gave birth to the 'permissive society' which, in turn, generated today's violent society . . . Permissiveness compounded by the economic failure and personal irresponsibility engendered by the socialist state leads inevitably to the violent society. (*The Times*, 14.11.85)

The views of Norman Tebbit, expressed during his 1985 Disraeli Lecture, may perhaps best be viewed as a statement of ideology rather than as a serious attempt to understand the social roots of violence within our society. Nevertheless it is the case that Tebbit's views constitute one more echo of a general theme which has been expressed frequently in recent years, both by politicians — particularly, but not exclusively, from those on the right of the political spectrum — and by senior police officers. In 1979, for example, the President of the Association of Chief Police Officers claimed that 'The mindless violence, the personal attacks and injury, and above all the use of violence in all its forms to further political creeds, are relatively new to the streets of this country' (*The Daily Telegraph*, 31.5.79). The view that British society is experiencing a new and dangerous upsurge in civil disorder and street violence appeared to be confirmed — at least in the eyes of some people — by the riots in many of Britain's larger cities in 1980 and 1981, and, in 1984, by the violence which was associated with the dispute in the coal industry. During the strike, for example, the President of the Police Superintendents' Association said that 'the peace and tranquillity of life have been threatened as never before' (*The Guardian*, 3.10.84). The strike, he said, had been dominated by 'appalling and intolerable levels of violence'; we have reached 'an all-time low and the nation needs time to recover its equilibrium'. The urban riots of 1985, the apparent increase in football hooliganism in that year and, above all, the events in May at the Heysel Stadium in Brussels, added to this impression.

Views similar to those cited above could be duplicated almost *ad infinitum*. What such views have in common is the idea that we have, in recent years, experienced a rapid and unprecedented escalation in the levels of violence and civil disorder and, associated with this, an equally dramatic process of moral decline. These perceived changes are further presented as representing a radical departure from the peace, tranquillity and responsibility which have traditionally been characteristic of the British way of life.

Such views have generally found little favour amongst historians and sociologists, for their training leads them to treat recent events in terms of a considerably longer time perspective than that normally held by politicians and police officers. Thus White (1981: 260–1) has assured us that 'riot is, and always has been, a part of the British way of life', whilst Kettle and Hodges (1982: 9–22), cite a large number of riots from the fourteenth century onwards in support of their argument that ours is a 'riotous history'. Tilly (1969: 4) has similarly noted that, 'As comforting as it is for civilized people to think of barbarians as violent and of violence as barbarian, Western civilization and various forms of collective violence have always been close partners.' Gurr (1969: 572) has pointed out that no country in the modern world has been free of group protest and violence for as much as a generation. Finally, Pearson (1983) has shown, with a wealth of historical detail, how, for hundreds of years, successive generations have voiced similar fears of escalating violence, moral decline and the loss of 'the British way of life'. He has also shown how each generation has been sure of its claim to remember better times when life was founded upon civility, reasonableness and an unquestioning respect for law and authority.

There is little doubt that historians and sociologists are correct in rejecting as spurious the novelty which is frequently attributed to the violent disorders of recent years. Nevertheless, such an argument is, on its own, inadequate. Indeed, it can be misleading, for in explaining the continuities of social life, it might be taken as suggesting that nothing ever changes. Pearson, for one, is clearly aware of this danger, for he writes that he is 'not trying to promote a "flat earth" version of history according to which nothing ever changes: social circumstances do change, and undeniably' (Pearson, 1983: 207). Let us start to become more substantive by looking critically at Pearson's thesis.

Although he reinforces his statement on social change by entitling one of his chapter sub-headings 'Novelty and Continuity', Pearson fails to examine in an adequate way the delicate balance between 'continuity' and 'change'. It is necessary to go beyond the well-documented argument that 'ours is a violent history', and to ask two further questions: first, how, if at all, has the *level* of violence changed over time; and second, what, if any, changes have taken place in the pattern or *structure* of violent disorders? Pearson fails to provide an adequate answer to either of these questions.

In relation to the first question, Pearson offers a highly impressionistic view. He writes:

> Each era has ... understood itself as standing at a point of radical discontinuity with the past. But when we reconnect these bursts of discontent into a continuing history of deterioration, must not the credibility snap — unless, that is, we judge ourselves to be in a worse condition than the poor, brutalised human beings who suffered the worst effects of the Industrial Revolution? If we listen to the documentation of history, rather than the pulse of our contemporary anxieties, is it not a little fanciful to believe that Britain's well-policed streets in the 1980's are more perilous than Henry Fielding's disorderly London, Engel's fiery Manchester, or the turbulent street life known to the original Hooligans? (1983: 210)

The argument that there has been a long-term tendency for levels of violence to be reduced is — particularly in the form in which Pearson expresses it — a very plausible one. However, plausibility is a poor substitute for empirical data. Indeed, Pearson's appeal to the reasonableness of his reader, for example, 'is it not a little fanciful to believe', is an implicit acknowledgement that he has not provided the data required to substantiate an argument of this kind. The problem of the changing levels of violence is therefore a problem upon which Pearson, despite the many strengths of his book, can shed little systematic light.

In relation to the second problem — that of changes in the pattern of violence — Pearson's position is both confused and confusing. He suggests, for example, that:

> Comparisons between late twentieth-century disturbances among youths and the riotous accompaniments to festivals in early modern Europe may seem to be stretching a point too far, however, in that they blur across too many social alterations. Surely, while there may be some momentary resemblance there is more to separate the unruly apprentice and the modern football hooligan — in terms of language, custom, material benefits, cultural horizons, and even bad habits — than to bring them together as instances of the same phenomenon? (1983: 221)

Pearson's question is clearly rhetorical. Nevertheless it serves to indicate not only the elements of continuity but also — and quite correctly — the equally important elements of discontinuity between these phenomena. Pearson, however, chooses to stress the elements of continuity, for he goes on to write that:

> The point can be stretched even further, back into ancient history. There are truly astonishing similarities, for example, between football rowdyism

and the violent disputes between hostile factions at the theatres and the hippodromes in Byzantine Rome and Constantinople when, more than a thousand years ago, the 'Blues' and the 'Greens' chanted their support for rival champions in chariot races, each faction grouped at opposing 'Ends' of the stadiums. (1983: 221–2)

The gross historical comparison continues:

> Disorders around popular entertainments in Rome during the first few centuries after the time of Christ were a particularly grievous matter . . . commonly ending in bloodshed. Around 500 A.D., when Emperor Anastasius had found it necessary to ban wild beast shows and pantomime dancing in order to quell faction violence, one of the more terrible theatre riots resulted in no less than three thousand deaths. (1983: 222)

As though suddenly struck by the enormous scale of the violence in Ancient Rome, Pearson (1983: 222) then suggests that the 'more modest punch-ups of our own time hardly bear comparison with such a spectacular disregard for human life'. Any differences which may exist between violence in Ancient Rome and modern Britain are, however, immediately cast aside, for in the next sentence he refers to 'formidably ageless continuities such as these' (1983: 222).

Pearson's failure to articulate adequately this delicate balance between 'continuity' and 'change' — that is to say, his failure to come to grips with the problem of changing levels and patterns of violence — is, inextricably linked with both the relatively unsystematic way in which he gathered his data and with his decision to write history 'backwards', for Pearson's analysis begins with contemporary Britain and works backwards to pre-industrial 'Merrie England'. What Pearson loses are the insights which could have been gained by the adoption of a developmental perspective. As Pearson notes, 'social circumstances do change, and undeniably'. Unfortunately, he appears not to see the full significance of this statement. Thus as societies change — as they become more complex, for example, and as this growing complexity generates new patterns of tension and conflict, so these newly emerging patterns of relationships are associated with the development of forms of social disorder which reflect, in part, previously established patterns of disorder, but which also have emergent properties of their own.

There have, of course, been a number of attempts to conceptualize variations in the stucture of collective disorders. Particularly noteworthy in this respect is the work of Rudé (1970: 17) who argues that the 'crowd' has to be studied

> as a historical phenomenon, and not as a stereotype that is equally suited to any form of society. Thus popular movements occurring in ancient times tended to be different in kind from those of the Middle Ages; and

these in turn tended to have distinctive characteristics that separate them from those that have arisen in 'pre-industrial' or industrial society.

Rudé's work clearly shows an awareness of the necessity to relate specific patterns of collective disorder to patterns of social development more generally. Nevertheless, from the perspective of a study such as our own, which is concerned with collective disorders in Britain since 1900, Rudé's framework has a number of limitations. In the first place, the distinction between 'pre-industrial' and 'industrial' is very broad and allows one to say nothing about variations in the levels and structure of collective disturbances whether between different industrial societies or within a single industrial society at different time periods. By 'pre-industrial', Rudé means broadly the period during which a society is adapting to the changes brought about by rapid industrialization which, in the case of England, he dates roughly from the early eighteenth century to about the 1840s; thereafter, the 'pre-industrial' crowd is increasingly replaced by the 'industrial' crowd. It is not very useful to describe crowd disorders from the middle or late nineteenth century simply as 'industrial' in character for, as we shall argue, there have been some significant changes in patterns of crowd disorders during the twentieth century in Britain, and a more sophisticated framework is required in order to enable one to analyse these changes *within* an industrial society.

A second, related problem is that the simple dichotomy between 'pre-industrial' and 'industrial', whilst emphasizing the significant differences between these types of disorder, tends to underplay the important degree of overlap between them. To some extent, Rudé himself is aware of this, for he asks 'what of the Negro rebellion that has been erupting in the northern cities of the United States since 1964? Hasn't this, in certain of its aspects at least, a distinctive flavour of the "pre-industrial" riot? I think the answer is yes.' (1970: 34) This problem can, perhaps, be overcome so long as we are careful to treat the models of 'pre-industrial' and 'industrial' crowds as ideal types which can sensitize us, not to changes of an 'all-or-nothing' character, but rather to the changing *balance* of 'pre-industrial' and 'industrial' aspects of crowd disorders in the nineteenth and twentieth centuries.

The work of Tilly is, in many respects, not dissimilar to that of Rudé. Tilly argues that collective violence has developed historically through three phases: firstly, 'primitive' violence, which is small scale, local, based on communal groups, and has inexplicit or non-political objectives; secondly, 'reactionary' violence which is also on a small scale but which is more overtly political, and in which the participants are commonly reacting to some change which they see as depriving them of rights which they formerly enjoyed; and finally 'modern' violence, which involves specialized associations with relatively well-defined objectives, organized for political or economic action. Like Rudé, Tilly sees the processes of industrialization and urbanization as being of major importance in generating a change in the pattern of violence. For Tilly (1969: 32) the transition from reactionary to modern violence is said to correspond roughly to the 'timing of industrialization and urbanization'. However, Tilly's scheme tends to suffer from the same limitations as Rudé's work for it does not provide us with the means to differentiate between types of violent disorders *within* an industrial society. Tilly's work has also been criticized by Gurr. More particularly, on the basis of his study of trends in violence in four major cities, Gurr (1976: 80) suggests that instances of 'primitive' violence abound in the twentieth century, thus contradicting Tilly's assertion (1969: 31) that reactionary forms of violence (and therefore the 'primitive' ones that are supposed to have preceded them) were well on their way to oblivion by 1830. Moreover, although the explicitly developmental aspects of Tilly's work are a pointer in the right direction, it would seem that his categories are perhaps both too broad and too rigid to enable us to conceptualize adequately the changing patterns of violent disorders in twentieth-century Britain.

Before concluding this brief introduction, it may be useful to comment on one other aspect of the study of 'crowd violence'. The 'tradition' in this field is usually represented as beginning with Le Bon, whose psychologistic approach emphasized the base, irrational nature of 'the crowd':

> A crowd is always ready to revolt against a feeble and to bow down servilely before a strong authority. Should the strength of an authority be intermittent, the crowd, always obedient to its extreme sentiments, passes alternately from anarchy to servitude and from servitude to anarchy. (Le Bon, 1960: 55)

This view of violent crowds still finds frequent voice today, for example, in the descriptions by politicians and tabloid newspapers of football hooliganism or the clashes between police and pickets in the 1984 coal dispute. The constant use of terms like 'thugs' and 'mob' suggests precisely the sort of easily manipulated, criminal, irrational and destructive elements that were the basis for Le Bon's psychology of the crowd.

Whilst most modern writers are critical of Le Bon, some still adopt a perspective which has overtones of his approach. Smelser (1962) for example, stresses the importance of social disorganization resulting from the disruption of traditional restraints on anti-social behaviour. The problem with this type of approach is that it can be used, not dissimilarly to that of Le Bon, to conceptualize collective violence as 'mindless', i.e. as a mechanistic response to social upheaval or 'strain'. The response to this by Rudé, Tilly and others has been to place emphasis on the 'social purpose' — or as we would prefer, the 'social purposes' — of the crowd, to show that collective violence may be part and parcel of the political process:

> Historically, collective violence has flowed regularly out of the central political processes of Western countries. Men seeking to seize, hold or realign the levels of power have continually engaged in collective violence as part of their struggles. (Tilly, 1969: 4)

Similarly Hobsbawn (1971: 111) has argued:

> ... there was a claim to be considered. The classical mob did not merely riot as protest, but because it expected to achieve something by its riots. It assumed that the authorities would be sensitive to its movements, and probably also that they would make some sort of immediate concession. For the mob was not simply some sort of casual collection of people united for some *ad hoc* purpose, but in a recognised sense, a permanent entity, even though rarely permanently organized as such.

Although various criticisms have been offered of Rudé's 'social protest approach' to the study of collective violence, particularly of his reliance on economistic explanations, such an approach continues to dominate the field. However, whilst we agree that it is not helpful simply to label all crowd disorders as irrational, it is just as important to avoid labelling them, in an equally simplistic way, as rational. Indeed, the very terms 'rational' and 'irrational' seem to be in important respects misleading, especially if they are seen as a crude dichotomy, for this can obscure significant dimensions of crowd disorders. In particular, it might be more fruitful to see crowds, not as 'rational' or 'irrational', but rather to explore the changing balance over time between what one might call the 'expressive' and 'instrumental' aspects of different types of disorders. At this point, it is enough simply to note by way of illustration that certain aspects of crowd disorders — most notably the 'quest for excitement' that is sometimes evident — can properly be regarded as primarily expressive without in any sense implying that they are irrational. The question of excitement is one to which we shall return.

Objectives and methods
Our own historical study of collective violence has attempted to avoid the sorts of pitfalls discussed above. More particularly, our project had the following major aims:

> • To document, since the beginning of the present century, the changing incidence of reported crowd violence and collective disorderliness nationally and in Leicestershire,[1] both generally and in a variety of different areas of social life.

- To document such qualitative changes as differing forms of violence, changes in the locations in which such violence tends to be found, and the differing class locations of those involved in such disorderliness.
- To document changes in the perception of violence as a 'social problem', and the effect such changes have had on the formation and implementation of policies.
- To document the development in this period of the mechanisms of social control, particularly changes in police organization and practice.

Much of our data regarding these problems has been generated by a comprehensive survey of the stories referring to incidents of disorder contained in the *Leicester Mercury* between the years 1900 and 1975 (up to 1914 it was called the *Leicester Daily Mercury*). For the years 1921–77, where the paper was still kept in bound volumes, we were able to read every copy that was printed. However, the paper for the years 1900 to 1921 had deteriorated so badly that it had been transferred to microfilm, making the task of the 'reader' much more time-consuming. Therefore we were forced to 'sample' the newspapers from this period, and decided upon a span covering one year in every five. We have, then, read the *Leicester Mercury*, hereafter called the *Mercury*, for the following years: 1900, 1905, 1910, 1915 and for every year from 1920 to 1977. We made a note of, and later, using a 'reader-printer', made copies of all the stories, whether 'local' or 'national', that referred to incidents of collective disorderliness. By 'collective', we mean 'involving three or more people', whether as spectators or participants, and by 'disorder', we mean 'violent actions directed at or against persons or property'.[2]

We have divided our data on collective disturbances into four general areas, namely those which occurred in the areas of politics, industry, organized leisure/sport and the community. These four categories are not of the same kind as those used by writers such as Rudé and Tilly. Nor are they designed to replace concepts which refer to the structure of collective disorders, such as 'pre-industrial' and 'industrial', or 'reactionary' and 'modern'. Rather the division of our empirical data into these four areas was used to sensitize us to the changing levels of collective disorder in different areas of social life. Is, for example, the trend of violent disorders the same in all four areas, or do they exhibit significantly different trends? The question of the changing forms which violent disorders take — for example, the question of the changing balance between what Tilly calls 'reactionary' and 'modern' violence, or between what we have called 'expressive' and 'instrumental' violence — is a related but slightly different question which can then be raised in relation to each of the four areas of social life.

The four areas of social life were constructed in the following manner. By 'politics' we are referring not just to collective disturbances in connection with the activities of political parties and at elections, but also to disorders connected with public demonstrations and protest marches which had political objectives. By 'industry' we are referring to collective violence that is related to the industrial protests of workers. 'Leisure/sport' refers not only to the disorderliness of spectators in and around stadia, but is a more general category which includes the broad spectrum of leisure activities such as fairs, carnivals, public dances, theatres and cinemas. The final category is entitled 'community' and has, by necessity, become somewhat of a 'catch-all' category. Generally speaking, the events that have found their way into the 'community' category are those relating to street fighting and brawls.

Additional data were gathered from a series of interviews with retired police officers. All had served in Leicester and had commenced their careers at some point before the Second World War, one as early as 1922. Officers from different ranks were interviewed, ranging from Constable to Inspector, and were questioned about their memories of particular incidents which we had noted from our reading of the local press. We also elicited their more general views on the role of the police officer and the methods of policing that had characterized the periods in which they served. It was hoped that this information would serve two purposes. Firstly, it would act as a check on the material we had gathered from the newspapers; and secondly, it would enable us to gather some information about aspects of social life that were either not covered or covered only briefly by the local press. For example, from our reading of the *Mercury*, the years of the Second World War appear to have been relatively 'quiet' ones, with few reported collective disturbances in Leicestershire. There are several possible explanations for this, such as the relative absence of large numbers of young males, the decreasing size of the newspaper, the priority coverage given to stories about the war and, perhaps, also a desire to minimize the reporting of social tensions at a time when there was a perceived need for unity in the face of the enemy. Our interviews with police officers who served during the war suggest that the latter consideration was not entirely absent, and that major violent disturbances were almost certainly under-reported — and deliberately so — in the local press in those years.

It is important to emphasize that these are *preliminary* findings. For the period 1900–75, we have collected newspaper reports numbering several thousands, and it has not yet been possible to analyse all of these reports for the whole of this period in as much detail as we would wish. In part, the preliminary nature of the present analysis accounts for the fact that, in relation to the four different areas which we have identified, we have sometimes chosen to high-light slightly different problems in relation to collective violence. We are nevertheless confident that the analysis presented does offer an accurate picture of some of the more important changes in the rate and structure of collective disorders in Britain in the course of this century. It should be noted that, from this point on, all references are to the *Mercury* unless indicated otherwise.

Violence in the community arena

Changes in the incidence of reported violent community disturbances in the course of this century are illustrated in Graph 1. As can be seen, the highest incidence of violent disturbances in this area was recorded for the early part of this century, with a significant decline in

GRAPH 1

Violent community disturbances in England, Wales and Scotland as reported by the *Leicester Mercury*, 1900–75 (five-yearly intervals)

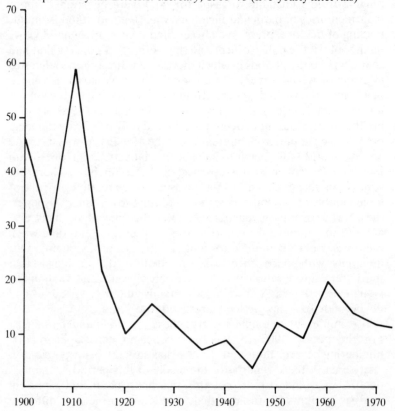

the level of violence in the period following the First World War. During the post-Second World War period there has been a tendency for the incidence of reported community violence to increase, although recent levels are still very much lower than those for the early part of the century.

In addition to recording the changing incidence of violent community disturbances, we have also been able to chart a significant transformation in the character of collective disturbances in this arena. Our argument is that, until the late 1930s, certain forms of street fighting, even if they involved the police, were regarded by both participants and spectators as almost a legitimate form of entertainment. This we suggest, was bound up with the existence of the 'street' as a principal centre of working-class leisure. Furthermore, the generally 'expressive' forms of violence that we have identified in that context must, in part, also be understood as attempts to resist 'outside' interference in 'street life' and this means that, in addition, they also had an instrumental component. We argue, in addition, that the years around the Second World War, which witnessed the beginnings of slum clearance and the dispersal of the inner city working class, were also characterized by the decline of the 'street' as a centre of entertainment. There was concomitantly a decline in the degree of legitimacy associated with the largely 'expressive' disorders.

Our task, then, is to describe the quality and pattern of collective disorder in the 'community' arena as reported by the *Mercury*. We shall concentrate particularly on the pre-Second World War period and on the distinctive character of both street disturbances in that period and the style and manner in which such disturbances were reported.

The information from the *Mercury* suggests that 'hooliganism' and 'hooligan gangs' were fairly widespread in Britain at the turn of the century, particularly in the poorer areas of major cities. These rival gangs did not only clash with each other, but also constituted a well-established threat to the more 'respectable' elements in communities, to the police, and to people who just happened to be passing through. That the authorities were concerned about the extent of such activities is suggested, for example, by the fact that, in London in November 1900, the Public Prosecutor took up a particular case 'in view of the very serious aspect street hooliganism had assumed in certain parts of the Metropolis' (23.11.1900). However, the police were rarely equipped to deal with the rougher districts of London and the Public Prosecutor's stance was really a token gesture. This can be seen in many of the cases reported in the *Mercury* around that time. In June 1900, for example, a 'police-constable was attempting to disperse a disorderly crowd in Chelsea when he was set upon' (7.6.1900). In October 1900, 'a youth, seventeen years of age, threatened to lay an officer's head open with the heavy buckle of his belt and when he was arrested the mob pelted the constable with stones' (23.10.1900). In December 1900, 'a constable, named William Thompson, was moving on a crowd of foreign loiterers in Union Row, off Commercial Road, East London, when one of them, a Polish Jew, attacked the officer stabbing him twice in the neck . . .' (1.12.1900). The policeman died almost immediately. It would be wrong, however, to assume that London was unique in this respect. In Birmingham in 1901, a coroner suggested that, such were the dangers in certain quarters of the city, that policemen should not be permitted to patrol the streets alone (31.10.1901). It would seem that he was not exaggerating for, following a 'stabbing affray' in that city the previous year in which two constables were injured, it was reported that there were nine constables who had been victims of violence lying disabled (30.6.1900).

Not surprisingly, public confidence in the ability of the police to deal with 'hooliganism', especially in certain parts of London, was not always high. Indeed, occasionally, a form of vigilante justice was resorted to, seemingly with the full approval of the newspaper:

> Mr. John Burn's cure for 'Hooliganism' was put into practice outside Christ Church, Blackfriars Road, late on Sunday night. Two young men of the working-class, while proceeding peaceably along the street, were set upon by a gang of six ruffians. One of the pair struck from behind was felled to the ground, and his companion was very badly beaten. But the passers-by turned on the Hooligans and in very little time every one of the cowardly assailants was lying in the gutter. Challenged again and again to stand up and fight fairly, they preferred to remain prostrate. But this did not save them from a sound thrashing before they were allowed to limp off into the obscurity of the back streets. (11.12.1900)

The form which newspaper reporting took in this period tells something about the then-prevailing attitudes towards violence. As can be seen from the above account, a 'sound thrashing' was, at least sometimes, considered to be a more fitting punishment than the possibility of police intervention. Indeed, the 'hooligans' were not turned over to the police but allowed to 'limp off into the obscurity of the back streets'.

If we move to the inter-war period and compare it to the situation after the Second World War, some aspects of this street-fighting and policing become clearer. In the inter-war years, many of the country's major cities seem to have been the site for disturbances involving gangs of a relatively highly 'organized' nature. A great many of the incidents that we have recorded involve the activities of established street gangs who had their own territories and who were prepared to repel rival gangs who tried to invade that territory, for example, in order to set up rival gambling organizations. The best known cases of this kind became known as the 'Sheffield Gang Wars' (Bean, 1981). In Sheffield, for four or five years in the 1920s, rival gangs contested the rights of various gambling operations, and, using very violent tactics, fought not only amongst themselves but also with the police. In that period, however, street gangs were a common sight in most major cities:

War Declared on Gangs in Glasgow

During the past six days over sixty people have been arrested in connection with street rowdyism. In some cases it has been alleged that bottles were thrown, and bayonets and knives flourished ... There are, it is stated, about 60 gang organizations in Glasgow. Those whose members are between the ages of 17 and 25, are known by such names as the Derry Boys, the Billy Boys, the Beehives and the Calamity Boys. (12.8.36)

Leicester also had its fair share of street gangs in the 1920s and 1930s. Several ex-police officers we have spoken to who patrolled the streets of Leicester before the Second World War, remember there being some well-known rival gangs who inhabited he Wharf Street area of town, causing it to become known as Leicester's 'Little Sheffield'. One of the ex-officers referred to what were known as 'bottle-gangs':

... [in] Wharf St., Bedford, Woodboy and Britannia ... well all that side it was the bottle gangs mostly ... They'd crack a bottle over the back of your head, they would. They weren't particular about knocking yer' duck off.

The *Mercury* also referred to gangs in this area which were involved in gambling and other activities: Gang Feuds in Leicester; Man Badly Assaulted By Crowd; People Alarmed.

Police Out To Break Up Warring Factions

The 'Mercury' understands that the Leicester police are taking every possible step to break up the rival racing gangs in Leicester, whose feuds threaten to rival those of the rowdies in Sheffield. Another outburst occurred last night in the vicinity of Russell Square, and a deadly enmity exists between them and another region of Bedford St. The men who compose these two gangs are of the racing fraternity, and beside engaging in bookmaking on courses within easy reach of Leicester, are leading the police a merry dance when they engage at 'pencilling' in the streets ... The gangs operating in the heart of the city are of the most dangerous type, and many are believed to carry fire-arms, knuckle-dusters, and other weapons of attack. (21.5.1925)

Highly organized gangs of this kind seem to have survived well into the 1930s. After that, however, their activities cease to be documented by the newspaper and it seems likely that, as gambling became easier both on and off the racecourse, and as the city-centre lodging houses were gradually demolished, they slowly disappeared. This is not to say that there were not disturbances involving gangs both during and after the Second World War but, rather, that it was the decline of this specifically 'economic' purpose — the protection of gambling operations, local 'cardsharpers', 'con-men' etc. — that distinguishes the disturbances which took place in the 'community arena' before the Second World War from those that took place after it.

There is another respect in which 'street-fighting' in the inter-war periods is distinguishable from its post-war equivalent: the public reaction to its occurrence. There are two aspects to consider: first, the response of witnesses on the street to the occurrence of a fight and, second, the response of the newspaper to public street-fighting. A clear indication of the attitudes underlying these responses is given by the fact that street-fighting in this period often attracted large crowds whose degree of involvement in the 'contretemps' would range from simple spectatorship to physical participation either by helping or hindering police officers when the latter had become involved. Quite often, as White (1979) points out in his article on Campbell Bunk, people would intervene to try to stop arrests being made. Consider the following three examples from 1930. In the first, in January, a policeman who intervened in a fight in Watford between some locals and 'ex-miners of the distressed areas', found himself surrounded by a hostile crowd and the man he was attempting to arrest was enabled to escape (23.1.1930). Then, in June 1930, it was reported that, in Glasgow, when two constables had attempted to arrest a man, they were attacked by a 'large crowd' and were so outnumbered that they had to send out an SOS (9.6.1930). In the previous week in Liverpool, the police had been stoned by showers of missiles hurled at them by a crowd in response to their raid on a 'gambling school'. The leader of this 'school' described what happened to him in the course of the raid and why:

> Sillitoe who declared that he was injured from his ankles to the whole length of his body up to the top of his head alleged that the baton was used very heavily upon him.
> He admitted that the crowd tried to rescue him, and the police beat him unmercifully as a warning to others. (2.6.1930)

After a similar case in Leicester in 1930 in which a police constable was attacked whilst trying to make an arrest, the Deputy Chief Constable made the following statement:

There seems to be a lot of these assaults on the police. Policemen on duty are surrounded by a hostile crowd, who instead of giving assistance, attack the constable. (3.11.1930)

The following case, which also occurred in Leicester in 1930, perhaps tells us even more about popular attitudes at the time towards both the police and violence:

Constable's Vain Appeal to Crowd

The constable stated that Blockley was shouting and laughing with three other men. He told them to move off and they did so, but Blockley stopped, arguing, and refused to go away. His shouting brought people out of their homes and a crowd collected.

When witness attempted to arrest him, Blockley struck him in the face and called to one of his friends. 'This man pinned my arm behind my back whilst Blockley hit me in the face several times', added the constable.

'I tried to blow my whistle but he pulled it out of my mouth. I called to the crowd for help, but no one came forward. I was struggling with them both for 15 minutes and Blockley tried to get away by pushing his fingers up my nose and forcing my head back. Then Police Constable Holden came along and I was able to arrest him.' (14.4.1930)

In this example, although the crowd did not actually harm the policeman, as was the case in the previous examples, they were unwilling to go to his aid. Even allowing for some exaggeration on the constable's part, it seems to have been a fairly lengthy dispute which the crowd were prepared to watch. This not only confirms the view that, in Leicester at least, the police could not rely on help from members of the public, but also suggests that, even when the police were on the receiving end of a violent dispute, street-fighting was seen by some people as an almost legitimate spectator sport.

This view is reinforced by the reporting style of the *Mercury*. Generally speaking, the reporting of street-fighting in the inter-war period consisted of a description of events without adopting any particular moral position. More interestingly, perhaps, the newspaper tended to convey a sense of the 'excitement' involved in street disorder. The following type of headline was not uncommon in the *Mercury* in the 1920s: Exciting Hinckley Street Scare; Allegations Against Three Men; Desperate Struggle (7.3.1927).

The report concerns a case in which three men in their twenties were involved in an incident in which a police constable was assaulted in Hinckley. Similarly another report from 1927, describing three separate fights which took place in Hinckley, all watched by large crowds, explained the actions of the combatants with the statement that, 'The by-election was responsible for causing them to get excited', and topped the whole story with the headline: More Battles of Bosworth; Arguments Settled With Bare Knuckles; Thrills for Crowd (2.6.1927).

The idea that street-fighting could often be exciting and entertaining is perhaps brought out most clearly in the following story:

Fought Four Navvies
Constable Entertains a Crowd

After spending their week's earnings in liquid refreshment four burly navvies entertained a crowd of 200 people in the Rushes at Loughborough on Saturday night by fighting amongst themselves. A young constable came on the scene and on witnessing the disturbance sent for assistance.

Loughborough's herculean constable P.C. Norman then arrived, and his part in the entertainment was recognized by the crowd as the star turn.

He took each navvy in turn, and as each one was rendered hors-de-combat he was handed over to the younger constable and taken to the Police Station. (3.9.1928)

The sense of excitement associated with street-fighting was also described by a retired police officer who had served in Leicester in the 1920s and 1930s:

Well they congregated you see. It was a marvel to me how they used to get to know. They used to come out of their houses and watch two people fighting, whether it were two men or two women. They thought that was good you know, a thing worth watching, if there were blood or anything floating around. That's how it was . . . That was their enjoyment . . . they got a kick out of it.

In conclusion, it can be seen both from the attitude of people on the street and from the style in which street-fighting was reported in the newspaper in the inter-war years, that such violence was often considered to be an 'interesting' or 'exciting' aspect of everyday life and not something that was to be particularly feared or overly condemned. However, the rise of other forms of mass entertainment, the beginnings of slum clearance, the effects of the Second World War on young males old enough to be conscripted and of evacuation on the rest, together with the gradual dispersal of the 'inner city' working class to the newer housing estates, saw the relative decline of the 'street' as a centre of entertainment and the growing condemnation of the largely 'expressive' forms of collective violence that we have identified as occurring there.

Violence in the political arena

Our data indicate that there was a relatively high level of violence in the political arena in the early part of this century. Following this, there was a long period in which there was a general decline in the level of political violence, although within the general context of decline, there were also some periods which exhibited a short-term increase. The generally downward trend is, however, quite clear (see Graph 2).

GRAPH 2

Violent political disturbances in England, Wales and Scotland as reported
by the *Leicester Mercury*, 1900–75 (five-yearly intervals)

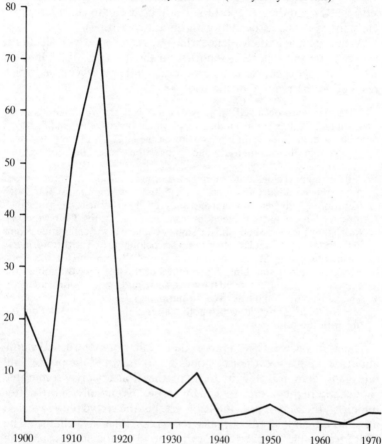

In order to understand not only the changing levels but also the
changing structure of political violence in the twentieth century, it
may be useful to differentiate between two rather different forms of
political violence. This distinction will also help us to understand the
rather different reactions to these two forms of violence on the part of
the police and other authorities.

The difference between these two forms of political violence may
be illustrated by reference to the events of 1910, in which year the
Mercury reported fifty-one incidents involving the use of violence in
the political arena. Almost all of this violence occurred in one or

another of two political settings: firstly, there was the violence which was associated with elections — there were two general elections in 1910 — and, secondly, there was the violence which was used by the suffragettes and their supporters. It will be useful to consider separately the violence associated with these two settings.

As an example of the violence which was associated with elections, one can cite the following report from the *Mercury* of 24 January 1910. The report concerned election riots in High Wycombe, which resulted in the reading of the Riot Act:

> Exciting scenes occurred, in consequence, it is said, of Liberals being victimised by dismissal from their employment because they had displayed party posters. A mob took possession of the streets and were dispersed by a charge of one hundred police with batons, after the Riot Act had been read by the Mayor . . .
>
> From eight o'clock until midnight, a crowd, numbering three or four thousand, paraded the streets, singing and howling against the Tariff Reformers. Between midnight and one o'clock on Saturday morning they tore down the wooden protections from the Conservative Club windows, which they then smashed, and did similar damage at the committee rooms in Crendon-street, and at other premises belonging to Tariff Reformers.
>
> But the Dump Shop near the old Guildhall came in for the worst treatment. After smashing the windows of this the crowd tumbled the contents into the street, piled them in a heap, and made a bonfire of them. The flames rose so high as to cause alarm, and the 19 borough policemen sent for the fire brigade, which both scattered the crowd and put out the fire with the hose.

The *Mercury* went on to report that 'Gangs of men rushed wildly about, making a great noise, stones were thrown at the police, and one gang demonstrated in front of the Conservative committee rooms, where they were repelled by a hose.' Eventually, shortly after midnight, the Mayor read the Riot Act, but the crowd merely jeered and hooted, and dared the police to 'make a Balaclava charge'. The Chief Constable gave his men orders to clear the streets, and the police drew their batons and charged the crowd. 'The mob stood for a moment, but as soon as the first men struck with the batons began to howl for mercy, the thousands took to their heels.' The streets were finally cleared about 1.30 a.m.

The riot in High Wycombe was unusual only in the sense that it involved particularly large numbers of people — between three and four thousand — for neither rioting itself nor the use of physical violence in relation to election campaigns were unusual. Election riots were also reported from Droitwich (7.2.1910), where the Riot Act was also read, and from Repton in Derbyshire, where three hundred boys from the public school wrecked the premises of the Liberal candidate after driving out its occupants, following which they pelted with eggs women who were believed to be supporters of the Liberal candidate. Schoolmasters and police were apparently 'powerless for a time to allay the tumult' (15.12.1910). In Lincoln, the Home Secretary, Winston Churchill, was prevented from speaking as a result of a riot in which there was 'desperate fighting' and in which the police were 'powerless' (3.12.1910) whilst in nearby Louth, what was described as a 'Tory Mob' which had attacked the Liberal Club was dispersed when the police charged with batons drawn (21.12.1910). Street, in Somerset, was said to have become 'a byword in the country for ruffianism and intimidation of the lowest type. So bad has the place become that it is hardly safe for sober and quiet members of the opposite party to live there, to say nothing of outsiders entering the place' (10.2.1910).

The throwing of missiles — often, but not always, aimed at candidates or newly elected MPs — was by no means uncommon. Amongst the missiles reported as having been thrown during the two election campaigns of 1910 were stones, bricks, pepper, eggs, snowballs, mud, apples and potatoes, whilst the Liberal candidate in Richmond had what was described as an 'evil smelling liquid' thrown over him (21.1.1910). The Press Association reported that the Unionist candidate for Pembroke had been shot at, the bullet passing through the windscreen of his car (11.1.1910). This report was denied by the candidate's agent the following day. Not all the violence, however, was directed against candidates. The Unionist candidate for Mid-Derbyshire was convicted and fined for assaulting a member of his audience during an election meeting! (10.2.1910).

From the perspective of the late twentieth century, elections in the early part of the century were relatively violent affairs. However, the data contained in the *Mercury* suggest that, at the time, the police and other authorities were not overly concerned about election violence, for a certain amount appears to have been expected, and perhaps even regarded as a normal accompaniment of elections. This point has also been noted by Richter (1964: 15) who, in his study of public order and popular disturbances, has suggested that one of the striking features of political disturbances in the early twentieth century 'was the calm unconcerned manner in which so many people in public office accepted them with no more alarm than any other bothersome but fully expected inconvenience of public life'. Richter's comments, though not meant to apply specifically to Leicestershire, would certainly seem to be an apt description of the response of the authorities within that county. During the elections in Leicestershire, there were no riots like those in High Wycombe, but there were a number of violent incidents. One election meeting was broken up when a 'free fight' developed (8.1.1910); another ended in 'uproar' as a result of the actions of over-zealous Tory stewards (10.1.1910); a Liberal worker was struck on the face by a piece of granite whilst driving his car (20.1.1910); a youth was knocked unconscious at another election meeting (12.12.1910); there were reports of stones and pepper being thrown at other election meetings (28.12.1910); whilst violence also occurred at all three of the suffragette meetings which were held during the election campaign in January. On the first two occasions, the women had to abandon their meeting and take refuge in the police station after their dray had been attacked by hostile crowds in Loughborough (5.1.1910 and 11.1.1910) whilst on the third occasion the women were able to complete their meeting, but they had to withstand the throwing of eggs and snowballs in order to do so (25.1.1910). These incidents do not, however, appear to have given rise to any great concern and, indeed, both the *Mercury* and the police singled out for comment not the violence which had occurred, but what they considered to be the good behaviour of the electorate during both elections. Thus during the election in January, the *Mercury* commended local electors for their 'good self-control' (19.1.1910), whilst the Chief Constable expressed his 'thanks and appreciation of the way in which the people had behaved'. Police and public, in the Chief Constable's view, had 'worked together most amicably ... and never in his experience had an election gone through more amicably as far as the general public were concerned' (26.1.1910). Following the December election, the Chief Constable went to Loughborough and similarly expressed his 'appreciation of the exceedingly good conduct of the populace in the town during the election' (14.12.1910).

The response of both the Chief Constable and the *Mercury* would seem to suggest that — possibly on the basis of their previous experience of elections — they had probably expected rather more violence than that which actually occurred. A further indication that violence was expected is provided by the fact that, prior to the announcement of the result of the poll in the city in January, a number of shops in the centre of Leicester boarded up their windows; in the event, however, there was no window breaking. According to the *Mercury*, both before and after the declaration of poll, 'feelings ran high' and there was some 'rough-shouting and pushing' and some 'over-boisterous' behaviour; there was, however, no 'absolute rowdyism' (19.1.1910). The concept of 'absolute rowdyism' is interesting, and the comments of the *Mercury* suggest that a certain amount of disorder was not only expected but, particularly if it did not reach the undefined level of 'absolute' rowdyism, acceptable. What was perceived as the relative absence of rowdyism and violence drew the following light-hearted comment from the *Mercury*:

Torchlight processions were the order of the evening for some time, but there is the disadvantage about a torch that it cannot be used as a weapon of offence without in some measure deteriorating as a means of light giving. (18.1.1910)

The relative lack of concern which the authorities showed towards electoral disorders appears to have been shared by significant sections of the 'respectable' middle classes. Indeed, there is evidence to suggest that such people themselves not infrequently resorted to the use of violence during elections. Thus it is clear that, on occasions, either the candidates or their agents employed as stewards people who were prepared to use 'strong arm' tactics. During an election meeting in Leicester, for example, there was 'uproar' because the Tory stewards were 'far too anxious to go for anyone who made an interruption' (10.1.1910). During the trial of a man who was charged with assaulting a police officer in London, it was said in the man's defence that he had gone on the drink after being 'enlisted', presumably in return for payment, to disturb election meetings (18.1.1910). As we have already noted, the Unionist candidate for Mid-Derbyshire, whom we may reasonably presume was not working class, was convicted of assaulting a member of his audience, whilst a Tory member of Salisbury Town Council was also convicted of assaulting a speaker from the Free Trade Union movement (19.1.1910). In Repton, the election riot did not involve a working-class mob, but three hundred boys from the public school. Moreover, the use of such violence was not in any way condemned by those in whose cause the violence was used. Thus the Unionist version of the riot at Repton was that the boys 'indulged the youthful propensity for mischief', whilst admitting that there was 'a miniature bombardment [of the Liberal committee rooms] with apples, eggs, potatoes and a stone or two', and that the Liberal women had been pelted, not with eggs, but with stones (15.12.1910). The view of the Headmaster of Repton, expressed in a letter to parents, was that reports of the riot had 'a very slender basis in fact. There is no occasion either for distress or anxiety' (20.12.1910). The implication was that the riot, whilst not perhaps being wholly acceptable, was certainly not something about which one should be unduly concerned.

An even more explicit condoning of electoral disorders — at least when these were caused by political allies — occurred in a court case in London in which a fifty-two-year-old nurse was charged with disorderly conduct following a disturbance at a political meeting. The *Mercury* reported the following conversation between the magistrate, Mr Lane, and the defendant:

Mr. Lane: Was it a Liberal meeting?
The Defendant: Yes.

Mr. Lane:	And are you a Conservative?
The Defendant:	Yes.
Mr. Lane:	What was it you objected to? You may be right, and if you are I'll let you go — [laughter]. What did you object to?
The Defendant:	Free Trade.
Mr. Lane:	Quite right; your politics are sound. You may go — [laughter] (10.1.1910)

It would, therefore, be wrong to imagine that political violence was the exclusive prerogative of working-class 'mobs', for the evidence suggests that middle-class people were on occasions also prepared to use violence, as well as other forms of intimidation,[3] and to condone the use of violence. Indeed, it appears that many members of the middle classes, who may well have condemned the use of violence in other contexts, were still prepared, at this time, to see the use of violence within the electoral context as being at least semi-legitimate.

This fact may, at least in part, help to explain the relatively low key approach to the problem of electoral disorders on the part of the authorities. However, for a more adequate explanation, we must examine this problem in developmental terms and this involves a brief analysis of the changing pattern of electoral disorders from the early nineteenth century.

As Stevenson (1979: 286) has pointed out, elections were one of the more persistent sources of popular disorder in nineteenth-century Britain. Following the passage of the First Reform Act, the first generation of reformers had pledged themselves to a policy of 'no treating' and had disavowed electoral violence but, as Gash (1953: 137–53) has argued, the First Reform Act had little immediate impact on the use of the traditional tactics of electoral intimidation and violence. These tactics continued to be a feature of elections throughout the Victorian and Edwardian periods. Richter (1964: 194), for example, has noted that there were disturbances at every general election in the period from 1885–1914.

This should not, however, be taken to indicate that there was no change in the pattern of electoral violence. In the first place, the development of a more centralized system of voting meant that violence tended to focus more on the open hustings during the campaign, and less on the actual polling, a development which was probably associated with the decreased effectiveness of violence and intimidation as means of influencing the final outcome of the vote. Second, one can also identify a process in terms of which violence, intimidation and other forms of electoral malpractice were coming to be seen — albeit very slowly — as less legitimate. This process was symbolized by, for example, the Corrupt Practices Act of 1883, and although the use of violence and intimidation persisted long after the Act had been passed, the level appears to have declined quite markedly in the three decades prior to the First World War. Thus, although the elections of 1910 seem to have been relatively violent affairs by the standards of today, Richter (1964: 194) has suggested that the 'significant fact regarding electoral violence in these three decades preceding 1914 is the reduced number of riots and the great lessening of violence and bloodshed attending them'. Although we believe that Richter underestimates the extent to which violent disturbances continued to be a feature of the elections in 1910,[4] we have no reason to doubt the accuracy of his general claim which is consistent both with the work of other historians and with our own findings indicating a long-term decline in the level of violence. As such, electoral disorders constituted a relatively long-standing or 'traditional' form of political violence, and one which had already begun to decline sharply by the early part of the twentieth century. Electoral violence was, therefore, a declining problem, and it was to play an increasingly less important part in the political violence of the twentieth century. A recognition of the declining significance of this problem, and of the fact that it was increasingly being brought under control is, perhaps, implicit in the comments of both the Chief Constable of Leicestershire and of the *Mercury* following the 1910 elections.

A second consideration which helps to explain the low-key response of the authorities to electoral disorders is that no one appears to have perceived such disorders as a threat to the established political order. It was 'regrettable' if a Conservative meeting was broken up by Liberal supporters, or if a Liberal meeting was broken up by Conservatives,[5] but neither the police nor the government saw such disturbances as a threat to the stability of the political system. In this respect, there was, as we shall see, a sharp contrast between electoral violence and other forms of political violence which have become *relatively* more common in the twentieth century.

A third consideration which probably helps to explain the tolerance of the authorities towards electoral disturbances is that relating to the idea — very widespread in the early part of the century — of the street as a centre of amusement, entertainment and excitement. Just as the street was the focus of children's games, so it was — much more than it is today — also the focus of a good deal of entertainment and excitement for adults. Within this context, the open hustings which were associated with election campaigns were seen as events which were a legitimate source of both amusement and excitement to the onlookers and, as such, they were also a semi-legitimate arena for 'letting off steam'. As the Chairman of the Loughborough Bench put it, it was to be expected that 'people got excited at such times, and there was a little horse-play' (26.1.1910). As a consequence, electoral disturbances — even some of the larger disturbances such as the riot at Repton — were likely to be seen as 'horse-play', as the 'youthful propensity for mischief', as 'over-boisterous' or 'over-enthusiastic' behaviour, rather than being defined as either criminal or subversive actions.

For much the same reason, it can be suggested, the police and the *Mercury* took a fairly permissive view of the violence which was used against the suffragettes. This permissive attitude is, for example, reflected in the relatively light-hearted style in which the *Mercury* reported the violence at suffragette meetings in Leicestershire. Under the heading **'Suffragettes at Loughborough: A Bad Start'**, the *Mercury* (5.1.1910) reported that a crowd had overturned the dray from which the suffragettes were speaking, and that the women had 'slithered' to the ground. The women were eventually forced to take refuge in the police station, for as the *Mercury* put it, in what one can only regard as an understatement, the women's 'position in the crowd was not a happy one'. Three weeks later, the suffragettes held a meeting in Leicester and the *Mercury* reported that after listening to a local parliamentary candidate, 'the crowd returned to the amusement of baiting the suffragettes'. Following the events at Loughborough, the wheels of the dray were on this occasion chained in order to prevent it from being moved, but despite this precaution, a hostile crowd succeeded in pulling the vehicle around the market area with the women on board. The *Mercury* reported that the 'sight of the women moving slowly across the market into the shadow of a gateway, standing on the dray and waving their hands, as if in farewell, was comical in the extreme, and the crowd roared with laughter' (25.1.1910). No arrests were reported from the Loughborough meeting and just one youth who had thrown eggs at the Leicester meeting was 'cautioned' and allowed to go.

We have argued that the violence which was associated with hustings and with other political meetings was a relatively longstanding or 'traditional' form of violence with a relatively high 'expressive' content, that it had already begun to decline sharply by the early years of the twentieth century, and that the police and other authorities adopted a relatively permissive attitude towards it. However, as this form of violence continued to decline, so another form of violence resembling what Tilly has called 'modern' violence, but which we would define as violence of a more 'instrumental' character, came to be relatively more important within the overall spectrum of political violence. As we have seen, though, this increase occurred within the context of an absolute decline in the level of political violence.

The suffragettes were one among a number of groups whose use of violence may be characterized as 'modern' in Tilly's sense, and it is significant that the authorities' attitudes towards the violence used *by* suffragettes showed little of the permissiveness which characterized their attitudes towards the use of violence *against* suffragettes.

The leaders of the suffragettes — most of whom, we might note in passing, were drawn from the 'respectable' middle classes — not only condoned but explicitly advocated the use of violence as a political tactic and there was a good deal of violence which was associated with the suffragette movement. Still confining ourselves to the year 1910, for example, the *Mercury* reported in January that a police officer had died as a result of injuries sustained while trying to quell a suffragette disturbance in Leeds (5.1.1910). Both the Home Secretary, Winston Churchill, and the Irish Secretary, Mr Birrell, were assaulted by suffragettes or their supporters (23.11.1910 and 28.11.1910), while attacks by suffragettes on public buildings, usually involving window breaking, were common. In November, between 300 and 400 women attacked the Prime Minister's residence in Downing Street (23.11.1910).

The use of violence by the suffragettes, unlike the violence which was used against them by hostile crowds, was not viewed simply as 'over-enthusiastic' behaviour, but as something much more serious which was deserving of condemnation. The *Mercury*, for example, argued that the suffragettes' cause would be advanced by public discussion 'rather than by window smashing and face slapping' (12.3.1910), whilst the attack on the Irish Secretary revealed an 'unreasoning frenzy', which 'filled the best friends of the franchise movement with unutterable disgust, and can only have the effect of further retarding the cause it is so fatuously expected to help' (24.11.1910). Moreover, magistrates normally regarded attacks on public buildings as serious offences. The fines which were imposed were relatively heavy by comparison with fines on those involved in assaults at elections,[6] whilst many women were given prison sentences (25.11.1910 and 8.12.1910). In addition, when some of the women went on hunger strike in prison, the House of Commons later agreed to the notorious 'Cat and Mouse' Act in order to ensure that all the women served their full sentence without having to be force-fed by the prison authorities.[7] The authorities clearly regarded the violence of the suffragettes far more seriously than the violence associated with elections.

A similar point can be made about police reactions to some other organizations which were formed for specific political purposes and which either used violence or — equally importantly — were perceived by the police as being likely to use violence. A clear example is provided by the growth of an unemployed workers' movement in Leicester in 1921. On Thursday 29 September a crowd of about 400 gathered outside the Relief Offices, believing relief to have been promised at a meeting earlier that week. When they found out they were mistaken, they became somewhat 'unruly' but were not violent:

> Throughout the proceedings there were moments when the crowd appeared to adopt a threatening attitude, but fortunately no untoward happening took place. (29.9.1921)

It is clear from a reading of the *Mercury* at this time that conflict of some order was expected. There is almost an audible sigh of relief in the newspaper articles when meetings pass off without incident. The realistic character of these fears was amply demonstrated the following day. The events of what came to be known as 'Black Friday' began with a march of the unemployed from the Trades Hall in St James' Street. It proceeded to the Haymarket and then on to the Rupert Street *Guardian* offices. Trouble first started to brew when the unemployed found out that they were not to be allowed to use the Trades Hall in order to hold a meeting. Before moving on to the Haymarket, they were addressed by local politicians who were apparently 'soundly booed':

> and but for the presence of the police it is probable that the hall would have been considerably damaged. (30.9.1921)

Moving on from the Haymarket, the marchers were met by the police at the corner of Halford Street 'and much vocal opposition was directed towards the men in blue'. The real trouble, though, started at Rupert Street where the marchers had gathered. The throwing of a stone through the fanlight of the Relief Offices was the 'flashpoint' (see Chapter 5 below). Unknown to the demonstrators, somewhere between thirty and fifty police officers had been seated inside the Relief Offices well in advance of any disturbance. When the window was broken, the officers drew their batons and set about the task of clearing the street:

> There was a mad stampede. The men in the front had no chance, and the police hit right and left with their batons ... One man, evidently a spectator, was standing near the corner with a cycle. A group rushed into him and they all fell in a heap. The cycle was smashed and some of the men were hit with truncheons. Horse police assisted their colleagues on foot, and soon the street was cleared. The spectacle presented was somewhat gruesome. Men were seen lying around in different parts of the streets bleeding and gesticulating while the police were still doing their duty at the Horsefair end of Rupert Street. Men were running in every direction and women were heard to scream as they witnessed scenes which have not happened for several years. Into shops in the vicinity and every point of

vantage in which shelter could be found did the unemployed and the
spectators who followed them rush. (30.9.1921)

Official figures indicated that ten people were taken to hospital
after this incident but, as the *Mercury* itself pointed out, many who
were cut and bruised were temporarily bandaged in the street or
received attention in local factories.

There are several interesting features in the report of this incident.
The first of these concerns the level of violence used by the police.
Obviously expecting trouble, they had hidden inside the Relief
Offices and as soon as the first stones were thrown by the crowd, they
started to clear the street as quickly as they could. It would seem that
little discrimination was shown when using the baton, for onlookers
and 'participants' seem to have been equally at risk. Second, the
Mercury's response to the violence involved was interesting, for
although the tone of the article conveys a certain sadness that such
scenes should be witnessed in Leicester, it nevertheless enters into a
full description of the events, particularly the actions of the police.
Here again, in its report, the *Mercury* seems to see no apparent
contradiction in suggesting that although 'the men in the front had no
chance' i.e. the police simply hit whoever they came across first, the
latter were described as 'still doing their duty'. The actions of the
police are seen as legitimate and we might note that, although the
police force may have been subjected to violent physical attack both
on this and other occasions, there was no question of their equally
violent response being greeted with anything other than approval by
magistrates and newspapers. Although in a similar situation, the
Recorder of Liverpool censured his city's police for their 'unnecessary violence' in controlling an unemployed demonstration, in
Leicester and most other towns, the level of violence used by the
police, although not explicitly condoned, does not seem to have been
the subject of disapproval or moral opprobrium.[8] The 'permissiveness' that was often shown to those outside the law during the
inter-war years, and which has been noted by Pearson (1983), was, as
we can see, also extended to the forces of law and order. It is
important to note that the actions of the police in Leicester do not
appear to have been in any way unusual. As Pearson (1983: 231–2)
has noted, 'If the British police nowadays have earned a reputation
for occasional brutality and a disregard for civil liberties, it is difficult
to uphold the view that this itself represents a novel deterioration.
Strong arm tactics against demonstrations of the unemployed were
common in the inter-war years.'

The comparison between violence which occurred at election hustings and violence which was associated with movements such as the

suffragettes or unemployed workers reveals some interesting contrasts. Whilst the former was seen essentially as an 'overspill' from an arena which was generally regarded as a legitimate source of entertainment and excitement, the latter was seen as much more directly involving the illegitimate use of violence in pursuit of political ends. The different contexts within which the two forms of violence were located were also associated with different responses to the violence on the part of the police and other authorities. In so far as the former was defined simply as 'over-boisterous' behaviour, it was not seen as a threat to political stability, and could therefore be seen as an 'irritation' but nothing more. In contrast, the latter was much more likely to be defined as subversive, and the subversive label was sufficient to justify a considerably more violent response as in the example of 'Black Friday'.

In summary, we are arguing that there has been a long-term decline in the level and seriousness of collective disorders in the political context. Concomitantly, there has been a decline in the physical vigour with which the authorities respond to them. Such a view, of course, does not rule out shorter-term fluctuations around this general trend. Moreover, within the long-run decline there have occurred subtler movements. In particular, we have highlighted a shift away from more expressive forms of political disorder towards more instrumental ones. Throughout this process there has been a tendency, at any point in time, for the authorities to respond more vigorously to the latter. It also appears that, in the course of this century the authorities and the media have become far more sensitive to political disorder in all its forms, which has helped to place stricter normative limits — both internalized and externally imposed limits — on what constitutes an acceptable public response.

That we seem at present to be at a point in the development of British society characterized by a rise in the level of political disorder does not undermine the soundness of this thesis. It is all too easy to be engulfed by the preoccupations and fears of the moment. In any case, the very fact that these disorders and the police reactions to them are currently generating such a heated public debate contrasts markedly with the not too distant past and testifies to the heightened sensitivities of the times in which we live.

Violence in industry

Our findings indicate a relatively high incidence of collective violence in industrial disputes in the early part of this century. By the late 1920s, the number of violent incidents had begun to decline and, for some forty years thereafter, the incidence of collective violence was at a consistently low level. By the end of the 1960s, the frequency of violent disorders appears to be on the increase, although this never begins to approximate the much higher incidence of collective violence earlier in the century (see Graph 3).

GRAPH 3
Violent industrial disturbances in England, Wales and Scotland as reported by the *Leicester Mercury*, 1900–75 (five-yearly intervals)

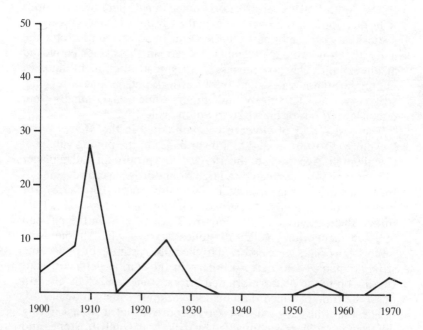

Moreover, not only is it the case that the number of violent incidents was very much higher in the earlier part of the century, it is also the case that the level of violence — as measured by the physical damage inflicted on both persons and property — was also much higher. In this section, we shall illustrate this point by reference to a number of twentieth-century industrial disputes, as reported by the *Mercury*. This will enable us not only to say something about the changing structure of violent industrial disputes, but will also throw some light on changing public perceptions of industrial violence, as evidenced by the changing style of reporting of the *Mercury*, and on changes in police tactics associated with the use of violence in industrial disputes.

In order to bring out some of the salient characteristics of industrial violence in the early part of this century, we shall focus on two industrial disputes, one of which is well-known to labour historians, the other far less so. The more famous is the strike of some 30,000 miners in the South Wales coalfield in 1910–11. Although violence was recorded from many parts of the coalfield, the violence is generally referred to as 'the Tonypandy Riots', on the basis of incidents which occurred in that village in early November. The other, much less well-known dispute, is that involving a lock-out of fishermen at Grimsby docks in September 1901.

The South Wales coal strike originated in a dispute over the price to be paid for working a new seam in the Ely pit, which was owned by a subsidiary of Cambrian Collieries Ltd. In an attempt to force the issue, the owners on 1 September, locked out all 800 men employed at the Ely pit. This action caused widespread resentment amongst miners in South Wales, and the local lock-out became a regional strike on 1 November. By mid-winter, some 30,000 miners were either locked-out or on strike in South Wales.

The first report of violence was contained in the *Mercury* of 2 November 1910. It related to a disturbance in the mining village of Cwmllynfell. According to the *Mercury*, the proprietor and manager of a local pit were assailed by a large stone-throwing crowd, some of the stones striking the proprietor. It was also reported that a revolver had been fired, though it resulted in no injuries. The strikers then turned their attention to the 'imported' workers down the pit, and 'greeted them with a volley of stones' as they left. Although the imported workers were escorted to the railway station by police, the strikers 'managed to make a breach in the station defences, and, rushing on to the platform, rained bricks, stones and clods of earth upon the train in which the pursued workmen sought refuge'.

The following day, the *Mercury* reported that a train carrying non-striking colliers was attacked by strikers at Tonllyd. 'Stones and other missiles were thrown, and many windows in the train were smashed. The passengers took flight, but were pursued by the strikers, and there was much wrestling and fighting. Many of the contestants were thrown to the ground and several had almost every scrap of clothing torn from them. At another part of the valley houses of several petty officials employed at the Powell-Duffryn collieries were attacked, and windows smashed' (3.11.1910).

Four days later, the *Mercury* reported that, at the Clydach Vale pit, the police — including some mounted police — had been 'powerless' to stop a large crowd of strikers who pelted 'blacklegs' and police with stones and other missiles. Several police officers were injured, and it was decided to draft in an extra eighty police from Swansea. In addition, an application was made to the military authorities for cavalry to aid the civil power (7.11.1910).

On the following day, it was reported that a crowd of 5,000 strikers had gathered outside the Glamorgan colliery, which was guarded by just twenty police. The crowd stoned the police, and then rushed them, sweeping them aside 'as though they were so many flies', and took control of the electricity power station inside the colliery. Later that day, police reinforcements, including mounted police, were called in and the strikers were dislodged, but only after skirmishes which resulted in many injuries to strikers and police. An inspector from Bristol was reported to have suffered serious head injuries, and it was agreed to send 300 Metropolitan police, including mounted officers, to the area (8.11.1910).

Incidents of this kind continued to be reported throughout November 1910 and, less frequently, in December. It was reported that, at Penycraig and Clydach Vale, strikers had broken into the colliery and put out the boiler fires, thus preventing the ventilating fans from working, whilst strikers also attempted to divert a mountain stream as a way of cutting off the water supply for the boilers (8.11.1910 and 11.11.1910). There were numerous reports of stones, bricks and other missiles being thrown at 'blacklegs', and at colliery officials and colliery property. Houses of colliery officials were attacked, windows, ornaments and furniture were broken and, on one occasion, furniture at a colliery official's home was removed and set alight in the street (21.11.1910 and 23.11.1910). On 14 November, it was reported that 100 pounds of high explosives, together with detonators and fuses had been stolen, whilst a week later, the *Mercury* reported that an attempt to blow up the house of a colliery official had been foiled by police action (21.11.1910). At Trealaw, it was decided to house colliery officials on the premises as the only means of offering them adequate protection (22.11.1910). The police were frequently on the receiving end of missiles thrown by crowds of strikers, whilst at the end of November, the home of a local policeman was attacked following an alleged assault on a small group of strikers by police (28.11.1910).

These events provided the violent context to the 'Tonypandy Riots' proper, the most serious of which took place on 8 November 1910, though there was a second outbreak of rioting in Tonypandy later in the month. The events of 8 November began with a conflict between strikers and police at the Glamorgan Colliery power station, where strikers were attempting to prevent 'blacklegs' from entering the colliery. The events which followed were described by the *Mercury*:

> At the Glamorgan Colliery power station the fight waged fiercely for a long time. Every window in the place and the surrounding buildings was smashed, and other extensive damage done. The police drove out the strikers and pursued them through the streets of Llwynpia. The rioters

pulled down a large hoarding and used the wood as staves. Colliers'
mandrils were also employed as weapons, and the men demolished a brick
and stone pillar at an hotel and assailed the police with the debris. The
vicinity was like a battlefield. Men were lying about unconscious with
gaping scalp wounds, and doctors were kept busy for some time attending
to the wounded. Over 100 severe casualties were reported, and many
more persons received minor injuries. About 20 policemen were hurt in
the affray, which surpassed in ferocity anything else of the kind that has
occurred in the coalfield.

. . . some of the strikers emerged without hats, but with gaping wounds
in their heads, and blood flowing freely. In one place a number of men
who took part in the conflict were observed lying on the ground bespattered with blood, and wounded in the head and face.

The strikers tore down a huge hoarding, and used the wood as weapons
against the police. Some of the latter lost helmets and batons, which the
strikers used themselves. Large stones were hurled at the police, who
retaliated with furious charges. Some of the combatants are seriously
injured, but no deaths have yet occurred.

When the strikers eventually withdrew to Tonypandy, there was
widespread looting, with 'practically every shop in the place being
entered by numbers of strikers, and everything of a portable character taken away, even windows being emptied, the shopkeepers being
powerless to prevent the depredations'. In Tonypandy Square 'not a
shop window is unbroken, and what remains of tradesmen's goods
lay scattered about' (9.11.1910).

Later in the month, further rioting broke out at Tonypandy railway
station after the police had refused to allow strikers to picket the
station and examine passenger trains for 'blacklegs'. It was reported
that, 'Showers of huge stones fell on the police, a dozen of whom
were injured. One is in a critical condition, while a Metropolitan
police officer, who was rendered unconscious . . . was in a grave
condition. A considerable number of strikers must have suffered
severely at the hands of the police, who had repeatedly to charge
them with their batons' (22.11.1910).

By the end of November 1910, reports of violent clashes between
strikers, 'blacklegs' and police had begun to decline quite sharply,
although isolated incidents of violence continued to be reported for
some time afterwards. By the end of November, however, 'order' of
some kind had been restored, but only after 800 infantry and 200
cavalry had been moved into the area and placed on standby. The
soldiers only came into contact with strikers on one occasion, when
they used bayonets to disperse a stone-throwing crowd.

How many people were injured in the riots is not known, but the
number almost certainly ran into several hundreds. After the events
in Tonypandy of 8 November alone, it was reported that there were

over 100 severe casualties, with many more people receiving minor injuries (9.11.1910). In a statement later in the month, the Home Secretary, Winston Churchill, found

> on inquiry that in the Tonypandy district 15 police constables were so severely injured in the recent colliery disturbances that they had to be relieved from duty and sent home to Cardiff, and elsewhere 40 other constables were less severely injured, and were relieved from active duty for a time ... In the Aberavon district six constables were injured and relieved from active duty, but all had since resumed it, although one was only fit for office work ... More than 30 Metropolitan constables were injured, some of them severely, and there were also considerable casualties among the local police. (22.11.1910)

These figures were issued after the second outbreak of rioting at Tonypandy, but before it was known how many additional injuries there had been as a result of that renewed rioting. Casualties amongst strikers are unknown, but were almost certainly very much heavier than those amongst the police. One striker, Samuel Hayes, died as a result of injuries received during the riots, and Keir Hardie claimed that Hayes had been 'killed by a policeman', though the inquest jury apparently found that 'the evidence was not clear as to how deceased received his injuries' (16.12.1910). That the police used considerable force, however, is indicated when early in December, the Chief Constable of Glamorgan, Captain Lindsay, presented a bill for 300 police truncheons, 'which he had had to obtain to replace those damaged at the Aberaman and Rhondda Valley riots' (12.12.1910).

Turning to the lock-out of fishermen and engineers at Grimsby docks in 1901, it is clear that, although the violence was spread over a much more limited period than in South Wales — most of the serious rioting at Grimsby appears to have taken place within a couple of days — there were nevertheless a number of important similarities between the two situations. As in South Wales, an important spark which ignited the riots appears to have been provided by the employment of 'blackleg' labour. In both cases the rioters adopted stone-throwing as a major tactic, there was substantial damage to property, and many casualties were reported following major clashes with the police. Finally, in both situations, the riots were only contained following the drafting-in of large numbers of policemen from outside the area, and after troops had been moved in and placed on alert.

In Grimsby, a dispute over wage rates resulted in a lock-out of fishermen and engineers in early July 1901. By early August, it was reported that 12,000 men were locked out and that 'destitution is increasing, the relief committee being besieged daily by necessitous applicants' (8.8.1901). Despite the obvious hardship suffered by the workers and their families, the dispute was almost entirely peaceful up to the middle of September, with just two relatively minor incidents involving violence reported towards the end of August. In the middle of September, however, the dispute took a new and considerably more violent turn.

On 12 September, the *Mercury* reported that the owners were seeking to engage Norwegian captains and engineers to sail their ships. Four days later, a meeting of workers was told that the owners had received an offer from someone in Norway to provide an unlimited number of hands at lower wages than those which had been paid to the Grimsby workers. They were presumably disconcerted by this news, for it was pointed out that if the owners accepted the offer it would mean 'almost the total exclusion of the Grimsby skippers and engineers from the vessels' (16.9.1901). The temperature probably did not improve the following day when it was reported that the first batch of 1,500 summonses was being sent out for non-payment of rates (17.9.1901), many of the summonses presumably going to fishermen, and engineers who had been on strike for two-and-a-half months.

The first serious outbreak of rioting was reported the next day. The trouble began when those locked-out became 'inflamed' after discovering that a 'blackleg' crew, together with two engineers from Bradford, had been hired to take out a trawler. A crowd of some 10,000 people surrounded the offices of the Owners' Federation and smashed 'every window in the place'. Then, some members of the crowd, 'upon learning that the owners were holding a meeting, broke inside, and in a few minutes had wrecked the whole of the interior. The offices had only been refurbished this week, and the damage done amounts to hundreds of pounds. The dock police, some dozen in number, were powerless to intervene.' The report went on to say that, 'Only the four walls of the huge building remain, and the whole of the interior, comprising most costly fittings, have been pulled out, strewn on the roadway, and smashed to atoms . . . Some members of the Federation, who were holding a meeting at the time only escaped the fury of the mob by smashing a window at the rear and jumping out' (18.9.1901).

More rioting was reported the following day, when a large crowd assembled outside the old offices of the Owners' Federation and stormed the building. There was, apparently, little furniture inside, and 'the crowd had to rest content with hurling bricks through the windows'. An appeal for order from the Chief Constable was greeted with ironical cheers, and the crowd, 'many thousands in number, went next to the office of Hagerup, Doughty & Co., and here the whole of the windows were smashed. The offices face the pontoon and hundreds of men climbed the pontoon roof and hurled missiles' (19.9.1901).

In the afternoon of the same day, the first contingent of police from outside the area, some eighty men from Sheffield, arrived and marched to the docks, where an angry crowd of several thousands had been stoning the offices of Gretten Brothers. However, as the police approached the offices of another company, they were 'greeted with a hostile demonstration. Stones were flying about in all directions, and the police had to duck to escape the missiles. It being evident that persuasion would be of no avail, they drew their bludgeons and charged the crowd, which dispersed in all directions ... though not before several men had fallen from blows by the policemen's staves, and a number of injuries had been inflicted on others' (20.9.1901).

During the evening, the police were further reinforced by a second contingent of seventy-seven officers from Sheffield, and by the arrival of 100 soldiers from the Lincolnshire Regiment, each armed with rifle, bayonet, and twenty rounds of ammunition. Further disturbances that evening led to the Riot Act being read by Mr Joseph Hewson, who was presumably a local magistrate. However, by this time the crowd was in a 'most infuriated state. No sooner did Mr. Hewson mount a wagonette to commence reading than showers of stones were sent flying in all directions', and the police drew their staves and charged the crowd. Following this incident, a fire broke out in one of the docks, the presumption being that the fire had been started deliberately, since it was in close proximity to a timber yard owned by Mr Hewson. Throughout the evening, there was a heavy police presence on the streets and, up to a late hour, the town remained 'in a turbulent state', but no further major incidents were reported (20.9.1901). The military, however, were not withdrawn until the end of the month, presumably as a precautionary measure.

It is difficult to give a precise estimate of the number of persons injured in the two days of rioting in Grimsby, but it is clear that there were many casualties. The *Mercury* indicated that a number of police officers had been injured, and there were fears that some children had been hurt, one of whom was reported as serious. An inquiry at the local hospital revealed that twenty people had been admitted as a result of injuries received in the rioting whilst, in addition, a 'large number' of persons were treated by local doctors. That there was a considerable number of casualties is also indicated by the fact that one of the offices on the fish docks was converted into a temporary hospital for the treatment of those injured in the rioting (20.9.1901).

It is useful to look at two specific aspects of the violence in Grimsby and South Wales: the role of the police and other authorities, and public attitudes towards violence and the control of violence as evidenced by the reporting style of the *Mercury*.

With reference to the former, it is clear that the local police had insufficient resources to deal with major disturbances involving several thousand people especially when, as in the case of the violence in South Wales, that violence was spread over quite a large area. Geary (1985: 28) has calculated that by 9 November 1910, the Chief Constable of Glamorgan had at his disposal some 1,400 officers, but of this total, some 800 had been drawn from the Metropolitan Police, so that the number of local police probably did not exceed about 600. If this was so, then police resources must have been spread extremely thinly on the ground in a situation in which violence could — and did — occur in a number of settings: at several different collieries in the area, for example, on the route taken by 'blacklegs' between the collieries and the railway station; at the railway station itself and at neighbouring stations; at other points on the line such as level crossings, where trains could be stopped; and in the villages and towns where the houses of colliery officials were at risk. This may well be why, during the first week or so of the riots, there were a number of reports which indicated that the police presence was simply too small to control large crowds of rioters, and on some occasions the police were quite obviously over-run. Thus the power station at the Glamorgan colliery, which had clearly been identified as a possible target for the strikers, was guarded by just twenty policemen. As we have seen, a crowd of some 5,000 simply swept the police aside 'as though they were so many flies'.

A not dissimilar situation existed at Grimsby prior to the arrival of police and army reinforcements in the town. Thus when rioters destroyed windows and furnishings at the offices of the Owners' Federation, it was reported that the dock police 'some dozen in number, were powerless to intervene' (18.9.1901). Moreover, those involved in the rioting may well have been aware of the limited police resources available locally. When rioting resumed on the following day, the Chief Constable arrived with a dozen officers, and begged the crowd to desist, stating that if they did not do so, he would have to send for reinforcements. His comments were apparently greeted with ironical cheers, and cries of 'Where will they come from?' (19.9.1901)

The events in Grimsby and South Wales would also seem to suggest that the collection of intelligence by police at the local level was probably still relatively unorganized and rudimentary. Thus in both situations the police appear to have been quite unprepared for the violence, at least in the early stages of the riots. Presumably they were either not expecting violence or, if they were, they judged incorrectly that they could cope without outside help.

Moreover, at least in South Wales, senior police officers appear not to have anticipated the possibility that the violence could spread after the first rioting had taken place. Following the first reports of rioting in Cwmllynfell, during which a revolver was fired, the Home Secretary, Winston Churchill, contacted the Chief Constables of Glamorgan and Merthyr Tydfil for a report on the situation. The former replied that 'no serious damage' had been done, whilst the latter replied: 'all peaceable and no disturbance in Borough' and added that 'I have no reason to apprehend any breach of the peace' (Geary, 1985: 26).

If, as seems probable, local police intelligence was deficient, this is perhaps not altogether surprising. In South Wales, for example, the Chief Constable of Glamorgan was a close personal friend of the manager of the Glamorgan Colliery with whom he frequently dined and whose advice he often took on policing matters. However, as Geary has commented, the employers 'proved a particularly unreliable source of information'. General Macready, who was in charge of the troops in the area, was later to describe the information he had received from the employers as 'worthless' (Geary, 1985: 36–8).

Given what has been said above, it may at first sight seem contradictory to suggest that Geary (1985: 39) is nevertheless probably correct to argue that the Tonypandy Riots were associated with a significant development towards a 'relatively sophisticated and centrally controlled intelligence network'. In fact no contradiction is involved. Thus whilst Geary provides persuasive evidence in support of his argument, it is important to emphasize, firstly, that this intelligence network came into existence as a *response* to the early violence, and that it did not exist in *advance* of the early rioting; secondly, that the initiative for the establishment of this network came not from the local police, but from the Home Office and War Office; thirdly, that the whole intelligence network was coordinated and controlled not locally, but centrally from London. It is equally significant that the major figures in this intelligence network — army officers who analysed reports, rumours and requests for troops, two Welsh-speaking CID officers from Scotland Yard, and a 'confidential' Home Office official — were all brought in from outside the locality, and that the central coordinator in South Wales appears to have been, not the Chief Constable of Glamorgan, but General Macready (Geary, 1985: 38–9). It seems that one of the functions of the Home Office official was to provide Churchill with an early warning of any serious confrontations. However effective this system may have become in the course of the strike, it seems clear that there was no such effective early warning system in operation at the beginning. Nevertheless, it is important to note that the development of a more organized and centralized system of intelligence gathering did mark a significant step towards a more interventionist policy on the part of government in an attempt to control not only industrial violence, but also the non-violent forms of social disruption which were associated with major industrial disputes.

The third point to be made about the police is that, at this time, police tactics were relatively crude, the baton-charge still being the standard public order tactic. This tactic was not only a relatively violent one, but, equally importantly, one which appears to have involved the relatively indiscriminate use of violence. As *The Times* (9.11.1910) commented during the Tonypandy Riots: 'That the police are using their batons with effect is obvious from the number of bandaged and bleeding ears which are to be seen. They have no time to discriminate and it is a case of "Whenever you see a head hit it!" '

Closely associated with this is that police action during riots appears to have been oriented primarily towards the administration of 'instant justice' in the form of a blow with a police baton, rather than towards the administration of justice through the apprehension of rioters and the bringing of charges in the courts. By the end of 1910, the *Mercury* had reported a total of nineteen people who had been arrested in connection with the riots, the charges against six of these being dismissed. When one considers that there were numerous violent disorders in South Wales, that they continued for most of November, and that a number of the riots involved several thousand people, what is perhaps most striking is the relatively small number of prosecutions which followed. In the case of the Grimsby riots, the orientation of the police towards 'instant justice' rather than towards the administration of justice through the courts was even more clear. Within the context of the large amount of damage which was done and the considerable number of injuries which were inflicted on both police and rioters, it is revealing that the *Mercury* reported, 'Acting probably on instructions, the police have not made any arrests' (20.9.1901).

'Instant justice' then was, at best, very 'rough justice' and there were numerous accusations — and some evidence to support those accusations — that police action on occasions amounted to the administration of violent injustice. We shall return to this point in the following section, in which we consider the manner in which the riots were reported by the *Mercury*.

At the outset, it should be made clear that the *Mercury* never supported the actions of the rioters and that, in general terms, it was sympathetic towards the police and the troops who were trying to restore order. However, having said this, what is particularly striking to the modern reader is the relatively even-handed and unsensational style, not only of the *Mercury*'s reporting, but also of its editorials on the subject. Thus whilst the *Mercury*'s prejudices occasionally showed through in its reference to the crowd as 'the mob', the use of such pejorative terms is not very prominent. A crowd of rioters is more usually referred to simply as 'the crowd' or 'the strikers', whilst on occasion a single relatively neutral term — 'combatants' — is used to refer to policemen, strikers and 'blacklegs' alike.

In general, the *Mercury*'s coverage of the riots was extremely detailed and often consisted of a 'blow by blow' account which managed to convey something of the sense of excitement which must have surrounded the events. It is important to emphasize, however, that these detailed reports were almost entirely descriptive of events. There is a general absence of comment on what happened. More particularly, no real attempt is made to denigrate either side in a dispute, and there is a general absence of questioning of the motives of either rioters or police.

Moreover, although the *Mercury* was generally sympathetic towards the police, there is no evidence to suggest that this prevented the newspaper from publishing news items which might have given rise to criticism of the police. In the description of the Tonypandy Riots, there was no attempt to conceal the level of violence used by the police, and no attempt to underplay the number or the seriousness of the injuries inflicted on strikers. Indeed, the report contains a vivid description of strikers with 'gaping wounds in their heads and blood flowing freely', and of other strikers 'lying on the ground bespattered with blood'. In similar fashion, following the Grimsby riots, the *Mercury* reported that there was 'considerable indignation at the action of the police in charging the crowd before the Riot Act was read'. After documenting the number of injuries, the *Mercury* commented, 'In not a few cases tradesmen who were quietly observing the scene were attacked. A regrettable feature of the charge was the number of women who suffered from the indiscriminate rush. In another instance an old man was twice struck with a truncheon, although he begged to be protected. Several children suffered in the melee, and a boy named Sproston was seriously injured' (20.9.1901). Quite clearly, the *Mercury*'s generally supportive position in relation to the police did not prevent it from publishing, in a more or less straightforward fashion, as much detailed information as it could obtain. Indeed, the *Mercury*'s lack of selectivity in terms of what it reported is one of the prominent features of the paper at this time.

The relatively even-handed coverage of the riots by the *Mercury* may also be illustrated by the way in which the paper dealt with the Tonypandy Riots in the three editorials it published. Whilst the editorials make clear the *Mercury*'s general support for the police and the troops, they are all characterized by a relatively low key approach and a degree of restraint which appears all the more remarkable given the levels of violence which were reported. On 8 November, for example, the *Mercury* devoted a short part of its editorial column to the subject and began, 'There are reports of exciting scenes in connection with the dispute in the South Wales coal field. Men, women and children have joined in demonstrations initiated by those on strike, and though some of them were good humoured, there is always a danger lest some untoward incident should create ill-feeling, and disturbances difficult to quell without regrettable use of force. And such untoward incidents are unfortunately reported.' The editorial added, 'Below all this unrest there are no doubt causes that ought to be seriously considered, but an atmosphere of violence is not favourable to this course.'

The following day, in another short section of its editorial column, the paper referred to the violence, which by this time included street rioting, looting of shops, wrecking of property and attacks on the police, and argued that there were clearly limits to what could be tolerated, 'and that those limits have *very nearly* been reached' (our emphasis). In the following paragraph, the *Mercury* did use the emotive term 'outrages', and argued that the likely effect of the violence would be 'to deprive men of the sympathy which might otherwise be extended towards them'. However, the editorial recognized that 'at the same time, men and women do not act in this way save under strong impulses, and to what are they due? It is essential to think of that even while taking the most adequate steps to preserve order, and public liberty' (9.11.1910).

In its final editorial on 10 November 1910, the *Mercury* said that the government could not reasonably accede to a request from the Miners' Federation to withdraw the military from the coalfields. However, once again, the editorial concluded that 'while order must be preserved we ought to search out and discover the causes of the trouble, so that they may be removed. The best way, in fact, of striking at effects is to get rid of the causes of them.'

The editorials were characterized by a general absence of sensationalism and, while the paper supported the preservation of public order, there is also implicit in the editorials a degree of sympathy for the position of the 'men', and a clear recognition of the need to investigate thoroughly the deeply held grievances which led them to behave in a violent fashion. Most particularly, there is a conspicuous absence of any attempt to attack the motives or the character of the strikers, or to denigrate them in any way. These points should be borne in mind as we examine the *Mercury*'s coverage of more recent industrial disputes involving violence.

Our data indicate that in the period following the First World War, and particularly from the mid-1920s, there was a sharp decline in the number of violent industrial disputes. They also suggest that the number of such disputes remained at a very low level for some forty years thereafter. This conclusion is consistent with that reached by Cronin (1979: 53) who, although concerned with industrial conflict generally rather than with the more specific area of industrial violence, has suggested that 'the real significance of the General Strike was that it served to bring in an extremely long period of industrial peace. Between 1926 and the mid-1950s, workers seemed to put aside the strike weapon in all but a few cases.' The establishment of a more 'orderly' system of industrial relations was associated with a changing pattern of relationships between government, trades unions and employers organizations which has generally been characterized as involving the institutionalization of industrial conflict or, as Middlemas (1979) has called it, the development of a structure of 'corporate bias'.

There is some evidence to suggest that, certainly by the late 1960s, this long-established pattern of institutionalization of conflict was beginning to destabilize and that, associated with this process, there was not only an increase in the total number of strikes but also — and more directly relevant to our concern — an increase in the number of industrial disputes involving the use of violence. In order to illustrate some of the differences between violent disputes which took place during this period and those which took place in the period around the First World War, we shall examine one of the major industrial disputes of the early 1970s, namely the national miners' strike of 1972 which was widely perceived at the time to have involved unacceptable levels of violence. As with our previous examples, our examination will focus on three interrelated problems, namely the amount and type of violence which was involved, the role of the police and the style in which the *Mercury* reported events.

The miners' strike which began on 9 January 1972 was the first national coal strike in Britain since 1926. The strike was called in pursuit of a wage claim, and followed a ballot of all miners which resulted in a 58 per cent vote in favour of strike action. The first few weeks of the strike were, by almost any standards, fairly peaceful. However, it is interesting to note that, in the absence of anything other than a few isolated and relatively minor incidents of violence, the *Mercury* still reported developments in a way which conveyed the idea that the strike was taking place within an atmosphere of violence. For example, just three days after the strike began, the *Mercury*'s major front page story was headlined 'Pickets Clash with "Blackleg" Safety Crew'. According to the *Mercury*, the Measham pit in Leicestershire was the scene of a 'confrontation' between pickets and five men who reported for duty on safety and maintenance work. However, despite the violent connotations of the term 'clash', a careful reading of the story indicates that the 'clash' or 'confrontation' involved nothing more than when the five men reported for duty, they faced 'the condemnation of their colleagues'. Despite the headline, there was no indication of any violence having been used, and the local secretary of the National Union of Mineworkers explained that the picket had been successful 'to the extent that a number of the employees who were on their way to work turned round their cars and went away after the miners had talked to them' (12.1.1972).

A week later, the *Mercury* carried another front page story on the strike. It appeared under the headline, 'Coal Lorry Drivers Intimidated, Say Hauliers'. The story began:

> Lorry drivers moving coal during the miners' strike have had their vehicles damaged and have been intimidated, and the owners of the trucks have had threats made to them that their premises will be damaged . . . it was alleged today. (19.1.1972)

The allegations were made by a representative of the Leicester sub-area of the Road Haulage Association, who claimed there had been 'at least eight cases of malicious damage to vehicles, ranging from the smashing of windows and the ripping out of fuel pipes to the letting down of tyres and the slamming of gates against vehicle radiators'. The rest of the front page story was given over to a detailed statement of these and other similar allegations. On an inside page, however, where the story was continued, the *Mercury* printed a statement from the local NUM secretary who emphasized the peaceful nature of the picketing and said that the allegations were 'completely untrue as far as Leicestershire is concerned'. The report gave no indication that any of the alleged incidents had been reported to the police.

On 27 January, the *Mercury* reported that a group of what later came to be called 'flying pickets' had come to Leicestershire from South Derbyshire, and that they had prevented the operation of a scheme, in which the Leicestershire NUM had agreed to cooperate, which involved the distribution of coal to the sick and elderly and to retired miners. The *Mercury* referred to the Derbyshire men as picket 'invaders' and, in an editorial headed 'Hard Men', it claimed they had achieved their goal, 'not by the peaceful picketing the law allows, not by persuasive argument with the Leicestershire pickets and the lorry drivers, but by callous intimidation'. The picket 'invaders' were, it said 'rampaging rebels' who 'should be brought to book'.

In the light of these comments, it is perhaps worth emphasizing that, nowhere in the *Mercury* is there any indication that the South Derbyshire men used any physical violence against either people or property.

On the following day, however, the *Mercury* was able to report what appears to be a rather more adequately documented instance of violence, though the participation of miners in the incident is not altogether clear. The paper reported that, in Bolton, the Employment Minister, Robert Carr, had been 'jostled' by what it called an 'angry demo mob' of 200 demonstrators, 'mostly miners'. The report indicated that, as Mr Carr left an employment exchange,

> The crowd surged forward ... and demonstrators banged on his vehicle with placards. Police struggled to clear a path.
> Two demonstrators ran alongside his car and hammered on the side windows as it stopped at traffic lights.
> Motor cycle police surged forward to clear them away and an outrider halted traffic to allow the procession to drive through at red. (28.1.1972)

Outside of Leicestershire, there were one or two other isolated examples of the use of violence which were not reported in the *Mercury*. In Nottinghamshire, a shop selling pre-packed coal had its windows smashed, and four pickets were arrested, two in Staffordshire and two in Dover (Geary, 1985: 71). Despite the relatively isolated and minor nature of these incidents, however, the leaders of the NUM were clearly becoming concerned at the damaging publicity and the NUM President, Joe Gormley, appealed for peaceful picketing (Geary, 1985: 71). The peaceful nature of the picketing had, in fact, been stressed by the local leaders of the NUM in Leicestershire from the very beginning of the strike. In denying the allegations made by the Road Haulage Association, the Leicestershire NUM Secretary said, 'Our pickets have been carefully chosen as men of stability and character. They wear armbands and they have been instructed to, and do, to the best of our knowledge, operate entirely within the law' (19.1.1972).

Occasional acts of violence continued to be reported. However, it was, perhaps, the events of early February 1972, when mass picketing closed the Saltley Coke Depot in Birmingham, which did most to create the image of a violent strike.

The mass picket at Saltley followed immediately upon an incident which appears to have contributed towards a significant increase in tension on the picket lines. On 3 February, Fred Matthews, a miner from Yorkshire, was killed by a lorry outside a power station near Scunthorpe. The non-unionist driver of the lorry drove his vehicle through the picket line at high speed, mounted the pavement and hit Matthews. The death of Matthews led to a good deal of anger amongst miners, and may well have been associated with an increased determination on their part to prevent lorries from crossing picket lines in future. In any event, the mass picket of Saltley began the day after Matthews' death.

The Saltley Coke Depot was of particular significance because it was the last big fuel store left in the Midlands and it contained a huge stockpile of 100,000 tons, and several hundred loaded lorries had been leaving the depot every day during the strike. The mass picket began on 4 February and ended on 10 February, but the most violent days were the three days of 7–9 February.

On 7 February, the *Mercury*, under the headline, 'Policeman Hurt in Clash with 500 Miners', reported that:

> A policeman and a civilian were injured and several miners arrested in clashes between police and pickets at a giant coke depot in Birmingham today.
>
> There were violent scenes as 300 police, arms linked, tried to hold back more than 500 miners attempting to stop lorries entering and leaving . . .
>
> Lorries from all parts of Britain were queueing when the gates opened this morning but the miners, hurling pies, fruit and eggs, turned most of them away.
>
> The first clashes came when two lorries broke through the picket lines.
>
> A young policeman, named as PC Rusk, was punched in the stomach and was taken to hospital by ambulance.
>
> A few minutes later helmets were knocked off as police struggled with strikers closing in on one of the departing lorries loaded with coke.
>
> A man lying down in the lorry's path was hauled to safety by police.
>
> He was released but, seconds later, lay down again in front of the second lorry which was leaving the depot in a hail of missiles, including half-bricks.

It should be noted that the *Mercury*'s coverage appears to have been based on reports which were probably received during the morning of 7 February, for later estimates indicate that, by midday, the number of pickets had increased to about 2,000, and that these were faced by some 400 policemen. Both the number of arrests and the number of injuries also increased during the course of the day. The final count indicated that twenty-one pickets had been arrested, and nine people injured, eight of them being police officers (Geary, 1985: 77).

On the following day, the depot was similarly protected by a cordon of 400 policemen who faced some 2,000 pickets, with the pickets periodically trying to break through the police cordon in an attempt to stop any lorry which tried to enter the depot. A further eighteen arrests were made that day, and eighteen more people, six of them police, were injured. The most serious injury appears to have been that sustained by a Chief Inspector who received a fractured thigh when a lorry accelerated towards the depot gates (Geary, 1985: 75–7).

On 9 February, the *Mercury* carried a front page picture of a policeman lying on the ground after a scuffle with pickets, and it reported a further twenty-five arrests at the Saltley Coke Depot. Four injuries were also reported, two of them to police officers.

It was on the following day that the Saltley Depot was finally closed following a huge picket involving some 15,000 people. Although the police numbers had been doubled to 800, it was clear that no lorries could get through, and the Chief Constable of Birmingham finally agreed to close the gates of the depot in the interests of public safety. Having closed what was a major centre for the distribution of fuel, the miners now found themselves in a relatively strong position. The strike was by now becoming increasingly effective, and the NUM was shortly afterwards able to reduce its picket lines to a token presence. The strike finally ended on 25 February on terms largely favourable to the miners following the report of a Court of Inquiry headed by Lord Wilberforce.

If we examine the amount and the type of violence which was associated with the dispute, it is immediately apparent that there were indeed a number of incidents which clearly involved the use of violence. Equally, it is clear that the strike involved a variety of forms of illegal behaviour, of which obstruction was probably the most common, although Geary's data also indicate that many pickets saw the immobilization of vehicles as a legitimate tactic. It is important, however, to place this violence in context and, in particular, it is important to bear in mind that, unlike the two earlier strikes, the miners' strike of 1972 was not a local affair, but a national strike which involved the picketing of a very large number of separate sites. Thus the miners did not only picket NCB offices and all collieries owned by the NCB: they also picketed private mines and quarries which produced coal, either as their main product or as a by-product. In addition, virtually all power stations appear to have been picketed, together with those sites such as docks and coal or coke depots which were central to the distribution of coal. Given this situation, it is clear that the violent incidents we have described were not typical of the picket lines and that the great majority of the picketing was conducted in a peaceful manner, a fact which was explicitly acknowledged by the Home Secretary, Reginald Maudling (Geary, 1985: 77).

A second point — though this does not emerge very clearly from the *Mercury* reports — is that there is evidence to suggest that most pickets made a clear distinction between the use of violence against people and the use of violence against property, particularly property in the form of lorries. This point is perhaps most clearly brought out in the interview data which Geary obtained from NUM members who had been involved in the strike, most of whom regarded lorries as a legitimate target for sabotage in a whole variety of ways. Violence directed against people was, however, a different matter, the general viewpoint being best summed up by one NUM officer who said:

> Violence to people doesn't really get you anywhere; then again, it depends on your classification of violence. Shouting at people, waving at them, and to some extent spitting on them, although I don't agree with that, just making a noise trying to upset or frighten them, yes, but not physical violence. (Geary, 1985: 92)

'Physical violence', in this definition, clearly did not include obstructing police or 'blacklegs', which was regarded as an acceptable tactic within the context of the dispute, but there appears to have been very little support for anything more violent than this.

Thus it seems that, although the pickets were certainly prepared to use violence in various forms, this violence was clearly limited by a more-or-less implicit but widely held belief on their part that, whereas certain forms of violence were acceptable, there were also limits beyond which the use of violence was taboo. That pickets generally accepted these self-imposed limits is probably important in understanding why relationships between pickets and police were generally characterized by a relatively high degree of tolerance and cooperation (Geary, 1985: 93–4). By comparison with the levels of violence used in industrial disputes earlier this century, the level of violence associated with the 1972 miners' strike — despite the fact that it was seen at the time as a violent dispute — was actually relatively low. The most revealing point is perhaps that, even during the most violent phase of the dispute outside the Saltley Coke Depot, the major form of violence appears to have been what has been described as 'pushing and shoving'. This type of action was not unusual during the strike, although it usually took place on a much smaller scale than at Saltley. It is also worth emphasizing that very few of Geary's respondents who took part in the strike either had experience of or were prepared to advocate personal violence in excess of pushing and shoving. The use of this form of limited violence is perhaps best put into perspective by Geary (1985: 78), who argues, 'the picketing at Saltley — often presented as an extreme example of industrial violence — consisted of large numbers of strikers pushing against smaller numbers of police. Such behaviour is hardly the ultimate manifestation of anarchy that it is often depicted to be.'

If we examine the role of the police, it is clear that the level of violence they used in the 1972 coal strike was considerably lower than that used by their counterparts at Tonypandy, for example. To a considerable extent, this was undoubtedly associated with the fact that the use of violence has generally come to be seen as increasingly less acceptable in the course of this century. Moreover, police actions have been modified in ways which partially reflect changing public sensitivities in this regard.

The long-term trend towards less violent policing has been associated with, amongst other things, greatly improved police intelligence and the development of a wide range of new crowd control tactics. The former frequently results in the police having advance information about when and where major confrontations — for example, between strikers and strike-breakers — are likely to occur. This in turn allows the police to visit such sites in advance, to remove objects such as stones or bricks which could be used as weapons, to choose the best place to station their personnel, and to ensure that sufficient numbers are available at the time and place required. It seems that many police forces now have a policy of numerically matching pickets (Geary, 1985: 102), a policy reflecting that it is now unusual for small numbers of police to be over-run by, or to be 'powerless' to stop, large numbers of pickets, as frequently happened in the early part of the century. In this respect, the events at Saltley on 10 February 1972, when 800 police were faced by 15,000 pickets and were eventually forced to close the gates, were highly atypical.

With reference to developments in police tactics of crowd control, it is clear that the baton charge of the early 1900s has become increasingly a tactic of last rather than first resort, and has been supplemented by a wide range of tactics designed to minimize the use of violence. For example, police officers on picket duty frequently attempt to develop friendly relations with pickets. If the rapport between pickets and police breaks down, and if pickets refuse to heed verbal warnings, the police may then resort to the use of physical force. However, this is most likely to take the form of using a 'wedge' — a formation of police designed to split a crowd into two — and of the cordon, of which there are several types, as methods of containing crowds. As Geary (1985: 108) has commented, 'These formations are not only relatively non-violent but can also readily be seen to be non-violent. It is difficult to convincingly portray a cordon of linked-armed police, possibly positioned with their backs to pickets, as brutal agents of the repressive capitalist state'. This is not to suggest that police action during the 1970s did not, on occasions, involve the use of higher levels of violence, and we should also point out that there were certainly a good many allegations of police brutality associated with the 1972 strike (Geary, 1985: 110–13). The point is that by the 1970s, police tactics of crowd control involved a relatively limited use of violence, especially if one compares crowd control tactics during this period with the baton charges of the early part of this century.

Finally, it is clear that the *Mercury* had abandoned the relatively low-key and restrained treatment of disorders which had charac- terized its reporting early in the century. As we have seen, by 1972 allegations of violence — allegations which were denied by local NUM leaders — were considered sufficiently newsworthy to be given front page headline status, whilst the *Mercury*'s style of reporting tended to create an image of violence surrounding the strike, even though the evidence of violent action, particularly in the early stages, was not very strong. Perhaps the clearest example of this is in the *Mercury*'s description of what appear to have been entirely non- violent 'flying pickets' from Derbyshire as 'invaders' and as 'rampag- ing rebels' who 'should be brought to book'. To a considerable extent, we can regard such front page treatment of even relatively minor incidents as evidence of a growing media and public sensitivity towards the use of violence, and it is certainly the case that an important weapon for anyone seeking to undermine support for a strike has come to be the presentation of strike action as violent action. That the miners' strike of 1972 should have been perceived, at least in some quarters, as a violent strike is indicative of just how much public sensitivity towards the use of violence has changed since the early years of this century.

Crowd disorder in the leisure/sport arena

Our data indicate that, in the course of the twentieth century, the incidence of violent disorders associated with leisure and sporting activities has fluctuated considerably, but that the general trend has been an upward one (see Graph 4). In this respect, the pattern of violence in the leisure/sport arena is significantly different from the patterns of disorder in the other three areas which we have described.

It should be noted that Graph 4 does not include football crowd disorders, which have been the subject of separate and detailed analysis elsewhere (Dunning et al., 1984, 1986, 1987). If football crowd disorders were to be included, the principal effect would be to raise the general level of the graph, particularly over the last two decades. In other words, the generally upward trajectory would be maintained. Indeed, for the last two decades it would become con- siderably sharper.

The major contexts in which reported sports crowd disorders occurred in the pre-1914 period were football and, to a lesser extent, rugby. In the context of the association game, there were many instances of crowd disorder that would be judged to be serious by

GRAPH 4

Violent sport and leisure disturbances in England, Wales and Scotland as reported by the *Leicester Mercury*, 1900–75 (five-yearly intervals)

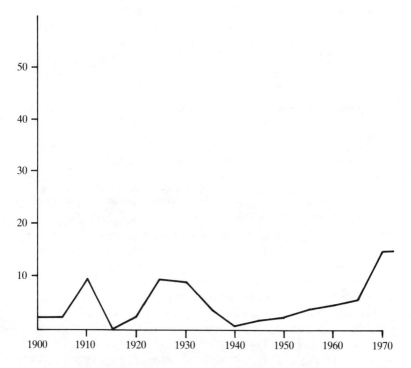

Note: This graph does not include football crowd disorders.

present-day standards. The *Mercury*'s accounts of these incidents are consistently devoid of sensationalism and characterized by an almost total absence of journalistic comment. The *Mercury*'s brief in this period seems to have been to cram as much news coverage into its pages as was physically possible. Attractiveness of presentation — at least as judged by the standards of today — was a low priority. Nevertheless, the blandness of its reporting style and the likely undeveloped nature of its sources of information would suggest a considerable level of under-reporting.

In this era, leisure for the working class tended to be community-based and street-orientated. Apart from the arenas of football, rugby and horse-racing (and, of course, palais and music halls), formally organized leisure pursuits and leisure establishments for the working class were virtually non-existent. Therefore, the number of incidents that fall into the leisure/sport category is deceptively low and this is primarily a function of our taxonomy.

Generally speaking, sports crowd disorders in the inter-war years do not appear to have been as serious as many of those reported in the pre-1914 period. This judgement does not only rest on a content analysis of newspaper accounts of incidents in the two periods, but also reflects prevalent views between the wars. For example, a *Mercury* editorial was fulsome in its praise of the 1928 Wembley Cup Final crowd. After praising the crowd, it continued:

> The comment arises, no doubt, from a legendary feeling that big sporting crowds are in some peculiar way predisposed to emotions and unseemly behaviour . . .
>
> Students of people in mass will probably tell us that we make merry nowadays without the discreditable manifestations that were at one time thought to be inseparable from these public rejoicings. Rejoicing and sobriety go hand in hand, and great crowds distinguish themselves with a sense of discipline that is creditable all round. May we infer that we are an improving people? (23.4.1928)

Moreover, this judgement on the decline in the seriousness of sports crowd disorder is made in the face of what might be judged to be, ostensibly at least, two countervailing processes, namely, the enormous expansion in organized sport in this period and the *Mercury*'s movement towards a more dramatic presentational style.

The inter-war years witnessed a vast expansion of the already well established spectator sports such as football, cricket and rugby. It also saw a rapid growth of other sports such as dog racing, speedway and licensed boxing. In the case of the former sports, they continued to be the scene of not infrequent crowd disorders, whilst the latter came to constitute new arenas for the occasional disturbance. In the present context two examples must suffice.

During the cricket match between Leicestershire and Glamorgan in 1930 there was a:

> minor demonstration . . . because it was thought that the umpires had too abruptly called time when Leicester wanted only one run in order to establish a first innings lead . . . as the players left the field, the spectators crowded the pavilion entrance and made a demonstration. (26.7.1930)

The second example is taken from dog-racing. In 1930, the *Mercury* reported:

> a scene of considerable uproar at Leicester Stadium on Saturday night, the crowd, or a section of it, demonstrated before the stewards' box at the close of the last race.
>
> 'It was the most vigorous protest by punters I have ever witnessed at the stadium', writes Sapline. 'There have at past meetings been angry shouts on occasions, but nothing worse than one usually hears at football or

cricket matches. On Saturday night, however, the anger of some of the people rose to such a pitch that there was every fear of a scene of violence, and for sometime after the racing, the police who were on duty at the meetings, along with some of the ground officials, had to stand around the stewards' box while the crowd hooted vigorously.' (30.6.1930)

The disorders that were reported in the *Mercury* in the inter-war years were given greater prominence than such events had ever received in the preceding period. This related to the transformation the paper underwent with regard to its general format after the First World War, resulting in a movement towards a more 'eye-catching' style of reporting. Notwithstanding these two countervailing tendencies, the judgement that sports crowd disorders in the inter-war period were less serious than those in the previous period seems to be a sound one.

The only disorders in the sporting context which offer a challenge to this general picture of a decline in the seriousness as opposed to the frequency of disorders were what came to be known as 'the race course riots' of the 1920s. By way of example, the *Mercury* reported a disturbance at Bath race course in 1921, between rival gangs from Birmingham and London:

> Numerous men were attacked in the open under the eyes of peaceful citizens. Three sustained injuries which necessitated treatment in hospital. The weapons used included sandbags, pieces of iron, formidable life-preservers studded with nails, and heavy sticks, while in one instance a revolver was produced. Over 200 Birmingham men are said to have taken part in the day's events. (18.8.1921)

In 1925, the Home Secretary said 'this terrorism has got to stop'. It was calculated 'that the total strength of the gangs is about 3000. All the gangs go about armed. Their favourite weapons are razors and knives, but on many occasions revolvers, daggers, life preservers, crowbars and knuckle-dusters have been used' (26.8.1925).

One might think that events of this order would be difficult to surpass. However, that was not the view of a witness who gave evidence in a court case in 1922. He expressed the opinion that the 'races were now a garden party compared with what they used to be years ago' (12.9.1922). This might be taken to be the implication of the work of the historian Vamplew (not dated), who writes:

> In general, before the 1880s, disorder was an expected feature of British racing. At most meetings the course executives would employ a few pugilists to protect the horses and other racing property, and a gateman or two to keep undesirables out of the stands. At society events police would also be in attendance to control the rough element with a strong hand. However, as long as the masses, in their anger or exuberance, damaged only themselves and did not offend anyone who mattered, those in charge were content.

Thus it would seem that during the inter-war years, the general picture of crowd disorder in the sporting context was less serious than in the pre-1914 era. However, it is important to emphasize that it was still far removed from the many romanticized views currently held of sporting events in that period.

The emergence and growth of institutionalized entertainment such as dance-halls and cinemas in the inter-war years served to provide a new situation in which disorder might arise. While street life was subject to increasing control, it continued to remain vigorous in this period as is indicated by the anxiety generated by the phenomenon of the 'Sunday night parade' or, as it was called in certain areas, 'the monkey walk'. It was the fashion for young working-class people to gather in the streets in great numbers on Sunday evenings and to engage in activities that were widely perceived to be hooligan in character. A growing appreciation that this phenomenon was in part a consequence of the almost total prohibition of recreational pursuits on Sundays gave considerable momentum to the movement for cinemas to open their doors on that day. The subsequent disturbances that occurred in cinemas on Sundays seem to provide clear evidence of the transfer of rowdyism from one sphere to another.

While the present-day disquiet about sports/leisure crowd disorders may have as its distant backcloth a romanticized view of the inter-war years, the principal benchmark used by most people would seem to be the decade and a half following the Second World War. One of the principal foci of this contemporary anxiety is disorder in the context of football matches. It is undeniably the case that the combined frequency and seriousness of these disorders, with the probable exception of the 'race course riots' of the 1920s, exceeds virtually anything that has occurred in a sporting context in this country since before the First World War. However, this should not lead us to embrace uncritically the presently dominant image of the 1945–60 period as one in which order reigned.

Apart from football, most of the reported disorder in the leisure/sport arena in this period occurred in cinemas and dance-halls. As far as the latter were concerned, police practice in Leicestershire as late as the mid-1950s seems to have been to station police officers in those halls at which trouble was not uncommon. One officer who served through the period told us:

> Say, Palais de Danse, Saturday night, or the Secular Hall the other side, which the Irish always used. There'd always be somebody drunk turn up and want to go in ... He'd start on the doorkeeper. Well, they had a system. There very often used to be a bobby on duty upstairs those days. We used to do picture houses ... and the dance halls, half past eight to half past eleven. And the Palais de Danse, two of you used to be there. If

there's anyone came on the scene, wanting to get in and abusing the doorkeeper, he'd just give us the tip and we outed him smartly. He didn't come back again!

It seems probable that fighting at dance-halls etc. may well account for such a large part of the reported cases of 'leisure/sports' disorder in this period because they were a police priority. In a similar way, the decline in the number of such reports, and the rise of the number of reports of football-related disorders from the late 1950s through to the present day, must be understood not simply in terms of shifts in media preoccupations or the changing relative 'roughness' of dance-halls and football crowds, but also as a result of changes in practical policing procedures upon which newspaper reporting is, to a degree, dependent.

The leisure/sports arena appears to be the only one in which there has not been a general long-term decline in the number of reported disturbances, and we would wish to argue that the general trends in at least three of the areas (politics, community and leisure/sport) are inter-linked. More particularly, it seems highly likely that the decline of the street in the first half of this century as a centre of working-class entertainment, has led (although not by itself) to a diminution in the level of reported disturbances in both the 'political' and 'community' arenas and that this, tied to the rise in the course of this century of institutionalized sport and leisure facilities, particularly for the working class, has tended to shift the focus for collective disturbances towards those sites which in our classification are described as 'sport' or 'leisure', rather than 'political' or 'community'. In this way, the declining levels of reported disturbances in two arenas are inextricably tied to the rising reported level in a third.

Conclusion

By way of conclusion, we should like briefly to comment on changes in the overall level of reported collective disturbances in the period 1900–75, and also to draw out some of the similarities and contrasts between the trends in the four arenas which we have identified. Our data indicate that, in the course of this century, there has been an overall decline in the level of reported collective disturbances within British society (see Graph 5). The patterns in three of the four arenas are similar to the general pattern or overall trend that we have identified. Thus 'community', 'industry' and 'politics' all have relatively high levels of reported disturbances in the early part of this century, with levels of reported disturbances tending to decline after the First World War. From the Second World War onwards, for at least a decade or so, the reported level remains relatively low but, thereafter, there is a gradual increase to a level which, although significant, does not begin to approach the much higher levels re-corded earlier in this century. It is only the 'leisure/sports' arena which does not fit this pattern.

The trends of collective violence in general and in each of the four arenas identified may be summarized as follows:

GRAPH 5

Reported rate of violent disturbances in England, Wales and Scotland in the *Leicester Mercury*, 1900–75 (five-yearly intervals)

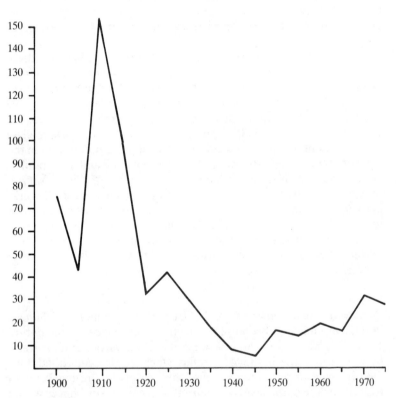

In the period from 1900–75 there has been a significant and gener-ally downward trend in the number of violent disorders within British society from the high point in the first two decades of this century. However, this downward trend has not been a smooth one, and there have been short-term fluctuations in the level of violence. The most significant of these upward movements has occurred in the period since the mid-1950s, particularly in the areas of 'community' and 'sport' and 'leisure'.

The level of industrial violence, which in this century has always had a relatively high instrumental character, has declined very sharply, and from a slightly earlier date than is the case in the other two arenas — politics and community — which follow this pattern.

The level of political violence has also decreased sharply from the early years of this century. We argue that this decrease is associated with the rapid decline of more traditional and more highly expressive forms of disorder, and that a growing proportion of the smaller number of disorders have been characterized by a more highly instrumental orientation.

The decline of violence in the community arena follows the general pattern of decline in the political arena. We also noted a sharp reduction in the level of organized, relatively highly instrumental gang violence in the mid-1920s, although the street remained a major site of more expressive disorders until the Second World War. Since the Second World War, there has been a more marked increase in violence in the 'community' arena than has occurred in either the political or industrial arenas.

The pattern of violence in the leisure/sport arena is markedly different from the overall trend for all violence, and from the trends for each of the three other arenas. The general trend here has been upwards — though unevenly so — with the marked increase in the last two decades being particularly associated with football hooliganism. In accounting for this generally upward trend, we point to the decline of the street as a centre of working-class entertainment and leisure and the concomitant increase in the provision of organized facilities for sport and leisure. This development has been associated with a shift of violence away from other arenas, particularly politics and community and with the emergence of sport and leisure facilities as a major focus for collective disorders.

Finally, it should be remembered that the material we have gathered on collective disorder in twentieth-century Britain is vast. We are still in the process of coming to terms with it. As such, many of the arguments contained in this paper are best understood as but tentative forays into little known territory.

Notes

1. It should be noted that, although at the outset this project was intended to be a study of 'local' crowd disorders, we discovered almost immediately from our coverage of the local newspaper that we would be collecting more stories relating to events outside of Leicestershire than to those which occurred within that county. This we feel, with hindsight, is actually an advantage, for it enables us to present a broader and more balanced picture of the period under discussion, without placing undue emphasis on one geographical area.

2. It was decided during the course of the project that stories reporting 'petty' acts of vandalism, e.g. the breaking of a school window, damage to trees in local parks etc., would be excluded. We took this decision because the sheer number of such articles would have made the 'cost' of including them prohibitive in terms of time, and because in almost all cases it was impossible to tell who, or how many people, had been involved.

3. There were, for example, a number of claims that Liberal working men had been victimized by dismissal from their employment for displaying Liberal posters. See *Mercury*, 24.1.1910 and 23.4.1910.

4. Richter (1964: 194–5) suggests that a 'careful survey' of Liberal and Conservative newspapers disclosed 'less than ten minor disturbances' during the election of January 1910. Our survey of the *Mercury* reveals a substantially greater number of disturbances than this, and it is by no means clear that all of these incidents can properly be described as 'minor'.

5. An excellent fictional — though not historically inaccurate — description of such events may be found in Robert Tressell (1982) *The Ragged Trousered Philanthropists*, St. Albans: Granada Publishing, pp. 533–4.

6. The Unionist candidate for Mid-Derbyshire, who struck a member of his audience with a 'violent blow on the jaw', was fined sixpence, whilst the Tory member of Salisbury Town Council was fined ten shillings for an assault on a Free Trade speaker In contrast, the usual fine on suffragettes for breaking a window or windows in public buildings appears to have been £5.

7. For the suffragettes' reaction to the 'Cat and Mouse' Act, see Midge MacKenzie (1975) *Shoulder to Shoulder*. Harmondsworth: Penguin, pp. 228–32.

8. It should be noted that, early in October, there was a meeting at the De Montfort Hall in Leicester which called for an inquiry into the police actions at the demonstration. The request, however, fell on deaf ears.

References

Bean, J.P. (1981) *The Sheffield Gang Wars*. Sheffield: D. and D. Publications.
Cronin, J.E. (1979) *Industrial Conflict in Modern Britain*. London: Croom Helm.
Dunning, E.G., Murphy, P.J., Williams, J. and Maguire, J. (1984) 'Football Hooliganism in Britain before the First World War', *International Review for the Sociology of Sport*, 19: 215–40.
Dunning, E.G., Murphy, P.J., and Williams, J. (1986) 'Spectator Violence at Football Matches', *British Journal of Sociology*, 37: 221–44.
Dunning, E.G., Murphy, P.J., and Williams, J. (1987) *The Social Roots of Football Hooliganism*. London: Routledge and Kegan Paul.
Gash, N. (1953) *Politics in the Age of Peel*. London: Longman Green.
Geary, R. (1985) *Policing Industrial Disputes: 1893 to 1985*. Cambridge: Cambridge University Press.
Gurr, T.R. (1969) 'A Comparative Study of Civil Strife', pp. 572–626, in H.D. Graham and T.R. Gurr (eds) *The History of Violence in America: Historical and Comparative Perspectives*. New York, Washington and London: Frederick A. Praeger.
Gurr, T.R. (1976) *Rogues, Rebels and Reformers*. Beverly Hills and London: Sage.
Hobsbawn, E. (1971) *Primitive Rebels*. Manchester: Manchester University Press.
Kettle, M. and Hodges, L. (1982) *Uprising: the Police, the People and the Riots in Britain*. London: Pan.

Le Bon, G. (1960) *The Crowd: A Study of the Popular Mind*. New York: The Viking Press.

Middlemas, K. (1979) *Politics in Industrial Society*. London: André Deutsch.

Pearson, G. (1983) *Hooligan: A History of Respectable Fears*. London: Macmillan.

Richter, D. (1964) 'Public Order and Popular Disturbances in Great Britain, 1865–1914', unpublished dissertation, University of Maryland.

Rudé, G. (1970) *Paris and London in the Eighteenth Century*. London: Fontana.

Smelser, N.J. (1962) *Theory of Collective Behaviour*. London: Routledge and Kegan Paul.

Stevenson, J. (1979) *Popular Disturbances in England, 1700–1870*. London: Longman.

Tilly, C. (1969) 'Collective Violence in European Perspective', pp. 4–45, in H.D. Graham and T.R. Gurr (eds) *The History of Violence in America: Historical and Comparative Perspectives*. New York, Washington and London: Frederick A. Praeger.

Vamplew, W. (n.d.) 'Sports Crowd Disorder in Britain, 1840–1914: Causes and Controls', unpublished paper.

White, J. (1979) 'Campbell Bunk: A Lumpen Community in London Between the Wars', *History Workshop*, 8: 1–49.

White, J. (1981) 'The Summer Riots of 1919', *New Society*, 57: 260–1.

3

Street life, ethnicity and social policy

John Edwards, Robin Oakley and Sean Carey

Introduction

The context

Street life, in the sense of presence on the street for purposes other than transit, is — with limited exceptions — generally viewed with suspicion or disapproval in contemporary society. Of course, attitudes do vary: some people romanticize street life, some view it as an escape from social pressure or oppression, and some see it as indicating moral decline or a subversive threat to moral order. Street life, moreover, may still take a variety of forms, ranging from carnivals and demonstrations to children's games and from street markets to prostitution, robbery and other kinds of street crime.

In the public mind, in recent times, the idea of street life has become particularly associated with 'youth', that is with the 'problem' of young people 'hanging around on the street with nothing to do'. However, the eruption of violence on the streets of numerous British cities in 1980 and 1981 gave rise to the association of 'presence on the street' with 'crime and disorder'. As with the preceding 'mugging' scares of the 1970s, the problem became identified with black people — and with 'black youth' in particular (Hall et al., 1978). While the crudest public equations of street disorder with black youth are to be found in organs of the popular and extremist press (Joshua and Wallace, 1983), the two are also associated in one manner or another in the thinking of a wide range of commentators, policy-makers and professional practitioners. Lord Scarman, for example, in his report *The Brixton Disorders*, writes of young black people as 'a people of the street': 'they live their lives on the street ...; they make their protest there; and some of them live off street crime' (Scarman, 1981: 11, 16). In Scarman's analysis, street life — at least in the Brixton area — is associated strongly with the black community; moreover it is viewed, if not as a cause, at least as a contributory or predisposing factor towards riot and violent protest.

It is often far from clear, however, what it is about street life that commentators believe is actually conducive to disorder. Street life as such, in its most literal sense, is not inherently problematic or disorderly: large crowds may gather on the streets, just as in other places such as parks or on the beach, without fear or fact of disorder. The gathering of people on the street or in other public places may be a necessary condition of riotous behaviour, but it is certainly not a sufficient one as numerous examples could show. What is distinctive about the 'street life' of young people, in the eyes of many commentators, is that — as 'hanging around' — it is essentially non-purposive crowd behaviour. In so far as this study focuses on street life as an example of non-purposive crowd behaviour therefore, it differs from the other studies reported in this book and from most other literature on collective and crowd behaviour. Such a view of street life is expressed by Scarman, who writes rather of the 'enforced idleness' of young people due to unemployment. On Scarman's analysis, not only does this condition bring people together on street corners, it provides them also with 'a continuing opportunity to engage in endless discussion of their grievances' (Scarman, 1981: 7). Street life, therefore, is not simply a matter of 'waiting for the action'; it entails a sharing of attitudes, a disposition to see the world in certain ways and to act accordingly. In Brixton, according to Scarman's analysis, it was young black people's experience of and disposition towards the police that held particular significance, and in this sense 'street life' appeared an important contributing factor to the outbreak of rioting on the streets.

This implicit theory of the relation of street life to riotous behaviour is based on a limited inquiry into one inner city area of London. Some further evidence exists to support the view that the experience of young people in Brixton is by no means unique across Britain's inner cities (Pryce, 1979). The incidence of riot, however, was uneven among cities in 1981 and also in 1985 and there can be no question of street life in this sense being a sufficient condition of disorder. What remains less clear, is precisely what this street life, alluded to by Scarman, consists of; and to what extent it is reproduced in all inner city areas, and across and within different ethnic groups.

The research
It is these issues relating to the confusions, ambiguities and assumptions surrounding street life that provide the impetus for this research. The major aims have been to explore the nature and variety of street life among young people in inner city areas, who participates in it and why, and its connections with crime and disorder. These have been pursued by means of intensive ethnographic fieldwork in inner city areas of north and east London, selected using census ward enumeration district data and other sources so as to provide a contrast both in area characteristics and in ethnic composition. In

addition, the research addresses the images of street life held by policy-makers, and how these have affected the policy response. This has entailed undertaking documentary content analysis designed to establish the social construction of street life as a social problem, and to identify the nature of the policy response. The intention has been to juxtapose a social problem construction of street life with an 'alternative reality' constructed as a result of the ethnographic field-work. In light of this comparison, policy implications of the research findings have been drawn out, and in turn, an assessment of the actual or likely effect of policies related to street life has been made.

The initial research design for the ethnographic fieldwork entailed the selection of three separate research areas, one for each of three broad ethnic groupings — Afro-Caribbean, Asian and white — so as to enable a clear-cut comparison in patterns of street life between ethnic groups to be undertaken. It became clear early on, however, that in no broad area was street life exclusive to one ethnic group and all areas were multi-ethnic to some degree. Moreover, the mixing or segregation of young people of different ethnic groups was a signifi-cant feature in its own right, as was the territorial relation between groups of different kinds. It became clear also that street life, even among young people, took different forms in different locations, for example estates, high street shopping areas and 'front-line' locations, and any area included a number of such different types of location. Not only did young people participate more or less in each of these, but they might participate in more than one location at different times or for different purposes. Moreover, in some cases young people moved outside their own area for various leisure purposes, and because of their mobility, it was not possible to define bounded areas within which strictly locally based fieldwork could be under-taken. As a result of these considerations, a broad zone stretching across north and east London was selected, covering parts of the boroughs of Haringey, Hackney and Tower Hamlets.

The main component of the fieldwork involved the use of partici-pant observation and informal interviewing over a period of two years, May 1983 to April 1985, as a means towards establishing the meaning and significance of street use among young people of dif-ferent ethnic groups in the research area. Participant observation was undertaken in a range of different settings encompassing off-street locations of both formal and informal natures such as youth clubs, unemployment drop-in centres, community centres, pubs, betting shops, cafés and pool rooms, as well as on the street and other open spaces. These activities on the part of the fieldworker set up a wide range of contacts and relationships with young people, many of which led to further contacts. Arising out of these contacts, approximately

100 semi-structured interviews were carried out with young people, and a further fifty with youth and community workers in their roles both as informants and as 'street-level bureaucrats', that is policy-deliverers 'on the ground'. No attempt was made to engage in random sampling or produce statistically significant findings: the purpose was rather to identify the main patterns in the attitudes and experience of young people according to area, gender and ethnic origin, and to explore some of the reasons accounting for such differences.

The research strategy for developing a picture of the policy view or, as we shall call it, the policy orthodoxy in respect of street life presented some initial difficulties. We began with the assumption that there exists a set of views or preconceptions — not necessarily coherent or consistent — about the character of street life that informed and influenced the policy responses to it. The problem was whether better access to this orthodoxy would be gained through interviews with policy-makers and influential people or through an examination of a wide range of policy documents. For a number of reasons including past experience, economy of resources and time, and ultimate productivity, the latter course was adopted and a trawl and content analysis of policy documents was carried out.[1]

Ethnographic findings

Street observations
Direct observation was the method used in the early stages to test whether some ethnic groups, and young black people in particular, frequent the street more than other groups. A direct count of num-bers of people actually present on the street was made in various different types of location, at different times of the day, week and year, and in different weather conditions, and analysed by age, sex and ethnic appearance.

Except in certain symbolic or commercial centres specific to one ethnic group such as black front-line or Asian commercial areas, there were no clear indications of disproportionate use of the street or other public spaces by members of any one ethnic group, allowing for age, sex and the demographic composition of the area. Indeed, with the exception of large, indoor shopping centres — frequented by younger teenagers of all backgrounds — we found that the tendency for young people to be hanging around was extremely small-scale and sporadic, and certainly far less than much social commentary and public imagery would suggest.

These findings suggest that the perception of young black people being more inclined to street use than their white counterparts owes more to selective perception or unwarranted generalization from specific types of location, for example the front-line in Brixton, than to the reality it purports to describe. They also suggest that a view of youth generally as routinely engaging in street life in a literal sense, as a form of crowd behaviour, is seriously misleading. This is not to deny that on some occasions, in some places, some groups do gather routinely, or that particular kinds of incidents may induce gatherings of people on the street. It is to question, however, that this behaviour is a regular daily occurrence in the lives of young people in inner city areas, and to question also that the streets as such are in some way routinely occupied by young people, to the disadvantage of others or indeed to themselves. The issue is rather one of under what circumstances and why do young people actually use the street, and what meaning and significance does it have for them.

Street life as life-style
In this context, street life means more than mere physical presence on the street, it denotes a way of life in which street use forms simply *one part* — significant or otherwise — of a regular routine for a purpose of some nature. And, as we shall see, in conventional usage it is associated with a number of other allegedly related phenomena. The issues to be explored consequently relate to the life-styles and experiences of young people in inner city areas. While the focus of attention has been with street use, and with the significance of the street and other public space in young people's lives, the research has also explored the wider context of young peoples lives and experiences within which the use and significance of the street needs to be understood. This is because street life in the more literal sense is inseparable from styles of life generally and from sets of attitudes, and because it is viewed in policy orthodoxy as being a component of a set of related phenomena all of which are to varying degrees considered to be morbid or pathogenic. Our concern must be with both sets of interrelated phenomena.

The most immediate concern has been to establish actual patterns of use of the street and other public space: types of area used, types of activity, their frequency, who participates, daily and weekly routines, use of different kinds of facilities, mobility, involvement in crime, relations with police, and the meaning and significance attached to these patterns by the young people. Then, providing a context for this information, and framing its interpretation, a wider range of data has been collected on the attitudes and experience of young people relating to their local neighbourhood, schooling, employment, domestic life, ethnic identity, politics, and to British society generally and their future within it. Throughout this analysis, a predominant concern has been to identify how far it is possible to identify distinct life-styles characteristic of particular ethnic or other social groupings, and what factors work towards or against the development of common patterns and shared experiences among young people of different ethnic origins (Brake, 1985; Pryce, 1979; Oakley and Carey, 1986).

For the purposes of this chapter we have concentrated on presenting a straightforward description and interpretation of our ethnographic findings, so that in the final section a direct assessment of the policy orthodoxy can be undertaken in the light of these data. The data include both behavioural and attitudinal aspects of street use, relationships to institutions and life-styles generally. In this way we have aimed to document a range of dimensions of potential alienation among young people, in the broadest sense in which that term is used. However, we do not address directly the theoretical and conceptual issues surrounding the notion of alienation since our purpose here is restricted to one of documentation and evaluation. (A further discussion of alienation and its application to black youth can be found in Gaskell & Smith, 1981; John, 1981; Solomos, 1982.)

The young people
The young people contacted in the research were young men and women in their teens and twenties, of Afro-Caribbean, Asian and white British origin, living in inner city areas on the north-east and east sides of London, referred to subsequently as Northside and Eastside respectively. Both areas display the main characteristics of economically declining inner city zones, though differ in specific economic and demographic features. Eastside has for over a century had a relatively stable working-class population, though one which over time has absorbed — though not without considerable tension and conflict — a succession of immigrant groups, the latest of which have been of Bangladeshi origin. Northside has a less settled population, more mixed in socio-economic terms though also multi-ethnic in composition, and lacks the distinctive, localized economic base characteristic of Eastside.

As noted earlier, no attempt was made systematically to sample young people according to age, area or ethnic group, although within the constraints of a small-scale field project, efforts were made to assess the significance of these variables within one or more contexts. Thus in Eastside, young people of school-age were contacted, as well as older age-groups, and people of all three ethnic origin groupings were involved. Many of the young people contacted were participants in a multi-ethnic group of mostly school-age youngsters who hung around together on a regular basis and whom we refer to as the

'Wall Kids' (Carey, 1984). In Northside, work was mainly under-taken with young people of Afro-Caribbean origin, enabling a comparison to be made so as to highlight the area variable. In view of their lesser involvement in street-based activities, fewer young women than men were contacted, although attempts were made to elicit attitudes towards street life among representatives of each ethnic group and in both areas.

The initial research design for the study presumed that it would be feasible to classify young people into ethnic groupings based on three broad categories of ethnic origin: Afro-Caribbean, Asian and white English. While it had been a purpose of the enquiry to identify variations in life-style within as well as between these categories, it soon became clear from the fieldwork that the categories themselves had several shortcomings, not merely that they inadequately represented the more specific ethnic origins of individuals, for example Bangladeshi, 'white' Irish, but that they took inadequate account of subjective ethnic identity. The three broad initial categories have nonetheless been generally adhered to, so as to enable the general patterns of similarity and difference between groups to be discerned.

Attitude to area

In the localities covered, young people of all ethnic origins expressed generally favourable attitudes to the areas in which they lived. There were both common and distinctive elements in this picture. The principal common element comprised 'knowing your own area', as opposed to the difficulty of getting around and the discomfort and possible dangers of other areas. Frequently what was evaluated was not any particular feature of one's own area but rather negative features of other areas.

These were cast in different terms by different ethnic and area groups. Young whites and members of multi-ethnic groups in Eastside contrasted their own neighbourhoods with those settled by the Bengalis, and while identifying strongly with Eastside in general, frequently expressed resentment about 'the Pakis', that is the Bengali intrusion. This was particularly marked among the young whites, for whom 'Pakis' extended to all Asians but not 'blacks', that is Afro-Caribbeans, and who seemingly blamed them for all the perceived ills of the area — poor housing, rubbish on the streets, strange cooking smells and unfamiliar languages.

Young black people in both Eastside and Northside were more likely to evaluate their area with reference to other areas of Afro-Caribbean settlement in London. Those in Eastside, while owning that 'people get along', found it 'a little bit boring', and more of a 'white area' than locations like Stoke Newington, Notting Hill and

Brixton where more expressive black life-styles manifest themselves and black people mix with one another. Northsiders felt more positive about their area in the latter respect, though were more likely to have experienced racial hostility from whites in some districts, especially if they had moved into the area from outside, and to see it as relatively unfriendly.

So far as young Bengali Asians in Eastside were concerned, attitude to area was dependent largely upon whether or not they resided within the main Bengali settlement area. In contrast to ten or even five years ago, this was now seen as a relatively safe area, and convenient for shopping and meeting friends. Some negative attitudes, however, revolved around the social control exercised by elders, relatives and friends. The locality functions not simply as a place of residence, but also as a 'status arena' in which reputations could be made or lost. Young men, and especially young women, experienced the constraints which gossip and rumour potentially, if not actually, exercised over their daily lives. Those who lived outside the main settlement area clearly recognized that their place of residence bestowed a relative freedom in terms of lack of gossip and control, but on the other hand was more likely to involve racial harassment and violence. The establishment of a 'home base' for Bengalis living in the area therefore had brought disadvantages as well as benefits to the community, in that the creation of 'defensible space' entailed in practice the confinement of Bengalis to the immediate locality, and among young people a feeling of constraint that, while appreciating the strengths and resources of the community, removed their sense of personal autonomy.

Schooling

Few of these young people living in inner city areas saw anything positive in their experience of schooling, often because it was not perceived to be linked to future employment. For most, school was either a painful and worthless experience in relation to their future lives, or an occasion for 'having a laugh' and filling time until they could leave at the age of sixteen. Among the white youths in Eastside in particular, a number of the males had informally left school aged thirteen or fourteen, or had been expelled for fighting or abuse of teachers. They had then spent their time on the streets — wandering around the market areas, helping on stalls, becoming involved in petty crime. In the case of girls, intermittent truanting or 'bunking off' was more common, though the more regular non-attenders were likely to involve themselves in home-based activities such as helping out domestically.

Those taking a more positive view of their experience of schooling and its potential benefit were both black females or Asian males, but in the case of these groups the evaluation was in strictly vocational terms. Older Afro-Caribbean males, especially if they had substantial experience on the dole, expressed more positive attitudes towards further education, and now wished to encourage younger blacks to respond more positively to the opportunities available to them in school. Bengali youths were inclined to express more pointed criticisms of the failure of the educational system. On the one hand these focused on their experiences of racism in school playgrounds, while on the other several thought that more could be done in terms of ESL (English as a Second Language) and a greater allocation of resources to meet the educational needs of children of immigrant families.

Employment
The impact of economic decline in inner city areas on the experience of, and attitudes towards employment among these young people has been far from even. While all have experienced severe economic disadvantage, the form this has taken varies considerably, and the young people's perceptions and attitudes vary accordingly. In addition to gender and ethnic group differences, area and community-linked factors are of considerable importance.

None of the young people contacted expressed objection in principle to employment in the sense of recognition of the need and obligation to 'earn one's living'. In their attitudes towards employment, however, many young people made clear distinctions between particular kinds and conditions of employment which they found acceptable or not. Basically all males, and many females, especially of Afro-Caribbean origin, held positive attitudes towards a secure job that paid a reasonable wage and involved tolerable conditions. All could articulate what would constitute 'rubbish jobs', a notion that was as much concerned with supervisory and managerial control as with material circumstances. What exactly constituted 'rubbish jobs' and a reasonable wage varied considerably. A common feature among these young people, however, was a very clear and forthright view that the Youth Training Scheme (YTS) was from their point of view a poor substitute for a proper job, and often in practice counterproductive for those participating in it. Not surprisingly, the YTS received a massive rejection from the young people contacted, who saw it neither as a substitute for, nor as an effective means to, 'proper jobs'.

The condemnation of YTS was strongest among white and black youth in Eastside. While few of either group were currently in employment, more of the black young people had had recent job experience, and more had been enrolled in YTS. They criticized it, however, as exploitative, boring, massaging unemployment figures and not leading anywhere. White young people, while expressing equally critical attitudes, had had less experience of this kind. In contrast to the young black people, the white Eastsiders tended to acquire income through access to the 'informal economy' via their families — for example through older brothers, neighbours and so on. Jobs of this kind were not permanent, but might involve moving furniture or some other kind of goods every so often for cash. Helping out with painting and decorating was also a favourite among this group. Some took casual employment for a few weeks if financial circumstances began to get desperate. None were under any illusions about the fact that well-paid, unskilled jobs were in short supply. Given their capacity to draw upon family- and community-based sources of income and support, they did not, however, view YTS as an economically worthwhile interim solution.

Young black people in Eastside, while sharing the community-based perception of YTS, were more inclined to have participated in the scheme, as already noted. By comparison with young whites, they were less able to draw on established networks of relatives and friends within the neighbourhood, especially those linking to small businesses which could absorb young people on an informal or intermittent basis. Only a few had some method of supplementing their dole income. They were more likely, therefore, to be 'forced' into work which they found unpleasant and did not like. Yet there was no evidence of these young people having 'unrealistic job ambitions', these being virtually identical to their white counterparts. Indeed, they shrewdly recognized the importance of being 'spoken for' in the local labour market. Significantly, however, the vast majority of informants in this area did not think that being black was a crucial barrier to getting a job, though some did think that it made the task harder.

Among young black people in Northside, more were in employment but attitudes were more sharply drawn. Informants made stronger accusations than did their Eastside counterparts of racial discrimination in job recruitment procedures. Where they held employment, it was often seen as unpleasant work taken strictly as a short-term means towards an alternative end. Their sense of being forced into jobs that were unpleasant was stronger than among black Eastsiders, and they felt more resentful about, and perceived more sharply, a racial dimension to their social and economic circumstances.

To a large extent what has been described above holds for both women and men. Two qualifications regarding Northside need to be added. The first is that in Northside several of the young women were out of the labour market since they were already single young mothers, and viewed their commitments to children as incompatible with employment. Second, among those women not yet involved with parenthood, a stronger commitment to stable employment was in evidence — more than among males, and among counterparts in Eastside. While on the one hand there was some resentment at a perceived masculine work-shyness, there was readiness also to recognize that black females were more acceptable than, and thus received less discrimination than, black males. At the same time, black females were more likely to have attained formal educational qualifications, and thus were more eligible for employment, especially at white-collar level. Despite this tendency towards a more positive experience of work, young black women in Northside were as dismissive, if not more so of YTS as any other group.

All of the foregoing relating to white and black young people is in some respects in sharp contrast to the experience and outlook of young Asians in Eastside. Among the latter, there were some shared attitudes with Eastsiders in general, and economic deprivation in a general sense was shared by all. In the main Bengali settlement area, however, young Bengalis were mostly either in employment or had recently been so, though largely in the garment industry. Working conditions and wages in many of the workshops were extremely poor, and many white and black Eastsiders were firm in their opinion that this was one industry in which they were unwilling to seek employment. For Bangladeshi youth, these wage-levels by comparison and in the absence of alternatives received more favourable evaluation, as did the conditions of work in a trade in which, together with the restaurant trade, the Bengalis had established a niche. Job-sharing was an important means of absorbing potential workers into the ethnic economy, and there was a general reluctance to register as unemployed. However, among informants who had spent a longer time in the UK, particularly in regard to education, there was a growing rejection of traditional jobs taken by parents, these being seen as economic responses that were no longer expedient or advantageous. Whether expectations of better jobs will be met is an open question. At the present time, however, most young peoples' lives were centred around regular employment, and work was a major component of the daily routine. Within this framework, YTS did not register as a meaningful option, since it made little sense in terms of young people's expected occupational careers, nor did it connect culturally or socially, especially because of the absence of an ESL component.

Among the young multi-ethnic group of street users, work was for most still a matter of hopes and expectations rather than a matter of experience or of attitudes based upon this. Hopes seemed closely geared to expectations, which in turn followed the long-established, community-based pattern of being provided for by relatives and friends, along lines already indicated above. YTS did not form a positive part of this outlook. Lads of Maltese, Cypriot and other white ethnic origin expected to disperse into traditional Eastside jobs as warehousemen, and girls into hairdressing, office or shop work. Those of Asian origin looked to find work in family businesses.

Routines
The major division in daily routines lay between those in employment or full-time education and those who were unemployed. Outside of this division a wide range of variation in routine among the young people was notable.

The differences between females and males tended to be prominent both among the employed and unemployed. Except where females were not living in their parental homes, their routines were more constrained by domestic factors than were males, principally in two respects — those of expectations of assistance with domestic chores and requirements of parental supervision. The degree and nature of impact of these varied according to a number of factors. In particular, being in employment or at school gave potential independence for young women from family supervision, as well as reducing the amount of time available for domestic work. There was no evidence that boys, of any ethnic origin or area within these inner city zones, were expected to make any significant contribution to domestic work.

For those in employment, the daily routine allowed only evenings for potential 'leisure' activities. Compared with the unemployed, however, those in work had at least some financial resources which, even if not large in quantity, were sufficient to enable drinking in pubs or local travel to clubs or friends, so that evenings — particularly in winter — need not necessarily be spent at home. The nature of these activities varied according to age and ethnic group, and within the latter there was also a wide range of variation corresponding to life-style and particular hobbies. Apart from visiting clubs, young black males used their wages to pursue hobbies such as sound systems, working out and playing pool, while young whites were more likely to make use of pubs. Young men of Asian origin were affected by a different set of influences on their use of leisure time, which included religious requirements, stronger control by community and kin and the threat of racial harassment. The latter was particularly important even with the most adventurous Asian youths who carefully selected their leisure sites so that they were least likely to meet

problems with white and black youths. Girls in all groups, by contrast, tended to pursue their weekday leisure activities in the home,
making more use of television and videos and entertaining female
friends.

For those in school or other full-time education, the rest of the day
was potentially filled with prescribed time spent outside the home,
although with limited resources available for leisure. Among those
below compulsory school-leaving age, and weather permitting, it was
common after school, and following essential homework, tea and a
change of clothes, for young people to go out for an hour or two for a
walk around or to regular hanging-out places to meet their friends.
Girls of this age outside the Bengali community in Eastside seemed as
keen to escape the home and spend time hanging around as their
male counterparts, though they reported more attempts to control
their behaviour than did the boys, and were usually subject to fairly
strict 'return-home' times. It was not only after school, however, that
time could be found during the day for leisure. 'Bunking off' from
school, practised regularly by both sexes, was engaged in by girls
specifically to create private space for disapproved purposes. While
boys might not hesitate to use the streets openly on such occasions,
girls were reluctant to do so not just because of the visibility, but
because of the different moral evaluations given to their behaviour.
Hence girls' bunking off from school was carefully situated in school
toilets, or in the flats of older friends and relatives, or at least well
away from the immediate neighbourhood or community. Creating
personal time in this way, or on the journey to and from school, was
one of the few ways in which girls from the well-supervised Bengali
community could engage in activities which would otherwise be
strongly sanctioned.

Among the unemployed, by contrast, the task was to fill the day
with purposeful activity and social contact. For most of the unemployed, and especially those who had been unemployed for any
duration, the daily routine developed a very different character.
Among white and black groups, and among females as well as males,
the day for most would begin about midday and finish correspondingly late in the evening or even later, if suitable social companionship was available. Individual routines would be established,
focused around getting up late, reading the paper, visiting girlfriends
and boyfriends, meeting other friends, listening to music, going to
clubs and unemployment centres and walking about. These
makeshift routines were constrained by the need for minimal expenditure, and involved attempts to spin out the potential pastimes of the
day so as to counter boredom and isolation as effectively as possible.
Staying at home all day was seen by many as the epitome of boredom:

'if I stayed at home all day I'd crack up', and 'this way I'll end up in the nuthouse'. Yet a number of those contacted *did* in fact spend most of their time at home and were socially withdrawn and depressed. The proportion affected by unemployment in this way is likely to be far higher than this research or surveys envisage due to their very invisibility. This was true of both black and white young people, though many of the latter drew on more long-established networks of kinship and neighbourly support, as could young unemployed Asians in the well-organized community environment of the main Bengali settlement zone. Furthermore, the weather was seen by many as having a major impact, precisely because of its power over one's capacity to escape from the home, especially when most felt there were few social centres of any kind where they could legitimately and with self-respect 'drop in'. Unemployment therefore had a varied impact on young people's disposition to spend time on the street, but even where that time was increased, no substantive change in life-styles were in evidence — merely a spinning-out and rescheduling of activities normal to the group.

Many young people in all of the groups, however, preferred to concentrate their limited financial resources for the weekend. All of the major activities of interest — shopping, sport, parties and visiting friends — tended to be concentrated in this period. This enabled the low-paid and unemployed alike to present themselves socially and attain self-respect at least once a week, subject of course to circumstances and life-styles. One good set of clothes would be sufficient for this purpose, and each item might entail considerable expense. Because of the costliness of some of these life-styles there were some among the unemployed who for weeks on end felt they could not appear publicly without losing self-esteem, and hence remained virtually isolated from their normal social circles. The commercial pressures, and the coexistence of poverty and relative affluence *within* communities due to substantial youth unemployment, were perceived by many of the young people as placing great strain on themselves and their friends, especially those who were unemployed, and as pressure towards engaging in financially oriented crime.

Street use
The street was seen as an activity space of central importance to young people by most of the groups in the study. All recognized the extensive use of the street by young people, even if they did not practise it themselves or necessarily approve of it. While it was appreciated that the street was used to some extent and in different ways by almost all categories of people in society, there was a recognition that young people's use was more distinctive, and tend to

involve an end in itself rather than the motive of transit. It was an unrestricted space in which youth could congregate and meet their friends outside adult supervision.

It was generally accepted that the street in the literal sense was too narrow a category to describe the space used and colonized by youth. Conceptions varied, however, between those for whom street life represented a style of life independent of home and other established institutions, and those for whom the street represented one among a number of possible activity sites, of which others, such as the home, the youth club, drop-in centres or the park were seen likewise as locations of no special symbolic or life-style significance.

Street use, in its frequency and its significance, varied considerably between groups, and did so for a variety of reasons. Women, for example, tended to make less use of the street than men during the day, and especially after dark. Fear of attack, in this case racial rather than sexual, limited Asian street use outside the main settlement area after dark. The unemployed, as we have seen, tend to make more use of the street than those in employment if only for opportunistic and time-filling reasons.

Among white young people on Eastside, street use was seen by all as an integral part of adolescence, and had been so for as long as anyone cared to remember. As several young people commented, if parents today took a different view of young people's use of the streets, it was not for their having behaved any differently when they were teenagers themselves. Perhaps the only difference between today and twenty to thirty years ago is that present youth unemployment stretches that practice in terms of age range. If the styles have changed, the basic position of young people vis-à-vis families and authority has remained largely unaltered, and the streets and other public spaces remain far more free and interesting than staying at home all day. On the one hand there are the established sources of leisure activity — the pubs, fish-and-chip shops, hamburger bars, cafés, betting shops and clubs — while on the other there are always the unpredictable events that either happen or that by one's own actions one can make or help to make happen. Hanging around in these kinds of locations is seen as full of potential, as well as pleasurable, sociable and preferable to most of the available alternatives. Meeting friends, watching for girls or boys, having a laugh, engaging in a little petty crime, taunting drunks or 'pakis', checking out and defending territorial boundaries — all these and many more were among the currently engaged-in activities.

The black young people on Eastside, while often not having a sense of the continuity of adolescent behaviour, participated in, and saw themselves as participating in, a local tradition. Only one informant in this area, an older woman of Jamaican origin, invoked cultural reasons for young black people hanging around on the streets; no others saw grounds for invoking a transplanted tradition to explain what was seen as normal adolescent behaviour for young Eastsiders. As with white youngsters, spending time on the street was seen as an integral part of the daily routine. The street was viewed as an interesting place where things could happen. As with whites, blacks and especially the unemployed, stretched the normal adolescent age-limits of street use beyond the conventional range, extending their participation well after school-leaving age. Most males in their early to mid twenties, while often obliged by unemployment to adopt life-styles that seemed even further to extend the duration of youth, nonetheless preferred to distance themselves from this extended adolescence, principally by using their flats or those of friends to pass leisure time.

In so far as there were differences between black and white young people in Eastside, these were of degree rather than of kind. Black youth were more likely to be unemployed, and to have experienced the streets as an alternative life-space than young white people. The latter seemed more secure in expecting they would graduate into the workforce and set up families of their own. Partly because of this greater exposure to street experience, and partly because of their black skins, young blacks reported more, and seemed more sensitive to, police harassment. In particular, they were far more likely to recount graphic accounts of encounters with the police, some — though by no means all of which — were perceived as racial.

In Northside, street use by young males tended to be more purposive in character. The street is one space among many where activities might be pursued. These were more specific in character, involving roller-skating, riding bikes, or sitting on a wall 'chatting up' girls. There was less casual hanging around in local street settings, and more deliberate action and movement from place to place. Where hanging around did occur it tended to be more confined to the enclosed estates, or focused on the pedestrianized shopping locations. As in Eastside, it was the younger teenagers rather than the older youth who spent time hanging around, particularly in the large indoor shopping centre.

The attitudes and experience of young women towards street use followed similar patterns in some respects, but differed in other ones. In Eastside, almost all school-age girls outside the Bengali community had positive attitudes, seeing the street as space where they could talk with their friends, have a laugh, and chat up the boys away from the prying of adults. Creating opportunities to spend time on the street, however, was not always easy since parents varied in their degree of supervision, depending not only on their attitudes, but also on whether anyone was at home to provide it. Girls varied too in the extent to which they were able to find time between school attendance and domestic chores, or were willing to practise some benign deceit. Those who had left school seemed to have turned quickly, and far more quickly than their male counterparts, towards seeing hanging about on the streets as a practice of little kids, and rather boring. It was an accepted part of growing up, in which hanging about preceded a subsequent phase wherein street use became more purposive involving shopping and visiting friends. The view of older girls in Eastside was that street life was basically harmless, allowing the younger kids some independence and the rest of the family some relief.

Young black women on Northside, by contrast, did not appear to be involved in hanging around to any extent, and older informants had not had this experience and disapproved of it. Several explained this lack of involvement by pointing to the firm parental supervision that most black girls received, especially in comparison with their brothers. While it appeared more common than in Eastside for them to have mothers in employment, they were nonetheless expected to be at home to do their homework and domestic chores, especially if there were younger siblings to look after. After leaving school, their determination to find respectable employment affected the extent to which many young women distanced themselves from the street scene. Among those who already had their own children, not uncommon among the older teenagers, the street was still seen strictly as a place of transit, for shopping expeditions with a similarly placed female friend. On such expeditions importance was attached to dress and appearance, but it was the home which was used as the place to chat, gossip and entertain.

The young people of Afro-Caribbean origin contacted during the study were aware of the location and significance of black front-line areas in London. Generally speaking, the existence of such areas evoked mixed feelings. Although one such area existed within Northside, none of the young people contacted within either Northside or Eastside had ever been regular participants. A number of the males, in both areas though, were intermittent visitors to one or more front-line areas in London, the Eastsiders tending to use the adjacent scene in Northside, and Northsiders using front-line areas elsewhere. The attitude towards such areas, among male and female informants alike, tended to be ambivalent, stressing that they were necessary, 'safe' areas in which blacks could feel at home, but they were not localities in which they wished to spend time. Nonetheless, all saw front-line street activity as intelligible given the paucity of life-chances in contemporary Britain, and saw too the hustling practices as a legitimate method of making a living and supporting a family.

The general perception was that front-line areas were strictly male spaces, with strongly defined categories of insiders and outsiders. Females, while sympathizing with circumstances giving rise to front-line street activity, tended to distance themselves from becoming involved. Male young people distinguished front-line areas as the territory of a specific section of blacks — the hustlers — and not a place they would hang out. As outsiders they might visit such areas occasionally to pick up a 'draw' (cannabis) if none was available locally, or if what was available was of bad quality. Only if they had friends there would they be likely to stay around longer. None of the teenagers reported having such contacts, though some of the older blacks had.

Street use within and around the main Bengali settlement area presented some marked contrasts. Within the centre of the area, in and around the main shopping street, a busy street life prevails, both in the street and in the shops and cafés. By comparison with other parts of Eastside, it is noticeable that almost all are older males. Females on the street are invariably in transit, usually in the company of men, and young people likewise are generally on the move. Those gathering and talking are almost always older men, whose presence generally dominates the street scene in this central part of the Bengali area.

The experience and attitudes of young Bengalis towards street use both reflects and challenges this pattern. Certain parts of the settlement area were defined by them as the exclusive preserve of older males. Other areas, principally those of the major local housing estates, were deemed more appropriate places for young Bengalis to hang around. Indeed, over the research period, a growing number of adolescents organized in semi-structured, though self-conscious, street-corner gangs began to appear, sometimes reflecting village and district alliances transplanted from Bangladesh. This seemed to reflect a growing awareness of Bengali male youths that this part of Eastside had become 'their' area. Such use of the street in the main settlement area may be expected to grow in the near future as it becomes an increasingly acceptable part of youthful, male Bengali leisure patterns. For many of the young people hanging around on the street was not a preferred activity. If it was pursued anywhere, it was done outside the main area, and in other Asian settlement areas in East and West London. Several of the young people claimed that to be seen hanging around on the streets by older relatives or friends could have serious consequences if the family was informed. This applied to males as well as females, and could affect marriage arrangements and the level of standing of the family in the community.

Among the younger Wall Kids, parental attitudes were still an important reference point. White and black members of the group of both sexes felt that their parents accepted hanging around as a normal activity for young people. The Asian and half-Asian members thought that parents did not approve, as it would lead to 'trouble' with the police or the opposite sex. The young people themselves took a more positive attitude towards street use, seeing the street as a place of autonomy and self-realization. It offered freedom from family and teacher control, and freedom to choose one's own activities and companions: to have a laugh with friends, to listen to music and dance and to try out new experiences. The latter included experimenting with drugs and solvents, but also with substances culturally proscribed for a particular ethnic group. The weather, when cold and wet, was seen as inhibiting by the female members, but males tended to assert that the streets were always preferable to hanging around at home. Despite this commitment to street use, all emphasized the desirability of being seen to behave respectably in public — even when messing about — so as to protect the reputation of other group members and of their families.

Pubs and other leisure sites
In theory, a variety of off-street leisure sites were available to these young people, ranging from clubs of different kinds, through pubs and cafés, to various forms of home-based entertainment. In practice, different groups had fairly specific notions of what they preferred and faced uneven provision of leisure facilities.

A range of attitudes to conventional youth clubs was encountered. The most critical were the school-age group and older white East-siders. In so far as conventional youth clubs provided formally orga-nized activities of a compulsory nature, they were seen by Wall Kids as 'shit' and 'full of wankers', although they recognized the rights of 'wankers' to have a conventional youth club. The objection of these young people to such clubs was not the activities, but the atmosphere — of adults in authority — too like school or home, and precisely what they came out on to the streets to escape. Hence their deroga-tory attitude to those of their peers who voluntarily submitted to adult direction outside school as well as within, as against asserting and realizing their own autonomy. Somewhat paradoxically, though proving the point, this group of young people did make regular use of a local youth facility, though it could hardly be called a club. In fact, minimal supervision was offered, and the kids were free to sit around, smoke and 'have a laugh' without being forced into compulsory activities. They saw themselves as fortunate in having access to this facility, but it was their very freedom to come and go as they pleased that gave them some commitment to it. They also liked to use a variety of other leisure sites, often as the whim might take them — amusement arcades, fish-and-chip shops, hamburger bars and, in the case of the older boys, without the girls, the pub. Again, the freedom of choice and the sense of variety and experimentation seemed important, just as did the possession of a regular hanging-out space on the street. Parties tended to be the main focus of weekend activities, and these were likely to separate out the group members from one another. In particular, the young males of Asian origin had access, often through kinship connections, to Asian party circuits covering a wide area. When the group was first contacted the girls were considered too young to accompany them but, one year later, attitudes changed and girls were accompanying boys.

White young people on Eastside, after leaving school, seemed to consolidate their negative attitude towards youth clubs including drop-in centres. Most saw these as places for little kids, while those of more adult status moved on to other leisure sites, preferably the pub. Generally speaking this was where older male teenagers tended to hang out, and in doing so they moved forward into the adult context of the local community. None the less, given unemployment, a number of young men considered that drop-in centres might be a good idea, especially during winter afternoons, although they did not feel that there were any centres geographically or socially accessible to them. Some of the girls did use drop-in centres frequented by black young people, and saw them as valuable places where one could have a game of pool, play video machines, meet friends and so on.

Black young people on both Eastside and Northside tended to take a more positive view of youth clubs and drop-in centres than their white counterparts, seeing them as offering valuable facilities. None of the black youths contacted made regular use of local pubs, and all looked to other kinds of leisure sites to meet their recreational needs which were often seen in far more precise and positive terms than those of their white counterparts. In particular, clubs were looked to for provision of sports facilities such as weight-training and gymnastic equipment, as well as pool and other pastimes. More importantly, they were appreciated, especially by the unemployed, as somewhere to go — places to relax and escape the pressure outside, whether it be from the boredom of unemployment, from home, or from the feeling of unease in the institutions of white society. Those in employment made proportionately less use of clubs, and tended to have leisure routines that resembled their white counterparts at work: visiting nightclubs, going to the cinema, watching TV and videos, but the places visited were often distinguished by a predominantly black clientele. This was seen to be as much a consequence of discrimination against blacks seeking to enter white nightclubs as of preference on black people's part. Many, however, could not afford to visit the legitimate nightclubs, and were obliged or preferred to attend more informally, though still commercially, organized 'blues'. Aside from being cheaper alternatives as forms of leisure, they also catered for the time available to those on the dole, in that they could continue through the night well into the daylight hours, and provide relaxation with a drink and a smoke, the satisfactions of which could be stretched out to fill the otherwise vacant hours. It was recognized, however, that such gatherings led to encounters with the police, who on Eastside in particular were seen by young black people as adopting a deliberate policy of breaking them up as soon as they had become established. Older males tended to regard 'blues' as activities engaged in by younger ones, and females said they participated relatively little.

Among the young Bengalis, youth clubs and community centres were perceived positively as the respectable alternatives to the street, and as means of keeping use of leisure time by young people firmly within the bounds of the community. They were recognized also as important channels for cultural transmission, as well as places to mobilize for appropriate political action, whether it be within the arena of institutionalized politics or for more direct action relating to rights of immigration or citizenship. Female Bengalis living within the main settlement area for the most part did not participate since their leisure activities were restricted to the home, unless there were particular activities such as a dramatic or musical performance and they were chaperoned by males.

Use of space
Among all groups, there was a strong sense of localism, and a limited disposition to travel outside the immediate area. As noted above, all displayed basically positive attitudes towards their own neighbourhood, chiefly on grounds that it was known, and seemed 'safe'. For different reasons, some of the young people moved outside their areas, although relatively infrequently. One of the major factors affecting them was financial, and those who had access to cars were far more likely to travel.

Throughout the groups contacted on Eastside, this pattern was especially pronounced. In the case of the Bengalis, there were particular factors accounting for this lack of mobility: the degree of self-sufficiency of the community, its cultural distinctiveness, the fear of racial attack and the restriction on women in the community. None the less, a similar 'boundedness' of comfortable territory existed among other Eastsiders. Most were fully content to use local leisure sites and to shop locally. Males rarely visited the West End, though females did occasionally for shopping, especially at Christmas. Most people thought it was important to have a night out once a week, though finance was a crucial factor. Some went out of the immediate neighbourhood because of a boyfriend or girlfriend. For others of minority ethnic origin, connections of kinship with families elsewhere in London entailed obligations to attend weddings or other celebrations at weekends from time to time.

As with their white counterparts the activities of young black people on Eastside were locally based. The fact that several of the young women had children, further restricted their mobility. Some of the young men also expressed reluctance at moving out of the area, perceiving a greater likelihood of being stopped by the police and held as an outsider. If black young people visited the adjacent front-line area for a 'draw', they did so during daylight hours for this reason. Likewise, although Northside was known for its large number of 'blues', most said they were reluctant to visit these because of the cost of a taxi home, and once again because they did not feel free from police harassment to walk home in the early hours of the morning.

Among black youth on Northside, similar considerations applied, and most activity took place within the locality. The greater sense of a distinctive black ethnic identity, and of a variety of associated black life-styles, produced more wide-ranging networks of social contacts among the young people, and a greater disposition to select clubs and other activities further afield. In this sense there was more movement around the area by young black people on Northside, though primarily for specific leisure and cultural events. This greater mobility extended to events organized on a London-wide basis, such as reggae and soul concerts held in Brixton or elsewhere, and to the annual carnivals in Finsbury Park and Notting Hill.

Crime

Participation in criminal activities varied on the three main axes — area, gender and race. Apart from being willing to discuss their own criminal activities, many young people had quite definite images of the criminality of different groups, and the reasons for their propensities. Where they were engaged in crime, however, it emerged invariably as petty in nature, and none of the young people contacted were, so far as could be ascertained, involved in crime of a serious nature in any committed or organized manner. While it is difficult to be totally confident about such a generalization, its reliability is founded firstly on the checks possible on young people's activities during a long period of participant observation, and secondly on the practice of only conducting interviews once a relationship of personal trust had been established.

The interaction between area and personal characteristics produced a complex pattern of experience. Perhaps the most striking difference occurred within Eastside where in different community contexts, sharply contrasting patterns of criminality emerged. In the main Bangladeshi area, self-report confirmed the general view that the level of street crime and public disorder was generally low. Values of family honour, combined with effective community controls, ruled out any likelihood that young Bengalis would involve themselves in petty crime. Of greater concern to some young Bengalis was the felt need for personal privacy and freedom, which required opportunities to move outside the community for activities deviating from community norms. Crime, however, did not appear to be on the agenda. None the less, some informants commented that among young people born in Britain and brought up in Eastside schools, a change in the present confidence in Bengali youth was likely to occur.

Among the more stable and established residential areas of Eastside, a strong sense of community co-existed with a very different pattern of experience and attitudes towards crime. Thieving and petty crime generally were perceived as an important part of the male life-style. This would range from burglary and theft to 'fiddling on the job'. When asked the reasons for engaging in crime of this nature, a widespread view was that it was a normal 'opportunistic' behaviour in which anyone would engage. It was also seen as a reasonable and relatively safe way of supplementing income on a modest scale. Some emphasized a connection between thieving and unemployment, but did not see this as a sufficient explanation of the prevalence of petty crime in the area. The general view, which reflected actual experience, was that petty crime was — and long had been — part of the Eastside tradition.

What has been said above was as true of the young black population of the area as for the young whites. Moreover, it appeared that young black people's experience of participation in crime was, if anything, lower than that of whites — especially at the level of the unskilled and unemployed. There was a clear view that to identify a 'black youth problem' with regard to crime would be incorrect as well as misconceived. In this and other respects young black people's behaviour was as much a product of the Eastside tradition as that of young whites. If for unemployed blacks, thieving was a crucial means to survival, this was a product not of ethnic origin but of area-typical response to the loss of a legitimate means of a livelihood.

In Northside, fewer black respondents reported participation in crime, yet more readily took the view that black youths were disproportionately involved in street crime. The reasons given placed criminal involvement firmly in the context of social deprivation. There appeared to be less of an established community perception of crime and its significance, and more of a willingness to identify issues in terms of media or politically framed images.

This seemed borne out also by the attitudes and experiences of young women in the two areas. Participation in criminal activities by young women was in general far lower than among men. Yet on Eastside the attitudes of women condoned petty crime within the community, whereas among young black women on Northside, there was considerable criticism of male youths for their perceived criminality and Rastafarian styles of resistance.

The one issue that clearly divided young white and young black people was that of mugging. Among young white Eastsiders, mugging appeared to be conceived as a separate category of crime from other kinds of thieving. The implicit distinction appeared to be made between deliberate acts against the person and acts against property. Young white Eastsiders felt particularly critical of what were seen potentially as crimes against 'us' committed by 'them', and 'them' was readily seen as blacks in the popular image.

Among the younger group of 'Wall Kids', petty adolescent criminal activities were practised routinely, especially among the females. This involved minor acts of vandalism, and the thieving of small items from shops — essentially for a laugh and to demonstrate bravado to peers. A few of the younger girls reported having been more purposive about theft, and sold stolen goods to neighbours and friends to supplement their income, 'we did it for the money: we used to shit ourselves'. This was usually done covertly and outside the control of the older male Asian members of the group, who saw delinquent behaviour as a threat to the benign status of the group amongst local and especially Asian communities. The sense of 'izzat', or honour was important in this context: 'if there's one stray sheep, it reflects on the rest of us'. Generally speaking, the ethos of the group was law-abiding, and group members saw themselves as a distinctive but legitimate component of the make-up of the local community. They did not perceive themselves to be in active opposition to any other groups or agencies, and there were no rivalries or fights sought with other groups of young people in adjacent neighbourhoods.

Police

Hostility towards, or at least strong complaint about the police was universal among the range of young inner-city residents. In almost all cases, the police were experienced as a negative force, unwarrantedly oppressing people and adversely affecting the quality of their lives. In most, though not all cases, these attitudes were based on direct personal experience which would be cited in detail and which, whatever the accuracy of those details, undoubtedly had had a strong emotional impact on the individual concerned. Given the power, if not legitimated authority, of the police, the latter is hardly surprising, and its significance and implications are not lessened by any doubt that might be cast on the accuracy of the reports. The crucial fact was that police harassment — as a topic, or life-event — loomed significant and large in these young people's lives. It was important to them, they talked about it, they were sensitized to it and they looked out for it. That is to say, it was not the actual level of police harassment that was so significant, but rather its magnitude and importance in young black and white people's lives.

Despite this general hostility towards the police, a clear distinction was made between the policing role and actual police performance. None of the young people articulated anti-police attitudes of an ideological kind, or rejected the policing role in general. On the contrary, most expressed forcefully the desire for what they felt would be proper policing. On the negative side, there was the view that the police should stop continually harassing innocent young people — a view born of the strong resentment arising out of direct or indirect personal experience. On the positive side, there was a strong feeling that police should spend more time catching 'proper criminals'. Such 'real criminals' were seen typically as 'rapists', 'child-molesters' and 'murderers'. While it was often commented that 'everyone agrees with a fair cop', the feeling was widespread that the police picked on young people, regardless of whether they had genuine grounds for suspicion, and for trivial offences while most of the real villains escaped.

The most striking feature of attitudes to, and experience of the police was its commonality in that these views and experiences prevailed regardless of age, sex, ethnic group or area. None the less, some differences of emphasis and interpretation were noticed. Whereas in Northside, personal experience was supplemented and no doubt embellished by gossip and rumour, in Eastside, among both black and white groups, the hostility towards the police was rooted not just in personal experience but also in local folklore. This portrayed the police not merely as harassing young people on the street, but emphasized more strongly the themes of brutality and police corruption. In the more residentially stable and ethnically mixed localities characteristic of Eastside, there was more of a sense of the community as a whole being in latent, if not overt conflict with the police. This reflected the stronger sense of possessive territoriality characteristic of most of Eastside, in which neighbourhood residents, and youth gangs in particular, exercised to some extent their own social control and experienced police intrusion not as protection but as a threat to their self-interest, or a challenge to be resisted.

Among young Bengalis, in the main settlement area, a more complex set of attitudes and experience was present. While in this area of Eastside there was a strong sense of a territorially based community, this was not associated with any generalized antipathy towards a policing role, but, on the contrary, was linked strongly to a feeling of need for police protection. This need was rooted in the vivid awareness, if not daily experience, of living in a protective enclave within an actively racist environment. Indeed the main complaint about the police was a familiar one: that they do little or nothing to either prevent or catch the perpetrators of racial violence.

It would be incorrect to state, however, that this was the only complaint, since several of the young Bengali males had also experienced 'stop and search' procedures. The pattern of these stop and search procedures in the case of young Asians was different, however, in that it occurred not whilst they were walking on the street but whilst driving vehicles, and in some cases after standard enquiries escalated into questions about passports and illegal entry. It was significant, though, that none of the young Asians participating in the newly formed street-corner groups on the local estates complained of police harassment while they were standing around 'doing nothing'. A general attitude, expressed forcefully, was that Bengali youths could no longer be seen as the passive victims of racist attacks, and that if the police remained unwilling to act, individuals or vigilantes would take the law into their own hands. 'Self defence is no offence' — initially used as a campaign slogan in 1978 — was common currency among the young Asians, and there had been a handful of isolated cases of Bengali youths making random attacks on white male youths in and around the main settlement area, quite deliberately as a tit-for-tat measure.

While young males generally reported far more street encounters with police than females, many of the latter of all groups, except within the main Bengali area had experienced 'stop and search' personally, and feelings of hostility towards the police were as strong, and sometimes stronger than those of males. Not only did these young women share or sympathize with the experiences of their brothers and boyfriends, but they experienced racist attack and police harassment in terms of masculine aggression, not least on account of its frequently overt sexist nature. Hence whereas most black and white males, and Asians provided they were close to the main settlement area, claimed they had no fear of walking the streets alone at night, most females outside their own street-corner gang area would catch a cab or arrange to be met by relatives or friends. The police, they felt, not only gave them double harassment as young and female, if not triple for being black, but also failed to provide the protection that freedom of movement and from sexual harassment and attack would require.

Among the group of Wall Kids, female members tended to be more hostile towards the police than males. Several females had experience of 'stop and search' on the street, or of being pulled up for minor acts of vandalism, and while they did not feel strong hostility on these accounts, they expressed a generalized negative attitude towards the police. Male participants of Asian origin tended to have similar attitudes towards the police as the Asian community. Where they had personal experience of street 'stops', they felt that they had been able to remonstrate reasonably effectively with the police. While they felt some resentment at being stopped, they recognized a need for stops on occasion, and by arguing successfully that they were doing nothing and up to no harm, they felt that they had maintained respect while avoiding police over-reaction. Members of the group made a clear distinction between police as a category and the local beat officer who passed regularly by the 'Wall' area. Their relations with this officer were friendly and polite, and they recognized that his tolerance of their use of what was strictly private property was dependent upon their good behaviour. The result of this implicit mutual understanding was that they regarded the one police officer with whom they came into contact regularly as 'alright really' and 'quite nice'.

Views of the future
Attitudes towards the future varied sharply between ethnic groups and between the sexes, as well as on other axes of social difference. There were sharp contrasts in terms of optimism and pessimism about the future, and of whether it was seen in personal or collective terms.

Females in all groups saw the future in a personal perspective and as centring around motherhood. There were significant differences, however, in perceptions of how motherhood would fit into the wider context of their future lives. Among young Bengali women, the responsibilities of motherhood were firmly contextualized within an established set of roles and personal obligations to other family members; and as a wife, the mother would assume a certain degree of economic dependence. Furthermore, the transition from young person/daughter to adult/wife was by means of a clearly structured process involving participation in the arranged marriage system. Many young black women, on the other hand, especially in Northside, did not see motherhood as entailing economic dependence, and saw their maintenance of a secure and decent job as the essential underpinning of a viable future. Their concern about employment prospects was more direct and in this sense deeper than perhaps any other group in the study, in so far as many of them were looking for a higher degree of personal autonomy in their struggle for survival in the inner city environment. White Eastsiders were also looking to employment as part of their future, but in all cases there was no sense of a career extending beyond marriage. Work was basically seen as the means to provide money and companionship for as long as it took to get married, and the only dissent from this view was in terms of taking one's time, and not rushing into marriage and motherhood or the reverse too soon. This attitude towards employment was shared widely among those of all ethnic origins in Eastside outside the main Bengali settlement area. There was no evidence of so-called un-realistic aspirations among these young women; on the contrary, most were only too realistic about their future employment prospects. Their perspective was firmly parochial, however, in that none considered seeking employment outside the area, and all envisaged making their future lives within it.

Among males the perspective was similarly local, with emphasis on getting a good job, and both black and white young people mainly perceived this in personal terms. It was notable that young Asians thought of the future more collectively, a future for their community — a notion which also encompassed Bangladesh. None of the young Bengalis thought that they would return to live permanently in Bangladesh, so they firmly defined Britain as the context of their future lives. It was widely accepted that Britain offered better educational and employment opportunities. Significantly, those who had ambitions of higher education defined them in terms of higher-level, tradition-oriented skills such as the study of commerce or accountancy. All, however, displayed a marked sense of responsibility towards one or more significant groups or networks — the 'community' in Britain or London, their immediate family unit, and the extended family in Bangladesh. Hence, there was a clear expectation that their personal futures would to a large extent be bound up with the future of their ethnic communities, both as regards employment and through the arranged marriage system. In this way, and through use of the educational system, young Asians saw themselves as exercising some control over their futures, and despite their uncertainty about the future of the rag trade and of the national economy, their expectations were on the whole optimistic.

The outlook of most young white and black males was by contrast pessimistic. These groups saw themselves more as individual victims of large-scale forces in society and their view of the future was accordingly open-ended. They had all seen the impact on other people's lives of being in or out of work, and well recognized the central significance of the wage — not merely in its material sense, but as defining one's worth and standing within the peer group and in family and other social contexts. Most perceived that government policy — employment schemes and building programmes — was a significant factor in determining and shaping their life-chances. This awareness arose from their own experience of such schemes, which likewise shaped their general attitude to them. While these forces — both of government policy and of a more underlying nature — were seen from the perspective of the local area, they were not perceived as locally specific in origin. That is to say, the locality functioned as the prism through which a national picture was filtered, with the effect that no real alternatives were perceived to exist outside the localities within which the young people lived. Hence while perceptions prevailed such as 'this country's on its way to the dogs', or 'It's getting really bad', no possibility was seen on any level of remedying this situation. It was in this sense of alienation — of alienation from a sense of capacity to control one's own fortune — that white and black young people showed to a substantial degree, and emerged in sharp contrast to those of Bengali origin. Their pessimism, while rooted in a personal mode of experience, was a direct reflection of an essentially political and economic marginalization in relation to the wider society.

The sense of resignation to this future was, if anything, greater among young white people than among young blacks. For, in detecting an element of institutionalized racism, in policing and in housing allocations for example, some young black people had a sense of shared predicament that was lacking among the whites, and that provided a more tangible explanation for their mutual plight. While this perhaps gave some strength in so far as it provided an object around which a potential collective struggle might be organized, appropriate action was conceived if at all in terms of resistance or, as in Northside, Rastafarian separatism rather than in terms of a political strategy for achieving change. Furthermore, this awareness alone was far from providing any power or basis for organization that might enable them to act collectively in a purposeful and effective manner to gain a greater degree of control over resources that could benefit their own lives.

Policy images

That street life is an amorphous idea has been amply demonstrated by the results of the ethnographic fieldwork. It remains none the less a potent spectre both in popular thinking and amongst policy-makers and commentators and those whose concern is maintaining civil peace. Precisely what form the spectre takes, however, is not always easy to pin down.

Our concern is threefold: to articulate the meanings both explicit and implicit that constitute the social construction of the concept of street life in policy orthodoxy; to examine how and why street life as a presumed social phenomenon is considered to be problematic for social policy and civil peace; and to describe and analyze the nature of the policy response to street life as a problem. The subsequent section will evaluate the actual and potential effectiveness of policy responses to street life in the light of our results.

It would be unrealistic to assume that policy-makers and implementors would have a coherent and well-defined conception of the phenomena to which the label street life has been attached. However it is none the less clear that there *is* a set of ideas and assumptions within and outside the policy-making community about such phenomena. These ideas are ill-formed, diverse and sometimes contradictory but they are important not only for what they tell us about policy-makers' conceptions of street life but also because they inform and influence the nature of policy responses to it. The fact that there are such policy responses and that they are seen to be necessary are reflections of the perceived problematic nature of street life. We shall call this collection of ideas and assumptions the 'policy orthodoxy'.[2] Furthermore, to the extent that street life is seen as a social problem it has to be socially constructed (Becker, 1963, 1966; Rubington & Weinberg, 1971: section 4; Golding and Middleton, 1982) by policy-makers, given some meaning, before a policy response to it can be formulated. This is a common feature of social problems that have a more amorphous nature. A sensible policy cannot be devised to counter an inchoate problem: it must first be constructed in such a way that a solution looks at least feasible.

Street life in policy orthodoxy

The concept of street life does not feature very often in policy documents. There is no reason why it should. It does appear, however, explicitly and implicitly, as part of a conglomerate of related concepts such as youth alienation, youth unemployment, intergenerational conflict, homelessness, youth identity problems, street activity, and in legal terminology relating to idling and hanging around. There is a set of interrelated notions within which street life appears sometimes as cause and sometimes as effect, and sometimes simply as correlate. We can characterize the interrelatedness of these ideas about street life as an effect as follows.[3] High levels of unemployment among youth, in part caused by and in part contributing to alienation and identity problems, combined with relatively high levels of homelessness exacerbated by conflict with parents and a weak family structure leads to youths having time on their hands, hanging around and killing time, which in turn is conducive to street activity and to street culture. The youth in question are almost always assumed to be male and often — though by no means always — predominately West Indian. There are many variations on this theme in the policy literature but space permits only this caricature. It is, none the less, more than adequate for our purposes.

It is clear that in policy terms street life cannot be treated in isolation from a set of other ideas and beliefs. It constitutes part of a package of beliefs about youth and black youth in particular.

Street life as a social problem
Street life is seen as problematical both from a social and a public order point of view. The two are of course inextricably linked within the policy orthodoxy. And it is because of its perceived problematic nature that a policy response to it is necessary.

There are two dimensions to the problematic nature of being on the street. Each is relevant to both social and public order aspects. Firstly, street life is problematic in itself as part of or as a consequence of a set of related morbidities. It is seen as a correlate of killing time, wasting time, hanging about for want of anything better to do, loitering, being up to no good (Home Affairs Committee, 1979–80(a), evidence from the Commission for Racial Equality; Scarman, 1981: 2.11 and 2.30). Whilst none of these per se constitute public order problems, they are seen as social problems with potentially harmful public order consequences. They are social problems not only because they lead to potential public order problems, but also because they do not conform to expected, or usual patterns of behaviour. Furthermore, to the extent that they are symptomatic of other, related problems such as alienation and disaffected youth, they bode ill for the future. Here is a group of young people, mainly men, who are not being socialized into the mainstream of society with its ordered progression from youth to manhood, from single to family man, from pupil to worker (Home Affairs Committee, 1979–80(b), evidence from Department of Employment; Environment Committee, 1982–3, evidence from GLC, Hackney London Borough).

The second dimension to the problematic nature of street life revolves around its potential consequences and associational patterns of behaviour. There are two consequential problems. Firstly, street life precipitates conflictual relations between youth on the street and the police (Scarman, 1981: 2–23, 4–66; Brogden, 1981; Home Affairs Committee, 1979–80(a), evidence from CRE and the Home Office). Such conflict is of course not a necessary consequence of street life, but street life does necessarily bring youth into more and more frequent contact with the police and therefore increases the likelihood of friction. Such friction could be harmful especially in so far as it involved an ethnic minority youth that was already alienated from the main institutions and patterns of personal development in society. It could at the very least lead to a hardening of attitudes and prejudices on the part of youth and of the police and distance them even further from the main law and peace-keeping institutions in society (Gaskell & Smith, 1985). This may then produce the second consequential problem: the danger of open conflict between youth and the police which, if sufficient numbers of young people were involved, either being already on the street or available and ready to be 'called out' at short notice, could result in a major threat to civil peace — a riot.

What are believed to be the mechanics of such an event are common currency, though this is far from saying that anyone really does understand the mechanics of riots and why the predisposing and 'trigger' conditions sometimes, though rarely, result in riotous behaviour and at most other times do not.[4] Thus we can place street life in the supposed pattern of events that may lead to rioting and as represented in diagrammatic form (see Figure 1) it can be seen that street life plays a significant part in the aetiology of civil unrest.

The other aspect of the second dimension of street life as problematic concerns associational factors and patterns of behaviour. There is an assumed relationship between involvement in street life and involvement in criminal activity. Indeed, one of the most common dangers attributed to street life in the policy orthodoxy is the exposure of youth to the temptations of crime and its important functional role in the development of a criminal career.

There is a number of aspects to the problematic character of street life in the policy orthodoxy. What they show, when taken together is that street life may be seen as a potentially serious problem. Street life is both pathological because it is a correlate of other pathologies such as alienation and crime and potentially dangerous because of the key role it plays in the aetiology of civil unrest. Street life is non-normal, pathological behaviour. Because it is pathological and problematic, it must be controlled and reduced.

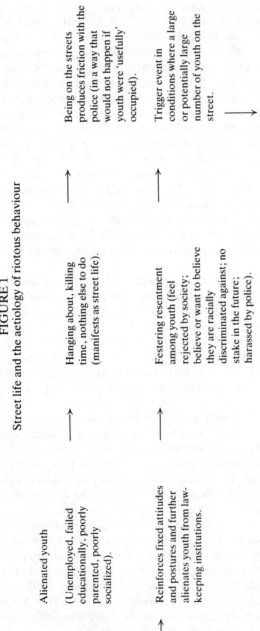

FIGURE 1
Street life and the aetiology of riotous behaviour

Alienated youth

(Unemployed, failed educationally, poorly parented, poorly socialized).

Reinforces fixed attitudes and postures and further alienates youth from law-keeping institutions.

Hanging about, killing time, nothing else to do (manifests as street life).

Festering resentment among youth (feel rejected by society; believe or want to believe they are racially discriminated against; no stake in the future; harassed by police).

Being on the streets produces friction with the police (in a way that would not happen if youth were 'usefully' occupied).

Trigger event in conditions where a large or potentially large number of youth on the street.

Riot.

The policy response to street life
As with the social construction of street life, the response to it cannot be treated in isolation from responses to related issues. Policy responses to street life will overlap with and include responses to other problems, but in general, a broad distinction can be drawn between policies of control and management, largely a policing function, and those designed to reduce or provide substitutes for it. The latter are generally social agency functions and it is with these that we are concerned.

Social responses to street life rarely have that as their sole and specific function but there are a number of provisions which at one time or another have been promoted in policy documents as at least contributory antidotes to street life. The most important of these have been firstly measures to reduce youth unemployment[5] such as the Youth Training Scheme and its predecessors, positive action policies and the enforcement of contract compliance, both aimed primarily at ethnic minorities but not specially youth, and the variety of provisions under inner city policies (Edwards, 1984; Higgins et al., 1983) and Section 11 grants.[6] Secondly there has been a range of alternative provisions such as youth clubs, drop-in centres, community centres, self-help groups and the like (Roberts, 1983: chs 10 and 12; Cashmore, 1982: 213–21; Cheetham et al., 1981: section 4). The logic behind such provision is clear in policy documentation — that youth will be less at risk and less likely to be up to no good if they are engaged in more constructive activities which sublimate their high spirits. Such measures including employment-related ones have also been promoted as antidotes to youth alienation (but see Gaskell & Smith, 1981, 1985; Cashmore, 1981; Troyna, 1979).[7] But so have such provisions as the careers service, outreach and youth and community workers, police liaison schemes and the provision of accommodation for the homeless and rootless.

The evaluation
As already noted, there are two components to our evaluation of policy orthodoxy about street life. The first is to compare the characterization of street life in policy orthodoxy with the picture that emerges from our fieldwork. The policy responses outlined in the preceding paragraphs will largely be influenced by orthodox beliefs about street life. The second part of the evaluation therefore is to use the comparisons made in the first part, to assess the immediate and potential efficacy of current policies in reducing or containing street life.

Policy orthodoxy and the view from the street

The phenomenon of street life. There are some broad areas of correspondence between policy orthodoxy and the view from the street — chiefly in respect of some of the correlates of street life — street culture, youth identity, unemployment (though only partially), attendance at clubs and pool rooms. But there are also significant differences which stem in the main from the oversimplified caricature of street life in the orthodox view.

We have already detailed the range of variations in street life and culture. Our present purpose is to note some of the more significant variations and complexities which the policy orthodoxy does not reflect and which in consequence may influence the relevance and effectiveness of policies. On the matter of street life, we found little evidence to support the conventional view of numbers of youths hanging around on the street and living out their lives on the street. The conventional view may more closely reflect the situation in some black front-line areas but these are few and involve only a very small (probably minute) proportion of youths of any ethnicity. There is a sense in which street life may be said to occur, but as we have demonstrated, it does not conform physically to the conventional view. Street life is a multi-variate phenomenon of which the physical manifestations are perhaps not the most important.

Among the significant correlates of street life in the policy orthodoxy that we are able to comment on from our data are youth alienation, attitudes to and experience of education, unemployment, aspects of self-identity, and — to a lesser extent — intergenerational conflict. Problems of identity among ethnic minority youth, in particular are often referred to in policy-related literature (CRE, 1980(a); HAC, 1979–80(a)) but less often spelled out in anything other than a superficial way. If by identity problems, is meant doubts about ethnic identity in a country where the majority are of different ethnicity, then there is some support from our data for a view that some young people do not see their nationality and their ethnicity as absolutely congruent. But again, there were wide variations — the Bangladeshis for example seemed to harbour no doubts — and much of what may appear to be identity problems, is probably more likely to concern cultural differences and the future prospects of black minorities in Britain. In any event, such ambiguities and uncertainties as we came across did not appear to pose problems to any great extent — at least for the young people concerned.

As we have noted, youth alienation is a very commonly cited problem in the commentative as well as the policy literature (HAC, 1979–80(a); CRE, 1980(a); Environment Committee, 1982–3; Scarman, 1981; CRE, 1980(b); DOE, 1977; HAC, 1979–80(b)). To the extent that attitudes to the police, to schooling, employment and the provision of surrogate work are indicators of alienation, as has often been asserted in policy documents[8] then our data can shed some light on the extent to which our respondents can be said to be alienated. Attitudes to the police were almost wholly negative though in all groups the hostility was directed not so much at the police as an institution but at some police practices. And the reasons for the dislike of the police expressed by Asians and Afro-Caribbeans were different. For the former it was a matter of the police being less than determined in their pursuit of those who tormented Asians; for the latter it was a direct response to what they saw as racial harassment. To the extent that these reasons were justified, and we make no comment on this, then they are not indicators of alienation from the law-enforcing institutions of society. In respect of education, as we have seen, attitudes varied both as between ethnicity and sex. Where a rejection of school and post-school education was in evidence, this occurred largely among white and Afro-Caribbean males, and much less so among females. Both male and female Asians had more positive attitudes to education. Again, employment as such was generally valued and the importance — and difficulties — of obtaining work were realistically assessed. Where more negative attitudes *were* expressed it was in relation to surrogate work schemes such as YTS, rejected out of hand by most respondents whether or not they had had experience of them. But this was not a rejection of work schemes as such, but because they were not perceived as leading anywhere; were jobs thought to be available at the end of them, they would have been endorsed. What these findings demonstrate, is that the blanket case for a disaffected and alienated youth — of any ethnicity — which is in varying degrees a significant component of the policy orthodoxy about street life, is difficult to sustain when set against our data. At the very least we are forced to argue that what our respondents said and did corresponded only very imperfectly with the orthodoxy. What we have said in respect of other components of the orthodoxy is equally true. The picture we must paint is both more complex and more variable. In respect of another variety of youth provision for example, our respondents had on the whole very positive attitudes to youth clubs and similar provisions. There is little indication here of massive rejection of state or voluntary provision and little evidence to support the view of an alienated and disaffected youth.

Finally, as to intergenerational conflict, we found little evidence of a young generation systematically at odds with its parents. Certainly, there were issues — attitudes to education and youth training schemes were two — over which respondents mentioned differences of opinion with parents, and a significant proportion of the male youth referred to life at home as boring. None of this would support an assertion of a serious breakdown in relationships or loyalties between the generations. Obviously, where family ties, mores and expectations are stronger and more rigid, there is a higher risk of intergenerational conflict, and this was the case with many of the Asian youth. If such conflict is to become a more widespread phenomenon then it will be among the Asian population.

The policy orthodox view of street life therefore would need to be qualified, amended and filled out in a number of respects if it were to accord with what we have learned. Certainly we have to conclude from our data that street life and street use to the extent that they exist do not constitute the public manifestation of a bewildered, 'lost' or alienated youth. The street is the space to be traversed between other activities and a place to meet friends and watch the world.

Is street life a problem?

Street life is significant in policy terms because it is seen as problematical and hence a phenomenon to which some sort of response is required. We must ask, therefore, whether the results of our fieldwork support this view. Do street life and its associated characteristics, in the multi-variate form that we have found, constitute a problem of some sort and, if so, what kind of problem and for whom?

The problematic character of street life from the policy-orthodoxy view has been elaborated. When we compare this with the picture that emerges from our fieldwork, we find that whilst there are some small areas of correspondence, street life on the whole does not present society with so alarming a threat of mischief and morbidity as policy orthodoxy would have us believe. First and foremost we were unable to discover the physical manifestation of street life as large or relatively large numbers of youths hanging about on the street. If street life is conducive to riotous behaviour, then the mechanics of this phenomenon at least must be different from those that orthodoxy supposes.

Apart from the variation in the mechanics of street life, is there any support for the view that it is actually, or potentially, problematical? We can best answer this by taking the particular problem manifestations in turn. Firstly then, street life is seen as closely associated and sometimes synonymous with hanging around, killing time and being up to no good. We found relatively little hanging around on the street and the variety of activities that youth do engage in — in a variety of locations and which we have taken to be the equivalent of street life — were by no means always or even usually purposeless. There *was* time-killing but it neither took place on the streets nor did it invariably or usually constitute a major part of youths' time. It must none the less be added that unemployment *was* a burden not least in giving little or no structure to time and leaving hours to be filled. It would not be true to say, however, that in consequence the hours had to be killed. Time filling was less purposeless than orthodoxy would imply.

Secondly, there is the question of whether street life and the associated phenomena of hanging around and killing time are symptomatic of or conducive to an alienated youth unsocialized into the roles of responsible citizenship. There is a problem of cause and effect in this supposed relationship. It would seem improbable that street life would in itself lead to youth being unsocialized. It may on the other hand be more probable that alienated or unsocialized youth would engage in street life. In any event, in policy orthodoxy street life, alienation and non-socialization are seen as somehow linked if only as interrelated variables within a complex whole. We have already mentioned the question of alienation but as to non-socialization, it did not seem from our evidence possible to make any firm connection with the activities we have called street life; at least, certainly not causal connections. Indeed, it would be difficult to say much that was definitive about so amorphous a concept as socialization. The future views of the great majority of girls and women in our study were of a very traditional and conforming kind. The pattern of future views of the boys and men was more variable however, being more conformist and assertive among Asian youth, more bleak and negative among whites and Afro-Caribbeans. In this respect, future views reflected the current employment situation of the different groups.

There is one respect in which we have to qualify these remarks, and it stems from the unfulfilment of hopes and expectations. The patterns of activities studied and which collectively we have called street life and street culture, are, paradigmatically, the activities of young people and youth. They are activities that fall by the wayside with the onset of early adulthood, employment, marriage and setting up home. Typically, they have been left behind by the early twenties. Yet there was evidence that for some Afro-Caribbean males — and indeed for some of their white counterparts — street life was being stretched beyond adolescence into early adulthood. These were men who have never been in work and probably see little likelihood of ever being so other than for short-term, marginal jobs. If one consequence of long-term or semi-permanent unemployment is the extension of adolescent life-styles into adulthood there may be as yet unforeseen results both for society and, more certainly, for individuals involved.

A third respect in which street life may be problematic as evidenced in the policy orthodoxy is that the nature of the activity is such that it brings young people into greater contact with the police, that this contact may well be conflictual and will lead to a hardening of antipathetic attitudes on both sides. This in turn, it is argued, will heighten the possibility of open conflict and civil unrest. To the extent that youths are on the street, and this seems numerically to be less the case than is supposed, then our evidence suggests there is some truth in the orthodox argument. As we have shown, attitudes to the police were almost entirely negative and a part of the reason for this so far as the white but especially Afro-Caribbean youths were concerned was experience of or rumour about harassment. But the mechanics of person-to-person contact on the street was only a part of the reason for antipathetic attitudes. More significantly there was an all-pervading belief about police attitudes to youth, and black youth in particular, which needed little contact on the street to sustain it. There was little evidence that reducing the street presence of youth would in any way alleviate the antagonistic attitudes that they held towards the police.

As to the mechanics of riotous crowd behaviour there is evidence that street presence by large numbers of youth, indeed even by small numbers, is not a necessary condition of riotous behaviour, though street life in its wider sense may be. None the less, it is the case that the street was one activity space among many and one whose freedoms and ephemeral excitements, other forms of provision such as clubs, pool rooms and pubs could not in any simple way displace. While older youths — especially the unemployed — preferred these off-street locations, they were still experienced as an extension of the street. Moreover, the younger teenagers of school age were largely uninterested in off-street provision, especially the more 'evangelistic' youth clubs. When these attitudes and dispositions are combined with the almost universal and strong dislike of the police that our respondents exhibited then it is highly likely that street events involving the police will very rapidly draw numbers of spectators and potential participants out on to the street.

The fourth and final problematic dimension of street life in the policy orthodoxy is its supposed association with other socially morbid and criminal activities. In short, street presence exposes youth to the temptations of crime and the company of criminals. We must be more circumspect in our assertions about this dimension. Criminal activity is less likely to be admitted to, talked about, or engaged in, in the presence of a fieldworker — even one who has, over a long period gained the confidence of his or her respondents. It is certainly true that some of our respondents were engaged in petty crime and took a fairly casual attitude to it, but we cannot judge the extent of criminal or semi-criminal activity. It seems likely however that much of this petty crime was opportunistic and was influenced neither in its aetiology nor its practice by the patterns of activity we have called street life and street culture. What we can say is that crime did not seem to be a significant or consistent component of the life-styles of our respondents and that the locations of their activities did not appear consistently to expose them to criminals or criminal ways of life.

The evaluation of policy strategies
The second part of our evaluation concerns an assessment of the policy responses to street life. These have been enumerated earlier but one point in respect of these policies needs to be repeated. We do not claim that the policies we have listed and which are commented on are a direct and specific response to street life as such. They are none the less policies designed to make some form of provision for youth, for example employment or alternative activities, or to bring help and structure to what are seen as unstructured lives. The *implicit* aim of many of these policies is to give youth something better to do than hanging around and killing time and the need for this must be seen to lie in the assumed problematic nature and consequences of street life — not least among which is the danger of riotous crowd behaviour. We have argued that our fieldwork results suggest that street life is, for a variety of reasons, probably not as problematic as orthodoxy might fear but we shall, for the purposes of policy evaluation, assume the veracity of the orthodox view.[9] It must be accepted that what we say about these policies in regard to street life does not diminish their importance in dealing with other issues.

Our evaluation of policies falls into two parts:

Part 1. What is the likelihood that policies designed to reduce youth unemployment will achieve any degree of success in this specific aim, in the light of our findings about attitudes to, and/or use of relevant policy strategies? And what are the likely levels of take-up and use of alternative provisions in the light of our findings relating to attitudes to and/or use of youth clubs, sports centres, community centres, drop-in centres and related kinds of provision?

Part 2. In the light of the ethnographic findings in relation to the self and group identity, alienation, leisure patterns, street use, mobility, location and time consumption and attitudes to police, is it likely that success under Part 1 would lead to a reduction in or alteration to street life, street use, street culture and alienation and a change in attitudes and hence, to a reduction in the likelihood of riots?

Part 1. The most important measure designed to reduce youth unemployment is the Youth Training Scheme (YTS). It is in part a scheme to provide training in a variety of job skills, and in part to provide young people with something to do during the daytime. It is not proper employment and the wages are very low. These aspects of YTS did not escape our respondents who without exception rejected it both on general terms and as something they, as individuals, would use. Indeed, it was one of the few things about which there was virtual unanimity. They are not typical of course. Many young people do make use of YTS schemes but for these inner city dwellers, YTS is exploitative and does not lead anywhere (but see OPCS, 1980; Cross et al., 1983; Coffield et al., 1983; CRE, 1980a; Dex, 1982; Roberts, Duggan and Noble, 1982; Roberts, Noble and Duggan, 1982). This last point is significant because it demonstrates that what is being expressed here is not an affective dismissal of any state policy, but an instrumental rejection of this policy because it is not thought to help you get a job. And getting a job, for most of our respondents, was important. It may be argued that if they were keen to get a job, they would not reject YTS before trying it and that their rejection of it is symptomatic of a general disinclination to work. There may have been an element of this among some, but our data does not support it. So far as YTS is concerned, however, it did not have nor seem likely to have much impact on our respondents. As a means of providing them with something to do or of keeping them 'off the streets' it is a failure.

Attitudes to education were strongly negative among white males and females and among male Afro-Caribbeans, They were more positive among Asians of both sexes and Afro-Caribbean females. Furthermore, most of those who expressed negative attitudes also left school at the earliest opportunity and, in combination, these might be seen as evidence of a degree of alienation — at least from the assumption that education is the beginning of training for the world of work (Willis, 1977). Such attitudes and actions further reinforce the view that additional education and training will not readily be used except by Afro-Caribbean females and Asians of both sexes.

It may well be that for some inner city youth at least, but especially whites and Afro-Caribbean males, a vicious circle has developed whereby education is rejected as being irrelevant to getting a job whether true or not. In consequence they leave school with minimal qualifications (Brown, 1984: ch. 6) and then experience difficulty in finding work. Where attitudes change with age, opportunities and access are still difficult to obtain. To the extent that this is the case, then perhaps policy ought to be directed to breaking the circle — or at least convincing those locked in it that it can be broken.

As to policies of positive action, positive discrimination and contract compliance, we can say that the amount of additional provision from positive action and positive discrimination policies is relatively small. In all probability these benefit ethnic minority youth at the expense of white youth — whose employment needs were just as great. Contract compliance, being in its infancy in Britain, has as yet had minimal impact on ethnic minority youth employment.

Whilst Urban Programme expenditure as Partnership Programme or traditional Urban Programme schemes is now substantial, the response at local authority or voluntary agency level remains project-oriented. Whilst individual projects may have some impact, the overall provision remains patchy and relatively small. This is even more the case with Section 11 grants which, though directed specifically at areas with high proportions of ethnic minority members, are few and small.

One final point in respect of the inner city response. Since 1977, the orientation of inner city policies has shifted towards regenerating the economic infrastructure and thereby creating more jobs. There is little evidence to suggest that this has benefited the sorts of young people represented in our study. Many of the jobs that have been created or drawn back into the inner city are high-technology jobs for which our respondents would, without further training, be unqualified.

The overall picture, therefore, so far as providing employment for our respondents is far from optimistic. Some provision is misdirected, other is on too small a scale, and the attitudes to YTS and schooling expressed by most, though in respect of the latter not all, would militate against widespread take up.

We have seen that, although opinions about and attitudes to youth club provision were varied, the majority of our respondents responded favourably. Ironically, the major criticism of youth provision came from the youngest of our respondents who rejected them as 'kids' stuff'. This may in part have been a result of the sort of clubs they attended which were oriented towards younger age groups and in part to the braggadocio that infected their talk. Other qualifications were made by white girls who tended not to use youth clubs after the age of sixteen or seventeen, and by Afro-Caribbean males some of whom said they wanted clubs that would remain open further into the night.

Apart from these qualifications it would seem that this form of alternative provision, at least, is valuable and made use of. Much of this provision is made under funding from the Urban Programme (and to a lesser extent under Section 11) and suffers from being limited and patchy. However, there did seem to be one form or another of club to which all our respondents could go. To the extent that these were fairly extensively used, they must be counted a success. However, simple use of the facilities is not our main concern. This is whether, if such provisions as we have discussed in Part 1 were successful in their immediate and limited aims, they would contribute to a reduction in street life, street culture and their associated characteristics.

Part 2. If surrogate work schemes were taken up, if more real employment suitable for inner city youth could be created and if alternative provisions and not only youth clubs were used, would there in consequence be a reduction in street life? This is aside from the question of whether street life poses a social and civil problem to which there ought to be a policy response. We have already questioned this assumption in policy orthodoxy.

The answer revolves around the nature of street life. We have shown that the mechanistic view of street life does not accord with the picture that emerges from our study. Street life is both more varied and more complex. It entails a set of beliefs and attitudes, a pattern of sub-culture and a set of activity patterns which are only partly played out literally on the street.

Given this alternative construction of street life, we must express considerable doubt about the efficacy of the policies we have discussed. They are, at least when compared with our data, based upon some misconceived premises about the nature of street life and its relationship to other activities. It probably would be the case that having reasonable jobs with reasonable incomes would effect some change in attitudes among many of our respondents and particularly Afro-Caribbean and white males and provide them with a future view that was less meaningless and bleak. And higher employment rates and take-up of YTS would offset some aspects of street life — but mainly by time-shifting some activities to out-of-work hours. There is little evidence however that a marked alteration in the complex of associated activities or in street culture would result. To the extent that street life consists in a complex of activities that take place not only or even mainly on the street, much of this would be likely to continue.

As to 'alternative' forms of provision — in the public, voluntary or private sectors — our evidence suggests that much of this, were it available, would be incorporated into the complex of activities that make up street life. Current provision is thus incorporated into the life-styles of youth; further provision would be too.

We base these claims about the relative ineffectiveness of YTS employment policies and alternative provisions to affect street life, on our belief — engendered by our data — that the policy orthodox view of street life is misconceived. It appears to us not to be aimless and purposeless activity to fill the void left by joblessness, alienation and inadequate alternative provision. It is, rather, a pattern of activities, beliefs and attitudes to which employment and youth provision are not alternatives but compatible activities. It is not a meaningless time-filling that will disappear when more constructive activities are provided. It is a life-style that has meaning and purpose, even if these are not immediately obvious to the casual observer. Having a job and leisure provision will add to it rather than replace it.

If our contention is true that street life is not the pressing social and civil problem that orthodoxy supposes, it may not matter to agencies of control that policies designed in part to solve it will fail. But lest this seems too sanguine an attitude, we would reiterate what we said earlier — that street life is *not* wholly unproblematical. Physical presence on the street, even if it is less than supposed, does bring youth into abrasive contact with the police and with other ethnic groups. Some of the activity patterns associated with street life may encourage criminal activities and criminalization of youth. But we doubt that street life per se is the main contributory function at work here. Furthermore, returning to the policy response, it should surely be of public concern that this has and probably will continue to fail. In the first place, it matters greatly to the youth, who do want real jobs: for them above all, the policies have been diversionary and a false promise. In addition, very substantial public resources have been channelled in these directions, but, we suggest, from the point of view of some objectives at least, to very limited effect. There are many other, and more important reasons for providing employment, educational and leisure provision to young people, and it is these, rather than some problem-defining notion of street life, that need to be addressed.

Notes

1. For a discussion of the use of policy documents as research data, see Edwards, 1986.

2. We do not wish to claim any special epistemological status for 'policy orthodoxy', it is merely a convenient term to characterize the everyday views and assumptions within the policy-making community as distinct from the possibly more lurid ones current in parts of the media and elsewhere — including the sociological community.

3. We shall consider another set of interrelated concepts where street life appears as cause, when we examine the perceived problematic nature of street life below.

4. We shall consider the relationship between riotous behaviour and the nature of street life as we have found it, later in this chapter. For further discussion of the nature and aetiology of riots, see Betz, 1974; Field, 1982; and Taylor, 1981.

5. For a discussion of attempts to get alienated youth into employment, see Roberts, Duggan and Noble, 1981.

6. In the fiscal year 1985–6 total expenditure under the inner city heading was £338m. of which £38.8m. was for specifically ethnic-minority relevant projects.

7. It is worth noting that in the policy orthodoxy, frequently occurring indicators or correlates of 'alienation' include: non-registration for unemployment benefit, non-registration with YTS (and its predecessors), rejection of work experience programmes, school truanting, disaffection with schooling and education, petty crime and vandalism and residential instability.

8. The Department of Employment in evidence to the Home Affairs Committee cited failure to register for unemployment benefit as an indication of alienation; the Department of Education and Science cited disaffection with schooling and truancy.

9. We none the less believe that any competent policy evaluation must start by questioning rather than assuming the nature of the problems to which the policy is a response.

References

Becker, H. (1963) *Outsiders: Studies in the Sociology of Deviance.* New York: The Free Press.

Becker, H. (1966) *Social Problems: A Modern Approach.* New York: Wiley.

Betz, M. (1974) 'Riots and Welfare: Are They Related?' *Social Problems*, 21(3): 345–55.

Brake, M. (1985) *Comparative Youth Culture.* London: Routledge and Kegan Paul.

Brogden, A. (1981) ' "Sus" is Dead: But What About "Sas"?', *New Community*, ix(i): 44–52.

Brown, C. (1984) *Black and White Britain: The Third P.S.I. Survey.* London: Heinemann.

Carey, S. (1984) 'The Multi-Ethnic Wall', *New Society*, 19 April: 99–100.

Cashmore, E. (1981) 'After the Rastas', *New Community*, ix(2): 173–81.

Cashmore, E. (1982) 'Black Youth, Sport and Education', *New Community*, x(2): 213–21.

Cheetham, J., James, W., Loney, M., Mayor, B. and Prescott, W. (eds) (1981), *Social and Community Work in a Multi-Racial Society*, New York: Harper and Row.

Coffield, F., Borrill, C. and Marshall, S. (1983) 'How Young People Try to Survive Being Unemployed', *New Society*, 64 (1072): 332–4.

Commission for Racial Equality, *Annual Reports 1975–1985*. London: Commission for Racial Equality.

Commission for Racial Equality (CRE) (1977) *Urban Deprivation Racial Inequality and Social Policy: a Report.* London: HMSO.

Commission for Racial Equality (1980a) *Ethnic Minority Youth Unemployment.* London: CRE.

Commission for Racial Equality (1980b) *Youth in a Multi-Racial Society.* London: CRE.

Cross, M., Edmonds, J. and Sargeant, R. (1983) *Ethnic Minorities: Their Experience of Y.O.P.* M.S.C. Special Programmes: Occasional Paper No. 5. London: Manpower Services Commission.

Department of the Environment (1977) *Policy for the Inner Cities*, Cmnd. 6845. London: Department of the Environment.

Dex, S. (1982) 'West Indians, Further Education, and Labour Markets', *New Community*, X(2), 191–205.

Edwards, J. (1984) 'U.K. Inner Cities: Problem Construction and Policy Response', *Cities*, 1(6), 592–604.

Edwards, J. (1986) *Positive Discrimination, Social Justice, and Social Policy*. London: Tavistock.

Field, S. (1982) *Urban Disorders in Britain and America: A Review of Research*. London: HMSO.

Gaskell, G. and Smith, P. (1981) '"Alienated" Black Youth: An Investigation of "Conventional Wisdom" Explanations', *New Community*, IX(2), 182–93.

Gaskell, G. and Smith, P. (1985) 'How Young Blacks See the Police', *New Society*, 23 August, 261–3.

Golding, P. and Middleton, S. (1982) *Images of Welfare*. Oxford: Martin Robertson.

Hall, S., Critcher, C., Jefferson, T., Clarke, J. and Roberts, B. (1978) *Policing the Crisis: Mugging, the State, and Law and Order*. London: Macmillan.

Higgins, J., Deakin, N., Edwards, J. and Wicks, M. (1983) *Government and Urban Poverty*. London: Blackwell.

House of Commons, Home Affairs Committee (1979–80a) Race Relations and Immigration Sub-Committee *Race Relations and the 'Sus' Law: Minutes of Evidence*. London: HMSO.

House of Commons, Home Affairs Committee (1979–80b) Race Relations and Immigration Sub-Committee, *Racial Disadvantage: Minutes of Evidence*, London: HMSO.

House of Commons, Environment Committee (1982–3) *The Problems of Management of Urban Renewal*. London: HMSO.

John, G. (1981) *In the Service of Black Youth*. Leicester: National Association of Youth Clubs.

Joshua, H. and Wallace, T. (1983) *To Ride the Storm*. London: Heinemann.

Oakley, R. and Carey, S. (1986) 'Street Life, Youth and Ethnicity in Inner City Areas', *New Community* 13, 2: 214–223.

Office of Population Censuses and Surveys (1980) *Young People's Employment Study*. London: OPCS.

Pryce, K. (1979) *Endless Pressure: a Study of West Indian Life Styles in Bristol*. Harmondsworth: Penguin.

Roberts, K. (1983) *Youth and Leisure*. London: George Allen and Unwin.

Roberts, K., Duggan, J. and Noble, M.M. (1981) *Unregistered Youth Unemployment and Outreach Careers Work*. Department of Employment Research Paper No. 31. London: Department of Employment.

Roberts, K., Duggan, J. and Noble, M. (1982) 'Racial Disadvantage in Youth Labour Markets', in Barton, L. and Walker, S. (eds) *Race, Class and Education*. London: Croom Helm.

Roberts, K., Noble, M. and Duggan, J. (1982) 'Youth Unemployment: an Old Problem or a New Life-Style?' *Leisure Studies*, 1: 171–82.

Rubington, E. and Weinberg, M. (1971) *The Study of Social Problems*. New York: Oxford University Press.

Scarman Report (1981) *The Brixton Disorders: 10–12 April 1981*. Cmnd 8427, London: HMSO.

Solomos, J. (1982) 'Black Youth, Economic Marginalisation and the State in Britain', in Korte, H. (ed.) *Cultural Identity and Structural Marginalisation of Migrant Workers*, pp. 29–45. Strasbourg: European Science Foundation.

Taylor, S. (1981) 'Riots: Some Explanations', *New Community*, IX(2): 167–72.

Troyna, B. (1979) 'Differential Commitment to Ethnic Identity by Black Youths in Britain', *New Community*, VII(3): 406–14.

Willis, P. (1977) *Learning to Labour: How Working Class Kids Get Working Class Jobs*. Farnborough: Saxon House.

4

Front-line supervision
in the British police service

Michael Chatterton

Introduction

This chapter looks at the function of intermediate-level supervisors in the police through an investigation of the role of the uniformed patrol sergeant. The focus of the chapter differs from the others in this volume, because it concentrates exclusively on the police organization, the position of patrol sergeants within it and their responsibilities and tasks. What has such a role analysis to offer to an understanding of collective behaviour particularly of the type investigated by Lord Scarman in 1981?

To appreciate its relevance one needs to understand what is meant by the front-line of the police organization, to recognize how vital these contacts are to the relationship between police and public, and to understand how the people in the front-line are trained and supervised.

If members of the public are dissatisfied with the quality of the service they receive because police officers do not deal with them in a civil, efficient and effective manner when responding to the wide variety of concerns, then this will produce a crisis of confidence. Suspicion and antagonism will increase and against this background any routine encounter between police and public may precipitate a riot.

The front-line of the police organization is defined as the section which interacts with members of the general public in normal and routine, settings (Smith, 1965; Jones, 1980). It is the first to respond to diverse demands they make on the police. Its mandate is so wide that it has to be available to be contacted about, and probably to attend to, *anything* concerning the behaviour of fellow citizens and the state of society which the public define as a police matter. (Banton, 1964; Bittner, 1970; Manning, 1977; Punch, 1979).

The front-line may provide 'first-aid' before specialist back-up resources are brought in but this 'first-aid' treatment should not be underestimated. The cost of a mistake at the initial contact can be heavy; fatal in some situations. Errors and mistakes can result from many things: genuine errors of interpretation; mistakes where constables misunderstand or are misled, because they do not know who to refer people to for help; because the constable does not treat the matter as important and cannot be bothered to get to the bottom of it (Chatterton, 1983; Holdaway, 1983). The professionalism of the police in handling routine and normal front-line incidents is as important as their professionalism in dealing with collective disorders. The insensitive and unskilled handling of routine beat incidents can contribute part of the fuel as well as the fuse for such collective disturbances (see Chapter 5 below).

Yet junior and inexperienced constables make up a very large percentage of the police officers in this front-line. On their shoulders falls the responsibility for servicing a multitude of demands and problems.

The cumulative effect of these front-line contacts on the public, the relative inexperience of the officers engaged in them and the complexity of some of the situations with which they have to deal, immediately draws attention to the nature and quality of the supervision they receive.

It is here that the role of the patrol sergeants is vital. Patrol sergeants are considered to be the first-line, quality-controllers in the police. Traditionally, they have been portrayed as street-supervisors and on-the-job trainers, closely monitoring and controlling the work of their constables on the street and at the incidents they attend. They are presented as the first-line of management who, because they are street-based, retain close contact with the constables on the ground.

Given this prevailing conception of the patrol sergeant's position in the police organization it is not surprising that Lord Scarman and others have argued that competently trained and directly involved sergeants could help overcome the difficulties associated with the youthfulness and inexperience of the constables:

> The need is not to remove young officers from sensitive areas — age in itself is certainly no guarantee of wisdom — but to ensure that they receive proper guidance and supervision in discharging their difficult, delicate, and indispensable function. (Scarman, 1982: 135)

Although Scarman recognized the role of the tutor–constable his views are unequivocal on the importance of the part to be played by inspectors and sergeants in training, monitoring and supervising the activities of constables on street duties. He made specific reference to the need for close supervision of stop and search operations. The Royal Commission on Criminal Procedure had charged supervision with a similar responsibility (1981: p. 29).

As far as supervision is concerned, the role of inspectors and sergeants is crucial. I am not wholly persuaded that its importance is sufficiently recognised either in the manning of Forces or in the degree of management training given to officers in these ranks ... I therefore recommend that greater attention be given to management training in the supervisory responsibilities of officers of inspector and sergeant rank. At the same time, these ranks must receive from their senior officers the support and recognition which is their due ... (Scarman, 1982: 135).

Like Scarman I initially focused on the training needs of the sergeant. There was already evidence that the organization, whilst recognizing the need to equip sergeants for a difficult task, was failing to provide the required training.

As early as 1967 a Police Advisory Board Working Party noted the importance of training sergeants for the challenges of Unit Beat Policing; training to equip them to perform the different type of supervision which the modern constable required. They recommended that a research project should be commissioned 'which might be expected to reveal those aspects of man-management which most require attention in the Police Service' (1967: 128).

My own contacts with sergeants suggested that their training was not preparing them for the responsibilities they had to carry and for the problems they encountered in their work.

Bennett and Wilkie reported a similar experience based upon their work at the Scottish Police College. They were particularly critical of a report, purporting to identify the training needs of sergeants, which contained no evidence of any research into the job of sergeants that might have provided the basis for the recommended training course. They stressed that an effective training programme had to address the problems faced by the person on the course (Bennett and Wilkie, 1983).

Despite their importance police sergeants, like first-line supervisors in other organizations, have tended to be neglected by researchers. This applies as much in the USA as it does in the UK. As Van Maanen commented:

> Sergeants have rarely been the explicit target of police studies. When they have been studied, it has been incidental to the broader examination of a particular police function ... The few studies concerned with general police administration have usually lumped sergeants into the lower order of police agencies and have concentrated instead upon the management activities, and perspectives of high departmental officials (Van Maanen, 1983: 276).

Child and Partridge described a similar situation in industry and at the time this research was being designed produced a text providing a more systematic look at the managerial functions and problems of

supervisors in manufacturing industry. They comment that supervisors have been relatively neglected both by academic investigators
and by the framers of industrial policy (Child and Partridge, 1982: 3).

The original intention was to identify the training needs of patrol
sergeants in order that courses could be designed which would help
them to exercise their street responsibilities more effectively. This
would help guarantee better service delivery by constables and this in
turn would promote more harmonious police–public relations, reducing the likelihood of violent street confrontations. If members of
the public have been well served by the police when they wish to
demonstrate they will be more likely to be peaceful towards the
police and less inclined to use the occasion as an opportunity to attack
them.

My earlier research in the late 1960s and early 1970s revealed that
sergeants spent a great deal of their time on the streets. In contrast
patrol sergeants now spend most of their duty time in the police
station. During the course of the project two other studies were
published which revealed that a similar situation existed in the
Merseyside and Metropolitan Police forces (Smith, 1983; Kinsey,
1985).

In view of the prevailing conception of the patrol sergeant's role
and the importance of street responsibilities many believed these
sergeants exercise, it was necessary to investigate how sergeants
divide their time between street and station work and to try to find an
explanation.[1]

Patrolling and incident-attendance patterns
To obtain a better understanding of the nature of the outside duties of
patrol sergeants, a distinction was made between *routine patrolling*
and *incident-attendance*.

Incident-attendance refers to those occasions when the sergeant
left the police station with the obvious and often explicit intention of
either attending an incident which had been reported over the radio
or to follow up an enquiry on the instruction of a senior officer.

A routine patrol was one where the sergeant left the police station
or the scene of an incident/enquiry, not to attend anything in particular but to show a presence on the streets and perhaps meet some of his
or her constables. Sergeants would announce their intention with
expressions like: 'let's go and get some air', 'let me get out of this
damned office for a spell', 'do you fancy a walk?', 'I think I'll go for a
spin'.

The time spent during each tour of duty on each of these functions
was recorded as well as the number of incidents the sergeants went to
and the number of patrols they left the station to carry out. Occa-

sionally, when a sergeant undertook periods of routine patrolling between attending incidents it was more difficult but not impossible, to calculate the amount of time spent on each type of activity.

TABLE 1

Percentage of tours where a specified number of incidents was attended and a specified number of patrols was made (152 tours)

	None	One	Two	Cumulative %
Patrols	21	44	25	90
Incidents	25	31	18	74

On most tours of duty (69 per cent) patrol sergeants were able to undertake at least one and sometimes two patrols during the tour (see Table 1). In 44 per cent they engaged in one period of patrol work and in another 25 per cent, in two patrols. In only one patrol in ten, however, did sergeants manage to do more than two periods of work. There was no patrolling undertaken on 21 per cent of the tours.

The number of incidents attended was also low. In just under half the tours the sergeants attended either one or two incidents. In only about a quarter of tours were more than two incidents attended. No incidents were attended in 25 per cent of the tours.

These data are incomplete because they take no account of the time spent on patrolling and incident-attendance. This had to be investigated, for it is conceivable that although a sergeant might only attend a few incidents and have made only one or two patrols, the time actually spent on this small number of patrols and incidents could account for most of his tour.

TABLE 2

Percentage of tours where a specified amount of time was spent each tour on patrolling and on incident-attendance (152 tours)

	None	Under 1 hr	Over 1 hr and under 2 hrs	Cumulative %
On patrolling	21	37	25	83
On incident-attendance	25	40	24	89

In 83 per cent of tours the patrol sergeants either did not go out on patrol at all or, if they did go out, they spent less than two hours patrolling in total. In 25 per cent of tours, they were patrolling for between one and two hours and they were out for under one hour in 37 per cent of tours.

A similar pattern emerges for incident-attendance. In 89 per cent of the tours they either did not attend any incidents or they spent less than two hours during the whole of the tour on incident-attendance. In almost two out of every three shifts sergeants attended incidents but altogether they were involved for less than two hours.

Perhaps the most surprising finding is that patrol sergeants did not undertake any patrols on 21 per cent of the tours and did not attend any incidents on 25 per cent of the tours. However, a word of caution is necessary. We must allow for the possibility that on those occasions when the sergeant did not undertake any patrolling during the tour, he or she might still have attended one or more incidents and vice versa.

Cross-tabulating time on incident-attendance against time spent on patrolling revealed that on 9 per cent of tours patrol sergeants were involved in work in the police station for the duration of the tour. Even on those tours when they managed to leave the station, the time spent on the streets was unexpectedly small given that these were street supervisors and not station sergeants. In just under two-thirds of all tours (61 per cent) sergeants spent a total of less than two-and-a-half hours on patrolling and incident-attendance combined. This means that on most tours they spent more time in the police station than they did on duties outside.

Further investigation revealed that even the limited time spent outside was not always used to supervise and monitor the work of constables. Some of the incidents they attended were licensing enquiries in which the sergeants visited public houses, clubs and restaurants to interview the proprietor about a licensing application. Invariably the sergeants went alone on such enquiries.

Even when the sergeants were out doing routine patrolling there was no guarantee that they would be working with a constable. Indeed there was a substantial number of patrols where the sergeant went alone and made no contact with any constables. No contact was made with patrolling constables in 34 per cent of tours where a patrol was undertaken.

On 63 per cent of relevant tours no constables were seen by an appointment arranged by the sergeant over the radio, through the Communications Room. On 53 per cent of the relevant tours the sergeant did not encounter any constables by chance as he patrolled the area.

On tours where the sergeant did meet one or more constables it was likely to be only a small fraction of the patrolling constables who were contacted. In only 14 per cent of the relevant tours did the sergeant meet more than two PCs by chance. In only 6 per cent were more than two constables contacted by prior arrangement during the course of the patrol. Taking into account that PCs sometimes worked together, even this small proportion exaggerates the number of occasions when a sergeant met a PC during his or her periods of patrolling because, in some instances, the sergeant saw two at the same location.

Why, then, did sergeants bother to engage in routine patrolling if it was not directed at making contact with their constables and spending some time with them?

I would argue that most of the time the sergeants were performing the same function as their constables — presenting a police presence on the streets. The rationale for routine patrolling is illustrated neatly by the following case.

> One sergeant who normally worked in the Enquiry and Charge Offices walked with one of the researchers at a fairly rapid pace around the perimeter of his territorial section. He was out for nearly two hours but saw no constables. Without being asked the reason why he had chosen to patrol the outer limits of the section, he volunteered the information that the patrolling constables tended to neglect these parts of their beats and it was up to him to make sure that a police presence was shown there.

About a quarter of the sergeants had another reason for patrolling which explains their attendance at certain types of incidents. The sergeants were asked whether a good patrol sergeant should try to make arrests regularly and also report people for offences. Although they thought it was less important for them than for their constables 24 per cent thought they should maintain a level of arresting not far below the one they had achieved as constables and 26 per cent argued similarly in the case of reporting people for summons. The majority considered that a sergeant should not be tied up processing prisoners and doing additional paperwork if it could possibly be avoided.

Incident-focused and constable-focused incident-attendances
Essentially incident-attendance can be based upon two types of rationale. One I shall call the *incident-focused orientation* and the other the *constable-focused orientation*. It is the predominance in practice of the former which explains how sergeants discriminated between calls and why the time spent on incident-attendance is so small.

There are certain incidents which sergeants attend because the way they are reported indicates they are serious enough to warrant the attendance of a first-line supervisor, probably an inspector as well as a sergeant. Sergeants anticipate that questions about the event will be asked subsequently by their senior officers, on the assumption that 'supervision' would have attended. Sergeants also attend anticipating that there will be a role for them to play at the scene. More often than not their assumptions are correct and they are able to play a direct part in dealing with the incident. For example, sergeants may find that there are so few constables present that they have to lend a hand and help to deal with it just as they would have done as a constable. At other incidents the sergeant will immediately take command, organizing the constables present, directing them to do specific tasks and arranging for personnel in other units, CID, Traffic Department, to attend.

Similarly, the patrol sergeant's role in helping at incidents such as fights in public houses, clubs and restaurants, where it is not unusual for several people to be detained on suspicion of being connected with an offence, can extend not only to directing his PCs to take responsibility for certain suspects, witnesses and property, but to organizing the interviewing, statement-taking and other activities in the police station afterwards.

When sergeants were asked to specify their contribution as sergeants and supervisors in such situations they were usually unable to do so. They acknowledge that often their contribution is based more on their experience of having dealt with such situations, possibly when they were PCs, than the fact that they are sergeants. They expect competent and experienced constables to do exactly what they do. The occasions they cite when the rank comes into play are those where the constables cannot agree on who is to do what, for example the report(s) on the incident. The rank can also help when it is necessary to gain the cooperation and assistance of another agency.

More importantly, these types of incidents provide the sergeant with an opportunity to become involved in the action as a central participant. Attendance is legitimated by the fact that there is a part to play. The sergeant's reputation in the eyes of the constables will be further enhanced if the sergeant proves to be a 'good copper'.

The term incident-focused orientation is used to refer to these assumptions and expectations and to the rationale for attending at incidents which they comprised. The incident-focused orientation explains why sergeants will suddenly reach for their helmets and coats, leave the work they are doing in the office and rush to the location of an incident which has just been given out in a radio message. In fact, it was possible to predict this response from most sergeants after hearing certain key words in the message.

The second rationale for incident-attendance is the constable-focused orientation. A key premise is that if supervisors are to undertake meaningful, realistic appraisals of their constables' capabilities as police officers and effectively exercise their responsibilities as on-the-job trainers, then they need to obtain information about how the PCs perform the numerous tasks demanded of them. The incident-focused orientation guarantees that sergeants will attend certain incidents and this will enable them to assess how effectively their constables perform at such incidents. They may even be able to undertake some on-the-job training, sharing their knowledge and expertise.

Sergeants will also learn about certain types of incidents and what action was taken from the constable's paperwork. The work to be done after the constable has attended the original event sometimes provides the sergeant with supervisory, managerial and training opportunities. What this means is that those incidents which sergeants feel obliged to attend and those which require subsequent enquiries and documentation, enable the sergeant to make some appraisal of the constables' performance. Because of paperwork requirements and the incident-orientation, the situations where constables invoke the law, report or arrest someone for an offence and those where there is a serious public disturbance or threat to life, are quite closely monitored and supervised by sergeants because they are personally involved at some stage.

However, constables will deal with an equal number if not more incidents where they do not invoke the law, submit crime reports or report offenders. Paperwork in connection with these incidents is kept to a minimum.

Normally, a brief recording of the original message is made by a member of the Communications Room staff. The PC then reports on the action taken at the incident. Normally these reports comprise short standardized phrases and expressions, which signify that it is unnecessary for anyone to enquire further; 'all quiet on arrival'; 'parties advised'; 'civil dispute'; 'not a police matter'; 'no further action'.

Although these incidents are reported over the radio, when viewed from the prevailing incident-focused orientation there is no need for the sergeant to attend. They are seen as run-of-the-mill, non-problematic incidents which the constables can be left to handle on their own. In contrast, because one of the basic principles of the constable-oriented approach is that a constable's competence can only be appraised across all types of incidents, proponents of this perspective believe that such incidents are equally important to them as supervisors. In fact attendance at such incidents is imperative, because there is little or no reliable feedback on paper. It is precisely because of the importance attached to on-the-job training and to the sergeants' responsibilities for monitoring constables, that advocates of this approach challenge the prevailing view that sergeants should only become involved with such incidents if constables actually ask for their advice and attendance. Constables need regular feedback, advice, guidance and practical instruction even though they may not realize it themselves. Moreover, the conscientious constable's motivation and commitment will begin to decline unless efforts and achievements are continuously recognized and rewarded. How can sergeants give meaningful praise and sustain motivation if they do not know how their PCs perform a large segment of their work? This rationale challenges a view that constables will appreciate being left alone to get on with the job. It is argued that being unsupervised is seen as a reward, a compliment to their skills and a testimony of their supervisors' faith in them. Such faith, according to the constable-focused orientation, is blind faith because it is not based upon current performance evaluation. Moreover, rather than bolstering motivation and morale it threatens to destroy them. The less competent constables unjustly receive as much recognition as their more able and conscientious colleagues because they are also left alone. This in turn leads to the undermining and discrediting of the formal appraisal system. Because assessments are based upon a narrow band of the constable's work, the constables who are conscientious and take pride in their achievements in the neglected areas, do not receive the recognition and reward they deserve. Those who are less competent unjustly receive as much recognition for poor performance in these areas. More importantly, the appraisal system fails to help them to identify the weaknesses in their work and how they and their supervisors can work together to improve their skills and performance.

Viewing incident-attendance patterns presented earlier using these two orientations, the data from the fieldwork lead to the inescapable conclusion that almost all attendances were founded upon the incident-focused orientation. This incident-orientation helps to explain why so few incidents were attended out of the total number dealt with during each tour of duty. The primacy of the incident-focused orientation means that a large proportion of the incidents dealt with by constables are unmonitored. The sergeants have little reliable feedback because the paperwork is designed to provide as little information as possible. There is no on-the-job training guidance or supervision. Appraisals of constables are based upon their performance in a relatively narrow band of policing incidents.

Why do sergeants adopt this incident-focused orientation? Is it that they do not define their role as being that of a street supervisor? Do they believe the supervision of their constables' work does not have a high priority? In fact, their role conceptions and the expectations they attribute to their divisional commanders support the constable-focused orientation.

The perceived importance of street supervision
Paradoxically, given the limited time available for street supervision, sergeants accept that they are held responsible for the consequences of their constables' actions. In most instances they claim the higher ranks hold them personally accountable whenever anything goes wrong, and more often than not they agree that a patrol sergeant should accept such demands. Like first-line supervisors elsewhere, sergeants believe that the 'buck stops with them'. They are the first line of management to face the problems that occur in the operational situation and they are the final level of management when those of higher rank wish to pass responsibility and blame down the rank system. They frequently act as the final 'back-stop'. Hence 94 per cent of the sergeants interviewed agreed that their main role is stepping in when the system breaks down and making sure the job gets done.

The sergeants were asked how much responsibility they believe the higher ranks expect them to carry for the quality of service delivery. Does the responsibility for ensuring that constables deal competently with all the calls for service they attend fall primarily on the patrol sergeant's shoulders? The majority, 87 per cent, thought it did and 81 per cent thought it was appropriate that they should be expected to carry the responsibility.

To fulfil this and many of the other obligations patrol sergeants are expected to spend more time than is currently available, working outside the police station directly supervising their constables and they recognize this.

Every sergeant interviewed thought the higher ranks expect a patrol sergeant to spend a minimum of 25 per cent of every tour of duty working with his constables; 98 per cent of the sergeants agreed. Many argued that two hours is not enough and that more time should be spent on street supervision.

To take account of the two different rationales for attending incidents and in order to highlight the constable-focused orientation, sergeants were asked about attending incidents with the primary intention of finding out how constables were dealing with them. They all thought the senior ranks would expect a patrol sergeant to make a point of routinely visiting a selection of incidents during every tour of duty, in order to observe what the constables were doing; 95 per cent of the sergeants also agreed.

Thinking prescriptively about their roles sergeants clearly espouse a constable-focused orientation. Further evidence of this is manifest in their responses to a question which asked about on-the-job training and the responsibility a patrol sergeant has in this connection. Some on-the-job training is done inside the police station. Teaching constables how to prepare reports and prosecution files, for example, and instructing them how to manage their enquiries, conduct interviews, and take statements are tasks which sergeants fit into their schedules of station-based work (see page 141 below). However, other instruction can only be carried out at incidents on the beat, in encounters with members of the public. The constable-focused orientation defines a sergeant's role as having watched a constable deal with an incident, the sergeant will discuss it when they resume patrol, or later in the police station. On-the-job training entails this kind of monitoring and assessment. Each constable's repertoire of skills is thereby identified and steps are taken to expand it. Did the constable know what options were available? What made the constable elect the course of action taken? Is the constable aware of the consequences of each option?

All the sergeants thought the higher ranks expected them to put a considerable amount of effort into on-the-job training, particularly for probationers. Most of the sergeants agreed that this should have a high priority.

Self-initiated work and the power to stop and search
In view of the importance attached within the service and the debate about police use of the powers to stop and search, sergeants were asked about their responsibilities for the production of self-initiated work. Although the majority (65 per cent) believed that the system attached too much significance to the quantity of self-initiated work by constables, they recognized the responsibilities they carried in this area. However, they qualified the extent to which they should become involved in supervising non-probationer constables. This is relevant to the issue of how the use of stop and search powers is monitored.

Traditionally, police forces have used the number of arrests and the totals of people reported for offences which constables produce on their own initiative as indicators of motivation and effort as opposed to those which result from incidents to which the police are called. They are particularly important during the probationary period and sergeants know that a probationer's output of self-initiated work will be noted by the higher ranks. If it fails to reach a satisfactory level it will result in a poor appraisal and all the sergeants thought their senior officers would hold them responsible. Most of them agreed (87 per cent) that it was part of a patrol sergeant's job to ensure this did not happen and that the rate of self-initiated production was maintained. Moreover no sergeant thought a patrol sergeant should be totally absolved of responsibility for the self-initiated work of more experienced constables.

What should a sergeant do if the level of self-initiated work production falls below a satisfactory level? A great deal will depend on whether the officer is past the probationary period. Most sergeants believed the higher ranks expect them to go out on patrol with their probationers looking for self-initiated work. The majority also subscribed to this view themselves (74 per cent). It is clear that they attach much more importance to this aspect of their on-the-job training role than the time they actually spend doing it. Again, it is usually justified by a constable-focused orientation. If a probationer continues to under-achieve despite warnings, they argue, the sergeant needs to go out with him or her. Is the constable able to translate legal training into practice or is he or she failing to spot offences? Is it a lack of confidence to report people or uncertainty of police powers in relation to particular offences? Is the constable shying away from these encounters because of a lack of ability to handle the conflict they sometimes produce with members of the public?

If the sergeant decides to go out with a non-probationer, it is more likely that the aim is to prove to the constable that offences exist and that as experienced police officers they both know that the low rate of production has more to do with the officer's attitude than with the number of offences being committed or knowledge of the law.

Although 76 per cent of sergeants thought the higher ranks expect them to do this, only 46 per cent were of the view that they should go out with experienced constables, looking for self-initiated work.

Of course, the monitoring of constables' self-initiated work activities is relevant to the use of stop and search powers and how professionally these are used. It is evidently the case that most patrol sergeants will resist the pressure to go out with constables when they are looking for self-initiated work and, by implication, using their stop and search powers. Unless the officers are probationers the use of such powers is unlikely to be monitored. This should be noted in the context of Scarman's recommendation and those of the Royal Commission on Criminal Procedure on the extended use of such powers and the need for effective monitoring systems (see page 124 above).

Disincentives to close supervision and monitoring

The reluctance shown by most sergeants to get involved in street supervision of non-probationers draws attention to possible tensions existing between the constable-focused orientation sergeants espouse as an ideal and other conflicting expectations which are as compelling and equally legitimate. This role conflict provides part of the explanation for the patterns of patrolling and incident-attendance described above. The relatively small amounts of time spent on these activities is a result of adaptive, avoidance behaviour.

One manifestation of the tension built into the front-line supervisor's role is apparent in the contradictory policy statements which recommend on the one hand, that the status of constables should be elevated and that they should be granted greater responsibility and autonomy and, on the other, that there is a case for closely monitoring and supervising their activities. A second source of conflict is that close supervision and monitoring require the sergeant to ignore and deviate from several of the unwritten rules which lie at the core of the occupational culture of the lower ranks. The sergeant may still identify with these rules and subscribe to them. After all, they protected and helped the sergeant to climb the first rung of the promotion ladder. Close supervision encroaches upon the cherished autonomy of the constables, threatens their valued discretion and heightens the visibility of their behaviour. Consequently it increases the probability of 'within-the-job' trouble (Chatterton, 1983).

Autonomy, low visibility and limited accountability
These are important to police officers in the front-line who believe they are working in an organizational and political environment which reacts punitively to mistakes. The greater the perceived risk of making a mistake the more imperative it becomes to control information about one's actions.

Some errors have more serious consequences than others, but any action is described as a mistake if it becomes an issue. Part of the craft of policing is to avoid this, which entails preventing others from gaining access to information which will enable them to create issues. 'Within-the-job' trouble arises when by omission or commission one of the lower ranks causes something to become an issue for the higher ranks. Conversely, where no issue is created, ie where no complaint is registered, no further enquiries are made into the incident by the complainants or their representatives, this is taken to mean that the officer's response was satisfactory. The police system operates in this sense with a management-by-consequences philosophy — no news is good news, no negative feedback implies good quality response.

This is hardly a rigorous and searching performance indicator. However, it enables police officers to appear effective by avoiding scrutiny. This means that they must take precautions to ensure that minimal information is fed back into the system about the way they deal with incidents.

Why should police officers feel vulnerable and threatened when their actions become more open to scrutiny? Why do they feel that so many of the decisions they take can so easily become issues?

Constables quickly learn there is rarely 'one best way' to deal with an incident. If the solution adopted does not work others, particularly when they have the additional advantage of hindsight, will suggest alternatives which would have been preferable. In the argot of police culture references are made to the 'shudder syndrome', the 'nine o'clock inquest', when the should-have-done-this alternatives are discussed and argued.

Not all constables have the same approach to policing and particularly to law-enforcement. On every section there are constables whose styles of law enforcement are different (Chatterton, 1976, 1983; Reiner, 1978; Muir, 1977). Some are legalistic in their approach. Others are less inclined to invoke their powers of arrest or to report people for offences. They will settle the affair in some other manner if they believe it is better dealt with in that way, or if they consider the offender is not to blame.

Constables know each other's styles and their actions are occasionally visible to colleagues whose styles are different. This is catered for by a powerfully sanctioned rule which proscribes the criticizing of a colleague's style, especially in public, irrespective of how one privately feels about it. Differences in style must be tolerated (Bittner, 1970). Outside the group, knowledge of the discretionary actions of a constable can make an issue out of a decision not to sanction a law-breaker. Should the officer have reported the offender and let his senior officers make the decision about prosecution? Does the mandate to enforce the law without fear or favour mean the constable has no discretion? Is it a disciplinary offence to ignore law-breaking? Were the grounds for the decision justified? Was the officer balancing blame or is he a male chauvinist taking the side of a wife-beating husband?

Constables develop strong proprietorial claims relating to what they regard as *their* beats, *their* incidents and *their* prisoners. There is an unwritten rule that the first officer to attend at the scene of a run-of-the-mill incident can claim the right to manage it. This norm is also supported by a line of common sense reasoning which recognizes that incidents can alter in character during the period of time the police are in attendance. Someone arriving later does not have the full story and may have to go over the ground again. This can be frustrating for the other parties involved and it may open up matters which the officer who was first there has settled or smoothed over. Because of the unfolding nature of encounters someone arriving late can misconstrue the nature of the problem and the character of the parties involved, leading to an inappropriate course of action being taken. The lower ranks accept the principle of 'situated expertise', which arises through lengthier contact with an incident (Chatterton,

1981). Sergeants who interfere offend this principle and risk making the wrong decision.

Controlling information

To control information about decisions and activities the constable has to take steps to ensure that complainants and other involved parties are convinced that everything has been done within the means to deal with the problem and to persuade them to let the matter drop. The constable must then decide whether to submit a report on the incident and carefully word it to ensure that the circumstances described justify the course of action reported and taken.

The advantage of low visibility and how this is sustained by producing the right kind of paperwork, have been recognized by other writers on this topic. Ericson (1982), for example, states that where the victim/complainant and the police officers disagree, the latter must work at getting agreement with his or her version of events. He argues that the power of the officer invariably enables this to be achieved, although conscious that the routines can be upset by the victim/complainant and the officer's superiors.

By attending incidents as representatives of management, sergeants break through this shield of low visibility, threatening the autonomy and limited accountability it protects. Moreover, because it has never been the norm for sergeants regularly to attend routine incidents unless constables were suspected of being incompetent or worse, such supervisory involvement is quickly construed as an expression of mistrust. Close supervision is associated with attempts to catch constables out, and a punishment-centred approach to management.

Manning has emphasized 'the centrality of trust' in the relationship between the supervisor and those supervised. The rationality of the administrator supports close monitoring and supervision, visits to incidents, detailed reports and formal appraisals. These are no part of the rationality of the operational personnel. Sergeants believe they are unnecessary. 'Supervisors claim that they are aware of what each officer is doing and why, and that they trust them' (Manning, 1980: 225).

Incident follow-up

Two instances of the administrator's rationality are to be found in one of the standard texts on police supervision. As a former police officer, Osterloh recognizes the unwritten rules regarding the preparation of reports and the selective reporting of the facts. However, he argues that 'the supervisor should insist on a positive reporting rule of relevancy rather than on a negative one of secrecy'. But even more threatening to the autonomy of the lower ranks is his proposal that the sergeant should:

> go directly to the client who has recently asked for police service. It is a simple matter to ring the doorbell of a person who lately has submitted a report, or otherwise has asked for assistance. Making a smiling inquiry of whether the customer was satisfied with the attention he has received will not normally open a can of worms. If minimal time has elapsed since the event, there still will be enough emotional impact to make the account the supervisor receives factual. (Osterloh, 1975: 81)

In the interviews sergeants were asked whether they thought the higher ranks would expect a sergeant to make visits on a regular basis to beat incidents after his PCs had dealt with them, to find out what they had done. The majority thought their bosses would agree with this proposal. However, most of the sergeants themselves disagreed with the suggestion and over a third expressed strong opposition to the proposal. In the opinion of sergeants such follow-up would be perceived by constables as checking up on them. Even if they were told that the sergeant was going to make it his practice to do such follow-up visits they would be seen as underhand and devious. The practice would betray the principle of trust.

Hence, asked whether they agreed with the statement 'my PCs would think I didn't trust them if I made a habit of attending incidents after they had finished dealing with them', 95 per cent of the sergeants agreed with it and 54 per cent strongly agreed.

Incident attendance, style and proprietorial rights
Attendance at incidents which are still on-going is also difficult unless the sergeant is self-evidently providing back-up. By breaking through the shield of secrecy, the sergeant faces the conflict between obligations as a representative of management and the rule about tolerance of style. Having been present at the incident the sergeant is now even more accountable to his or her superiors for the way it was handled. Yet the PC's style may be different from that of the officer. Most sergeants recognize that attendance at incidents which require the exercise of discretionary judgements whether or not to enforce the law, inevitably means that they will have to insist on the constable dealing with the matter in accordance with their style. Virtually every sergeant thought the higher ranks would expect this and, in fairness to themselves, 78 per cent thought they were entitled to insist on this. They recognized, however, that it would offend their constables and many admitted that they would not have liked it if their sergeants had done it to them when they were PCs.

In practice, sergeants would find this a difficult position to adopt. It might lead to a constable challenging their right to order them to make an arrest or to report someone for an offence. This would then precipitate the kind of issue, for example over whether this was a disciplinary offence, or whether the order was a lawful order, which sergeants and PCs are anxious to avoid.

A similar dilemma arises in connection with attendance at other incidents where the issue of discretionary law enforcement will probably not arise. In an earlier study I found that sergeants who were notorious for being directive at incidents were nicknamed 'oarsmen' by their PCs because they 'stuck their oars' into their PCs' incidents (Chatterton, 1981). In the interviews sergeants were asked about their preference for a directive or passive role at incidents. Did they think they were expected to stand by at incidents, observing their constables and only interfering if something threatened to go seriously wrong, or the constable sought their advice and assistance? A minority thought those higher up would expect this. The majority thought their bosses would expect them to adopt a more directive style. Just under half thought that if they attended at incidents then they would have to get involved in dealing with them. Having attended, they would be held as accountable as the constable. In any case, they argued, it is difficult to avoid being drawn in because members of the public expect the sergeant to take charge and constables will tend to defer to the presence of their supervisor.

The 55 per cent who thought they would act as a 'fly on the wall', appreciated these problems. The difficulty with their preferred approach was that it made them feel redundant at incidents. They describe it as feeling 'like a spare part, standing around doing nothing'. They thought their constables would be self-conscious knowing their sergeant was looking over their shoulders and that they would resent it if it was to happen regularly.

Overcoming the disincentives to close supervision
There are very powerful constraints within the work environment discouraging sergeants from engaging in close supervision and monitoring of the performance of their constables on the beat.

On the positive side there is little incentive to attend run-of-the-mill incidents and to apply the constable-focused orientation. The organization discourages sergeants from enquiring into their officers' work. Unless the officer's performance becomes an issue, for example, the subject of one or more official complaints, the sergeant is implicitly encouraged to leave well alone. By prying into the officer's conduct issues may even be created. No rewards are currently offered to sergeants who might put into practice the constable-focused orientation. Senior officers do not ask for the kind of detailed, systematic appraisal of constables' performance which would require the intimate knowledge of their work produced by the constable-focused approach to supervision. Sergeants believe they know what the higher ranks would say they expect, but in reality they know they are offered no inducements to supervise in this manner. If sergeants are to be blamed for not spending more time on street supervision the higher ranks of sub-divisional command should be held even more culpable. Closer monitoring and street supervision require changes in the organizational structure, not just in the behaviour of sergeants. The appraisal system, for example, needs to be taken apart and a new system of inspection and feedback, together with rewards for both good constable and supervisory work devised. Sub-divisional commanders should be required to keep in much closer touch with their front-line supervisors and use the information they obtain about constables' performance to plan with their sergeant and the patrol inspector the constable's professional and career development.

On the negative side there are also powerful factors discouraging sergeants from adopting the approach advocated by Scarman and others. Sergeants are only too aware of the fact that close supervision breaks the bonds of trust and penetrates the shield of secrecy. Moreover, it obliges them to face role dilemmas and to take risks relating to directive/passive involvement in incidents, the question of style and the uses of discretion.

The time spent by sergeants in the police station provides an escape route from these latent role conflicts, particularly as the official reward system seems to offer tangible benefits to sergeants who undertake such tasks.

Station-based activities

Consultations about incidents and enquiries
When patrol sergeants are in the police station they are not totally divorced from the work their constables are doing outside. Sometimes constables report back on the outcome of certain incidents they have been sent to and seek advice. The same applies to the enquiries they are following through. Sometimes they explicitly seek the sergeant's advice. At other times the approach is more subtle. A total of 1,064 interactions of this kind occurred during the tours analysed; an average of seven each tour.

Constables initiate consultations
The first important point to note about these interactions is that the majority were initiated by the constables. Only 22 per cent were initiated by sergeants. This is consistent with what was observed

during the other tours of duty. It is unusual for a patrol sergeant to ask what has happened at any of the incidents to which the constable has been despatched. In practice sergeants allow constables to control information about their incidents and leave the decision about sharing it to them. The same norms and understandings operate with regard to station-based enquiries as with incident attendance. A sergeant who asks probing questions breaks the shield of low visibility, threatens autonomy and style and immediately confronts the dilemmas discussed above.

Sergeants routinely assume that if their constables encounter problems they will radio through a request for advice or ask them to attend the incident. No contact is interpreted to mean there are no problems. This is a very different approach from the constable-focused orientation the sergeants espoused in the interviews. In 43 per cent of those interactions where constables did report back to their patrol sergeants, the sergeant asked for additional information about the incidents. Perhaps more significant is the fact that in half of these cases the sergeants were able to suggest additional steps which would need to be taken before the incident or enquiry could be satisfactorily closed.

These data indicate that although the sergeants rely upon their constables to take the initiative, once they are given the opportunity to advise or comment they are willing and able to do so in a significant number of cases. In how many of the other cases which are not brought to their attention might sergeants be able to suggest improvements? If we knew the answer to that question we would be able to say whether the adoption of a constable-focused orientation would improve the quality of policing received by the public.

It would be a mistake to discount the importance of those instances where the sergeant suggests nothing additional to what the constable has already done. These are also important exchanges. They give the constables confidence in their own capabilities and the chance to receive positive feedback. They are consequently relevant to job satisfaction and morale and sergeants recognize this. In the course of the study sergeants commented about the reassurance a constable had received from such consultations. Yet this realization of the significance of positive feedback and tacit support does not lead sergeants to take the initiative by enquiring about other incidents.

Disguised consultation
The nearest sergeants come to this are the cases of disguised consultation (Blau, 1963). For example, a constable might come into the office ostensibly seeking permission to go outside the boundaries of the sub-division in order to carry out an enquiry. The sergeant will

ask about the enquiry and advise the constable on any needs before granting the request. It was never quite clear whether constables intended to elicit the sergeant's advice about these incidents but it allowed the more experienced constables to receive advice without losing face. The sergeants certainly used it as if it was a form of disguised consultation.

Serial supervision
The extent to which sergeants can get involved in their constables' work and manage the way that they deal with incidents without actually going out with them, is most clearly demonstrated by a pattern of consultation which I shall call serial supervision. Just under half of the discussions of incidents and enquiries that took place during a sample of tours had been preceded by a discussion of the same incident between the same sergeant and constable. Just over a third had been discussed earlier at least once during that particular tour of duty.

Sergeants refer to this sequential involvement as 'pavestoning'. They instruct the constable how to proceed with the first stage of an enquiry and then in the light of what happens, how to undertake the next stage and so on. Others describe it as having the constables 'on a wire', casting them out to collect information, reeling them back in to assess what they have gleaned and then deciding where to cast them out again.

Although these discussions take up the time of sergeants and keep them in the station longer than they would otherwise be, they do enable them to keep in close touch with a proportion of the incidents their constables are involved with, particularly in those instances where serial supervision occurs. Although it is station-based activity, such consultation does qualify the incident-attendance data presented earlier because sergeants are not quite as remote as those data appear to suggest. In fact the discussions, and particularly serial supervision, appear to be a form of adaptation by office-bound patrol sergeants to the need to provide their constables with some supervision and guidance. The fact remains, however, that most incidents and the way they are handled are unmonitored and unsupervised.

Paperwork
Sergeants maintain that paperwork is the principal reason why they are obliged to spend so much time inside the police station. Most of the sergeants interviewed argued this and said that they found it annoying; about a quarter found it very frustrating, almost half frustrating while another quarter a bit frustrating. Other research indicates that this is a problem elsewhere. In Merseyside 26 per cent

of the sergeant's time was spent on administrative duties and paper-work, 6 per cent on crime paperwork, (Kinsey, 1985: 55). The PSI report on the Metropolitan police reported lower percentages; 13 per cent on other paperwork and administration and 1 per cent on paperwork connected with crime (Smith, 1983: 43). Involvement with paperwork is the single most time-consuming, station-based activity performed by patrol sergeants.

Yet it would be a mistake to argue that time spent advising con-stables about items of paperwork, and checking them, is wasted time. There is a tendency within the literature to devalue paperwork pro-cessing, and to treat it as a bureaucratic and administrative process divorced from the main goals of policing. Nothing could be further from the truth where many items of paperwork are concerned. The system and its members achieve organizational and personal goals through paperwork. Through items of paperwork the police system liaises with the courts. The preparation of quality prosecution files enables the police to place offenders before the courts. Items of paperwork, strategically prepared, comprise part of the shield pro-tecting the autonomy of the lower ranks, as was noted above. The management and organization of the processes of paperwork produc-tion is complex because police officers must follow through the initial incidents by making enquiries, taking statements and arranging for other forces to obtain evidence. The constables have limited control in these other arenas, which can make such post-attendance proce-dures quite protracted and, correspondingly, difficult to manage (Chatterton, 1985).

'Paperwork' is, therefore, the gloss term covering a wide variety of occasions and decisions. Many of these processes are as constitutive of policing as patrolling a beat, answering a radio call and chasing and apprehending an offender (Chatterton, forthcoming).

Sergeants accept their responsibilities for ensuring that the quality of their constables' paperwork is maintained at a high standard. They know this is something the higher ranks expect and they acknowledge its importance. They are also responsible for making sure that reports and files are completed within laid-down time limits. These time limits are not universal and can, therefore, vary across sub-divisions, depending upon the preferences of the higher ranks. This will alter with the introduction of the Crown Prosecutor system and the new time restrictions it imposes. An important part of the sergeant's on-the-job training role, therefore, is to provide constables with guidance on the preparation and management of reports and files.

Serial supervision of paperwork
As proved to be the case with incidents, the same file and report may

be discussed several times in the preparatory phases and afterwards in the untoward eventuality of it being returned as inadequate.

There were 817 discussions or consultations about files and reports in the sample of tours analysed, an average of five per tour. Just under half of these referred to files and reports that had been discussed by that sergeant and that PC on at least one other occasion. In 19 per cent of the cases the file had been discussed earlier on that particular tour of duty and in a further 25 per cent of the discussions the file or report in question had been discussed by that sergeant and PC during a previous tour of duty.

Constables evidently expect their sergeant to be on hand to give advice on paperwork. Whilst they are in the police station the sergeants are able to help PCs with this important part of their work and, thereby, exercise the responsibility for paperwork.

Attitudes of police personnel to paperwork are multi-faceted and reflect the variable complexity and importance of the items subsumed under this term. Not all paperwork is viewed positively by sergeants. For example, they are angered when items of paperwork are returned and this is unnecessary because the missing item of information could have been obtained just as easily by the person returning the documents. Sixty-nine per cent of the sergeants agreed that this happened far too frequently. Half of them reported that they found this very frustrating.

Other station-based roles

Sergeants find they are distracted by many requests for advice, information and assistance. These diversions lengthen the period of time needed to check through statements and other items of paperwork. It is important to be able to read the whole of a statement, or the contemporaneous notes of an interview without being distracted. Sergeants were compelled on numerous occasions to go back to the beginning of the script after they had been interrupted.

In the absence of a detailed description of a typical period of duty it is difficult to convey the ceaseless activity and continuous stream of enquiries and requests which sergeants deal with whilst they are in the police station. This is particularly the case on the day and afternoon tours when the constables are also at their busiest dealing with outside incidents and when the potential for incident-attendance is, therefore, at its highest.

Sergeants claim they are 'the back-stops', as noted earlier, and this is confirmed by some of the things for which they accept responsibility in the station as well as outside. They follow up and remedy problems that arise through administrative oversights, poor forward planning and breakdowns in communication. Without their intervention, the consequences would have been serious. In a large percentage of these cases the sergeant could have justifiably argued that the problem was not of his or her making and therefore should be absolved of responsibility for dealing with it. The fact that sergeants are prepared to step into the breach on these occasions reflects their commitment to the service, but particularly to their officers who, more often than not, will be the people to suffer. It also testifies to their vulnerability to having responsibilities and tasks thrust on to them.

This is evident in other tasks which sergeants are expected to perform. Consequential time-consuming 'back-stop' activities are juxtaposed with trivial, menial tasks which it does not even need a trained constable to perform. The number of routine messages sergeants take and relay is considerable and definite savings on sergeants' time could be achieved if such 'errand-boy' tasks were delegated to someone else within the organization.

Sergeants have their radios on as they work in the station. This also produces interruptions and requires the sergeant to make decisions about, for example, which constable to send on an assignment when the Communications Room find that there is no one available, or if an assignment has arisen which will entail the constable going off the beat for some time. The sergeant will use the radio to find out where the constables are, what they are doing and when they will be free to resume duty. If this fails to produce someone to deal with the incident, he or she will then scour the station.

Sergeants combine these deployment tasks with various others, such as liaison with other departments in the force, other forces and other agencies. These commitments, together with the consultations over incidents and paperwork with their constables, keep them fully occupied whilst they are in the station, legitimizing their presence there and excusing their absence from the streets.

Conclusions and implications

Types of policing and riots
In this chapter police work in the front-line has been recognized to be a broad spectrum of activities undertaken in response to a diverse range of public demands, reflecting a variety of personal, interpersonal and moral general social problems. Not every writer on the relationship between policing and riots accepts this conception of the police role. According to one account riots are the product of 'a vicious circle of cumulative causation' (Lea and Young, 1982: 12; Kinsey et al., 1986). They arise as a consequence of the adoption by the police of 'high profile strategies' and 'aggressive policing' styles,

such as stop and search, in response to rising crime rates. These result in the alienation of the community, who then withdraw their support for the police and refuse to provide them with information about crime and offenders. This drives the police into greater reliance on aggressive, military style policing. Another effect is the 'mobilization of bystanders' — when the police go to arrest any member of the community this is seen 'as a symbolic attack on the community, per se' which leads to collective resistance and possibly a riot.

In this account the complex reality of police work is simplified and distorted to give an appearance of theoretical elegance to the vicious spiral thesis. No attention is paid to the many thousands of encounters and incidents where the police meet members of the public as victims of crime, complainants about vandalism and rowdy youths, as relatives of drunken or mentally confused, or lost, or dying, or dead people, as aggrieved parties in road traffic accidents, as offenders against road traffic legislation and so on.

It is not unreasonable to suggest that the quality of service delivery at these incidents will contribute as powerfully to feelings of alienation or, conversely, positive attitudes as those incidents selected by the exponents of the vicious spiral thesis, that is the purely adversarial law-enforcement contacts. In fact, there is no evidence to indicate that the victims of burglaries would object to the use by the police of stop and search powers in a professional manner, if the one stop in twelve which produced a result detected their burglar and led to the recovery of their property (Smith, 1983).

The thesis is flawed on other counts. The writers are vague about the era when the golden age of consensus policing existed in urban areas (see Chapter 2 above). Research carried out in the 1960s demonstrates that members of the public rarely acted as police informants. The police were certainly dependent upon the public's cooperation which enabled them to produce a significant proportion of the arrests they made for crime. However, these complainants who provided the information were the victims of crime or their friends and associates. They had a personal stake in the apprehension and arrest of the suspect (Chatterton, 1975, 1987). Even in those instances where the arresting officer attributed success to 'crime enquiries', on further investigation the apprehension of the offenders in three quarters of these arrests was possible because the victim and offender were related to, or connected with, each other in some way. In the case of assaults against the person the proportion of such relational crime arrests is even higher (Chatterton, 1983).

The failure of these writers on policing and riots to acknowledge no other police/public contacts than adversarial ones, seriously damages their thesis and their claims to objectivity. What is more disturbing is the suggestion that the police should not attach as much priority to such work as they do at present (Kinsey, 1984). The evidence for this proposal should be rigorously examined. Data from crime surveys such as the one conducted by Kinsey (1985) in Merseyside cannot be used to assess public expectations and evaluations of the police with respect to incidents that do not have a law-enforcement outcome. An investigation of this type of work might proceed in a similar fashion to one on crime by asking a representative sample whether they have been the victims of any of the kinds of problems dealt with by the police. This would reveal the extent of unreported, non-crime victimization and the reasons for not involving the police. Such research would also tell us how satisfied those who called the police are with the response (Ekblom and Heal, 1982). People could be given a meaningful choice between crime work and other front-line work and asked to state their priorities in a realistic way. In the absence of such data no one can claim to know how the public rate in importance the two kinds of work.

In practice it is often difficult to define at the outset, from the information that is initially provided, the precise nature of an incident (Southgate, 1986). In many instances, it would be problematic for the police to decide that they need not attend and direct the call to other agencies. Even service calls may require the presence of a police officer should events take an unexpected violent turn and the use of force becomes necessary (Bittner, 1970; Waddington, 1986). Having argued on both pragmatic and theoretical grounds that the police should continue to provide a comprehensive front-line service, it follows that one should be concerned to ensure that this service is of a high quality. Police officers must be trained for this work and their activities monitored, which entails supervisors implementing the constable-focused orientation in practice.

The identification of skills and organizational reform
In contrast with the thesis just described, the present approach begins with a proposition that the quality of police performance in encounters with members of the public affects the probability of violent, large-scale confrontations occurring between police and public.

This view is shared by the author of a Home Office report on police/public encounters, published after the present study was completed. Almost any contact can, in principal, go wrong at some point if one party reacts inappropriately towards the other, or is perceived as doing so (Southgate, 1986: 1).

The study was designed to identify the policing skills necessary to equip police officers to handle encounters professionally. Attention is drawn to the fact that policing is not only about enforcing the law but also involves the exercise of discretion and dealing with many issues that do not fall within the criminal law, or the law as a whole.

Training courses should help officers develop the skills to perform this complex role. The project provides case studies of beat incidents to assist in making skills-training realistic and practical.

Southgate recognizes that although training centres have a vital part to play, the work environment is also very important. Several factors which have been shown to be relevant to the practice of supervision are cited as instances of pressures in the work environment, for example, supervisory standards, rewards and sanctions, peer values and work procedures. The study concludes that unless conditions within the work environment are altered, then no amount of training will change the way things are done.

In this chapter I have described how a study originally designed to identify the training needs of sergeants came to focus on organizational factors which shaped the sergeant's role and resulted in them spending far less time supervising constables on the streets than their title and the formal prescriptions of their role suggest. Most of the time patrol sergeants are not supervising the beat work of their constables. They believe they should be spending a lot more time doing it. They realize it is the only way they can realistically fulfil the expectations of the higher ranks and their own idealized role perceptions. They accept the constable-focused orientation and its implications for beat work supervision. In reality, however, such supervision takes second place to a number of other obligations and commitments. The conclusions of this study echo those of Southgate, by drawing attention to the need for organizational change and for more research into the skills of policing and how to teach them.

As more and more responsibilities are thrust on to the shoulders of sergeants, they are being deflected away from those activities which should take priority. It is tempting for those above them in the rank structure to delegate more responsibility to them. The effects of the Police and Criminal Evidence Act, 1981, are still being monitored but I would predict that it has increased the work of the sergeant rank. The Crown Prosecutor system will similarly make a different set of demands which will not only add to sergeants' responsibilities but remove some of the limited controls they have been able to exercise. In many areas the sergeant will have to contend with tighter time deadlines for the preparation of certain items of paperwork. These expectations will conflict with the pressure to have police officers out on the streets for lengthier periods of time. Already the procedures introduced under the Police and Criminal Evidence Act governing the processing of people in custody, are keeping constables longer in the station and away from their beats. If the demands

by Crown Prosecutors lead to more time being spent on file preparation to cover every conceivable line of enquiry this will further limit
the deployment capabilities of patrol sergeants and lead to greater
role conflict and corresponding stress.

In view of the numerous demands and conflicting expectations
facing sergeants at the present time, and the tendency of the organization to overload them there is clearly an urgent need to examine
the span of control. It is unrealistic to expect patrol sergeants to
discharge the responsibilities placed upon them and exercise a span
of control over ten to twelve constables. The number of constables
for whom a sergeant is responsible should be reduced by half that
number to perform the kind of role described. The authors of 'Managing the Police' are not exaggerating when they refer to 'the crisis in
first-line supervision in the police service' (Bradley et al., 1986: 183).
Although resources for this rank are important, as Scarman recognized (see page 125 above), this is only part of the answer to this
crisis. There will remain the inherent difficulty of achieving a system
of close supervision, given the resistance described. Can it be recon-
ciled with 'the rationality of the lower ranks'?

The problem of close supervision

There are no easy, ready-made solutions to the problem of close
supervision. It will certainly not be overcome by the time-honoured
method within the police service of directives from the higher ranks
instructing sergeants to spend a specified amount of time on the
streets each tour and requiring that they visit each constable before
and after refreshments in order to sign their pocket books.

What has to be explored is the substance of the supervision and
on-the-job training that might occur at such incidents. The rationale
for attendance as documented in the constable-oriented approach
would be accepted by most sergeants. Moreover, most constables
would not object to having the sergeant more closely involved in their
work if they could see some personal advantage. This might take the
form of praise and recognition for a job well done, or suggestions and
advice about how the same result could be achieved more quickly
next time, or a different approach adopted altogether. Within the
occupational culture there is such a precedent which could be extended. In an earlier study (Chatterton, 1975) undertaken when
sergeants had more time to spend on the streets I found that the most
respected sergeants would not challenge a constable's right to his or
her style. However, they would not hesitate to advise the officer
against adopting it in a particular set of circumstances if they considered that the means or the resources were insufficient to deal with
the matter successfully in that way. From my experience constables

did not resent this type of advice. They did not define it as interfering or 'sticking your oar in'. This was because the sergeant gave them something which they could see was valuable. It enabled them to avoid 'within-the-job' trouble. Was it also accepted because the advice concerned means rather than ends, methods rather than outcomes?

This traditional concern with the 'how' of incident-handling, usually when the incident involved an offence, could be extended to incorporate the methods and skills employed in dealing with a variety of other incidents. If sergeants were trained to look into other areas of constables' performance to assess how they rated on specific skill dimensions, and if they could thereby identify both skilled performance and training needs, then this would remove a good deal of the resistance which could otherwise be expected.

I do not want to portray an image of the patrol sergeant arriving at an incident with clip board and pro forma in hand and then placing ticks and crosses against a check list of skills. However, this is perhaps no more ludicrous than suggesting that sergeants should be made to attend constables' incidents just to be bystanders and to feel like 'spare parts' with 'nothing to do'.

Sergeants do define themselves as on-the-job trainers, as we have seen. Yet they are totally nonplussed if asked to be explicit about this on-the-job training role. Ask the average sergeant to put the name of one constable on a sheet of paper. Ask him to list that constable's training needs, to indicate what steps have been taken over the previous month to improve the constable's skills, methods and knowledge, to give an assessment of improvement and what evidence there is for asserting this — in my experience one will find that few sergeants are capable of doing this. Those who do make some attempt invariably fall back on paperwork skills and/or law enforcement situations and teaching about police and legal procedure, evidence and the law. These are undeniably important areas of police work and such training is essential but, as I have stressed they only represent a part of policing.

If such a system of skills assessment and training is to be of use and for it to have 'street-credibility', the skills will have to be identified precisely. Use of such glosses such as 'demeanour' and 'attitude' is a waste of time. The time and effort put into identifying skills and making them concrete and explicit and then training sergeants to use them, will be considerable. It will result, however, in training in management and supervision becoming more relevant and produce much needed changes in the formal appraisal system. Unlike the present 'pen portraits' on appraisal forms which are stereotyped and predictable, the sergeant and the higher ranks could offer praise and encouragement based upon concrete evidence. They could decide which aspects of performance need to be improved and work out a learning/teaching plan or contract with the constable. One amazing feature of the appraisal system operating in a number of the forces with which I am acquainted is that sergeants are not present when the constable has the appraisal interview with a senior officer. Only 18 per cent of the sergeants interviewed thought it was a good idea to be present, which speaks volumes about how the appraisal interview is viewed and about its purpose.

If information about a constable's work was to be fed back in such a practical and constructive manner this would go a long way towards eliminating suspicion about sergeants 'checking up' on incidents. Because sergeants would be expected to know much more about their constable's work than at present, such involvement would become routine and not reserved for the rare cases where malpractice is suspected. Even going to incidents after they have been dealt with would conceivably become more acceptable if constables learnt something which was of interest and assistance to them.

It woud be unfair to complete this chapter without acknowledging that many sergeants feel that they intuitively know how their constables perform on the streets. Some are able to identify those constables who are capable of smoothly negotiating their way through the most hostile and heated situations and others who seem to generate antipathy and resentment, wherever they go. The problem is that the *language* for explicating these intuitive notions is only just beginning to be developed. Before patrol sergeants are prised away from their station desks there is a need to tease out these intuitive ideas and identify the specific skills and techniques which will help to promote harmonious police–public relations by improving service delivery in all types of police–public encounters.

Note

1. The project started in February 1983 and ended in March 1985. During the first ten months an observational study of patrol sergeants on one sub-division of an East Midlands police force was conducted. Once the confidence of the sergeants had been established it was possible to make detailed, contemporaneous notes of all actions and decisions taken during a tour of duty. In the second year of the study an assistant was appointed and the research was extended to other parts of the division.

The qualitative data were supplemented by quantitative data from structured interviews with forty-six sergeants and from an analysis of the field notes on 152 tours of duty.

I am grateful to those officers of all ranks in the Derbyshire Constabulary who assisted with this project. Special thanks are owed to Mr Parrish, former Chief Constable, and Mr Smith his successor. Mr Smith continued to support the project after taking office and I am particularly grateful to him for providing me with an opportunity, on three separate occasions to present the findings and conclusions to personnel in the research division. Constable G. Towle and his associates in the Derbyshire Police Foundation have supported the project from its inception and I thank them. I would also like to express my gratitude to Sir Stanley Bailey CBE, QPM, Chief Constable of Northumbria Police; Mr R. Cozens, former Chief Constable of the West Mercia Constabulary; Mr B. Irving, Police Foundation; Mr A. Leonard, deputy Chief Constable, Sussex Constabulary, and formerly Assistant Chief Constable, Derbyshire; and Mr M. Plumridge, Police Staff College. Their encouragement after two police forces had denied me access to conduct the study was invaluable. Without their support I would not have been able to follow my ideas through to fruition.

I am indebted to Gary Armstrong for the time he put into the fieldwork, his skills as a participant-observer and for his diligence in faithfully and punctually recording his material.

References

Banton, M. (1964) *The Policeman in the Community*. London: Tavistock Press.

Bennett, S. and Wilkie, R. (1983) 'Managerial Problems of Scottish Police Sergeants', *Police Studies*, Spring.

Bittner, E. (1970) *The Functions of the Police in Modern Society*. Washington DC: US Government Printing Office.

Blau, P. (1963) *The Dynamics of Bureaucracy*. London: University of Chicago Press.

Bradley, D., Walker, N. and Wilkie, R. (1986) *Managing the Police*. Brighton: Harvester Press.

Chatterton, M. (1975) 'Organizational Relationships and Processes in Police Work: The Case Study of Urban Policing'. Unpublished PhD thesis. Manchester: University of Manchester.

Chatterton, M. (1976) 'Police in Social Control', in King, J. (ed.) *Control Without Custody*. Cropwood Papers. Cambridge: University of Cambridge Institute of Criminology.

Chatterton, M. (1981) 'Practical Coppers, Oarsmen and Administrators: Front-Line Supervisory Styles in Police Organisations' (unpublished MS).

Chatterton, M. (1983) 'Police Work and Assault Charges', in Punch, M. (ed.) *Control in the Police Organisation*. Cambridge, Mass.: MIT Press.

Chatterton, M. (1985) 'Resource Controls: Issues and Prospects', *Policing*, 1(4).

Chatterton, M. (1987) 'Assessing Police Effectiveness — Future Prospects', *British Journal of Criminology*, 27(1).

Chatterton, M. (forthcoming) *Managing Paperwork*.

Child, J. and Partridge, B. (1982) *Lost Managers, Supervisors in Industry and Society*. Cambridge: Cambridge University Press.

Ekblom, P. and Heal, K. (1982) *The Police Response to Calls from the Public*. Research & Planning Unit Paper, 9. London: Home Office.

Ericson, P. (1982) *Reproducing Order: A Study of Police Patrol Work*. London: University of Toronto Press.

Holdaway, S. (1983) *Inside the British Police*. Oxford: Blackwell.

Jones, J.M. (1980) *Organisational Aspects of Police Behaviour*. Aldershot: Gower.

Kinsey, R. (1984) *Merseyside Crime Survey, 1984*. First report. Edinburgh: Centre for Criminology, University of Edinburgh.

Kinsey, R. (1985) *Survey of Merseyside Police Officers*. First report 1985. Edinburgh: Centre for Criminology, University of Edinburgh. Commissioned by Merseyside County Council.

Kinsey, R., Lea, J. and Young, J. (1986) *Losing the Fight against Crime*. Oxford: Blackwell.

Lea, J. and Young, J. (1982) 'The Riots in Britain, 1981: Urban Violence and Political Marginalisation', in Cowell, D., Jones, T. and Young, J. *Policing the Riots*. London: Junction Books.

Manning, P. (1977) *Police Work, 1977*. Cambridge, Mass.: MIT Press.

Manning, P. (1980) *The Narcs Game*. Cambridge, Mass.: MIT Press.

Muir, W.K., Jnr. (1977) *Police Street Corner Politicians*. Chicago: University of Chicago Press.

Osterloh, H. (1975) *Police Supervisory Practice*. London: Wiley.

Police Advisory Board (1967) 'Operational Efficiency and Management', in *Police Man Power, Equipment and Efficiency*. London: HMSO.

Punch, M. (1978) 'Participant Observation with the Amsterdam Police', *The Police Journal*, L1(3): 251–60.

Punch, M. (1979) 'The Secret Social Service', in Holdaway, S. (ed.) *The British Police*. Edward Arnold: London.

Reiner, R. (1978) *The Blue-coated Worker*. Cambride: Cambridge University Press.

Reiner, R. (1985) *The Politics of the Police*. Brighton: Wheatsheaf Press.

Royal Commission on Criminal Procedure (1981) *Report*. Cmnd. 8092. London: HMSO.

Scarman, Lord (1982) *The Scarman Report*. Harmondsworth: Penguin.

Smith, D.E. (1965) 'Front-line Organisation of the State Mental Hospital', *Administrative Science Quarterly*, 10(3): 381–99.

Smith, D. (1983) *Police and People in London: III. A Survey of Police Officers*. London: Policy Studies Institute.

Smith, D. and Gray, J. (1983) *Police and People in London: IV. The Police in Action*. London: Policy Studies Institute.

Southgate, P. (1986) *Police-Public Encounters*. Home Office Research Study, No. 90. London: HMSO.

Van Maanen, J. (1983) 'The Boss: First-Line Supervision in an American Police Agency', in Punch, M. (ed.) *Control in the Police Organisation*. Cambridge, Mass.: MIT Press.

Waddington, P.A.J. (1986) 'Defining Objectives: A response to Tony Butler', *Policing*, 2(1).

5

Flashpoints of public disorder

David Waddington, Karen Jones and Chas Critcher

Introduction

'Flashpoint' refers to the idea, prevalent in American studies of the ghetto riots of the 1960s, that an apparently trivial incident can spark off disorder. It has been frequently used in media coverage of public disorder, and received further endorsement in Lord Scarman's report on the Brixton riots.

> The incident which *sparked off* the disorder on Saturday was nothing unusual on the streets of Brixton ... Why, on this occasion, did the incident escalate into a major disorder culminating in arson and a full-scale battle with the police? ... The tinder for a major conflagration was there: the arrest outside the S & M car hire office was undoubtedly *the spark which set it ablaze* ... Deeper causes undoubtedly existed, and must be probed; but the immediate cause of Saturday's events was *a spontaneous combustion set off by the spark of a single incident.* (Scarman, 1981: 37 — emphasis added)

We set out initially to discover whether flashpoint was merely a metaphor or whether it explained how disorder begins. The term suggests that a given incident may set off widespread disorder if there is a background of pre-existing social tensions or grievances and if news of the event spreads rapidly to other people who are drawn into the original conflict and escalate it.

Our research had as its initial objective the analysis of the dynamics of disorder to see how far they approximated to the flashpoint model. We also wished to investigate whether flashpoints were as unpredictable as the term suggests. Were flashpoints amenable to explanation in spite of their unexpectedness, and if so, could an outbreak of disorder be foreseen? This question has both theoretical importance and practical implications.

The case studies

We began by looking for events which appeared to be or to contain flashpoints. We hoped that one original feature of our study would be precisely its emphasis on the role of local factors in explaining the presence or absence of disorder. When the study began in 1983, Sheffield, unlike other major British cities, had experienced no recent inner city rioting, violent demonstrations or police-picket confrontations.

This had two implications for our research. Firstly, it meant that we had to account for the absence of disorder leading us to pay attention to what sustains order as well as what provokes disorder. Secondly, since we could not rely on any major incidents of disorder occurring in our two-year research period, we undertook a retrospective study of past events which either did result in or could have provoked disorder. One was the national steel strike of 1980 which for some time centred on the picket of a private Sheffield steel firm, Hadfields. The second was a confrontation between black youths and police in the city centre shopping precinct known as the Haymarket which took place in the immediate aftermath of the inner city riots in 1981.

During the study we were alert to any potential flashpoints, and one emerged with the visit in 1983 of the Prime Minister to Sheffield; we were able to study the run-up to the planned 'Thatcher Unwelcoming' demonstration, the event itself and its aftermath.

However the research was then transformed by the miners' strike, the most bitter industrial dispute in post-war Britain. It seemed inevitable that flashpoints would occur: Sheffield housed the headquarters of the NUM, and the South Yorkshire coalfields were among the most militant. We were strategically placed to monitor events as they occurred, in the ways described below.

In April 1984 two consecutive rallies were held to lobby members of the union's national executive meeting in Sheffield. A month later, a coking plant at Orgreave on the outskirts of Sheffield was the focus of a mass picket which turned into a pitched battle between police and pickets. In the mining village of Maltby in June 1984 and in Grimethorpe in October there was widespread community resistance to the police presence.

Our case studies consisted of three pairs of actual or potential flashpoints in three different types of situation:

Demonstrations	'Thatcher Unwelcoming' vs NUM rallies
Picketing	Hadfields vs Orgreave
Communities	Haymarket vs Maltby/Grimethorpe

This chapter deals only with the first pair of events, the two demonstrations. Work in preparation (Waddington et al., 1987) will incorporate all the case studies.

Methodology
The data we gathered about each of the case studies varied. Retrospective study of past events precludes direct observation. Most of the information was gained through interviews, both structured and

open-ended, with participants in the events. These were assumed to be subject to selective recall, though their accounts were supplemented with documentary evidence such as legal statements.

The two demonstrations were studied at first hand. Participants, both demonstrators and police, were interviewed, and official statements and reports analysed. For the Thatcher demonstration, we carried out a survey among the crowd during the event, and another of public opinion after the event. In these as in all the case studies we monitored the media coverage. Media accounts are used in some cases as evidence: we have also carried out an analysis of the accounts themselves and their political implications (Brunt et al., 1987).

Existing theories of disorder

The concept of flashpoint, for reasons outlined below, led us away from frequently offered but less promising explanations which attribute disorder to a single cause, whether extremist agitators, copy-cat behaviour or mob psychology. All of these explanations have a long history but little else to recommend them.

Early theories of crowd behaviour can be seen as a pseudo-scientific elaboration of the common sense assumption that members of a crowd become incapable of any but the most primitive forms of reasoning:

> Whatever be the ideas suggested to crowds they can only exercise effective influence on condition that they assume a very absolute, uncompromising and simple shape . . . It cannot be said absolutely that crowds do not reason and are not to be influenced by reasoning . . . However, the arguments they employ and those which are capable of influencing them, are from a logical point of view of such an inferior kind that it is only by way of analogy that they can be described as reasoning. (Le Bon, 1952: 61–2)

From this early school of crowd psychology, only Tarde (1901) retains any interest in that he sought to investigate the relationships between public opinion, collective action and the newly emergent means of opinion formation, the mass circulation press, questions which we discuss elsewhere (Brunt et al., 1987).

The fusion of sociology and evolutionary biology known as sociobiology draws upon common sense notions of innate aggression, and sees the dynamics of crowds as providing an expression for collective aggression underpinned by universal instincts such as territoriality (Ardrey, 1970, Tiger and Fox, 1974). The attempt to explain complex social phenomena such as wars, strikes, gang fights and political demonstrations by reference to 'instinct' seems crudely reductionist; it also fails to explain why untrammelled aggression is not the norm in society.

Modern psychological approaches such as the social-facilitation approach (Geen and Gange, 1977), which holds that individual behaviour is merely accentuated by the presence of an audience, and the game theory of Olson (1965) who suggests that individuals within a crowd act on calculations of 'payoff' from the action and of probable support from others have tended to go to the opposite extreme of the 'group mind' thesis, denying that collective phenomena are any different in kind from individual actions. Such approaches see collective behaviour as merely an aggregate of individuals' actions based on cost-benefit calculations, thus over-emphasizing the instrumental aims of action (Potter and Litton, 1985).

A more fruitful approach stems from the work of Moscovici (1985) who has stressed the importance of collectively held social representations as sources of motivation and identity. Reicher (1984) shows the importance of social representations of 'the community' in explaining the collective actions taken by the residents of Saint Paul's, Bristol during the riot of 1980. But this needs to be supplemented by a sociological explanation of the social conditions which promote the emergence of the shared sentiments in the first place.

Sociological approaches have tended to be equally one-sided. The sociological common sense proposition (New Society, 1982, Downes, 1970) that deprivation leads to rioting, while containing a kernel of truth — the rich and powerful have other ways of expressing dissent — has been rightly criticized by Field and Southgate (1982) for its failure to explain why, if this explanation is correct, riots only occur at some times and places and not others.

More convincing, though restricted to inner city contexts, has been the hypothesis that the nature of police-community relations may be crucial in making disorder more or less likely (Kettle and Hodges, 1982). One study put forward an analysis which has proved all too prophetic.

> For whatever reasons, a small number of difficult encounters do occur, and these can easily form the basis for a collective community suspicion of the police (or, indeed, spark off disorder) ... Once this happens, bad relations can become self-perpetuating. (Tuck and Southgate, 1981: 44)

The 1985 riots in Handsworth, Tottenham and Brixton seem to confirm this prediction. However, there remains the need to explain why such 'difficult encounters' are more frequent in black inner city areas. Also, such an explanation refers mainly to community disorders, and cannot necessarily be generalized to other forms of disorder. This was also a feature of other sociological approaches to specific examples of disorder — football violence (Marsh et al.,

1976), picketing (Kelly and Nicholson, 1980), demonstrations (Halloran et al., 1970), urban riots (Bowen and Masotti, 1968) — which did not set them in the context of a wider model of disorder.

Such a comprehensive model of disorder has been developed by Smelser (1962) who views collective behaviour, whether orderly or disorderly, as amenable to analysis in terms of the same theories and concepts used for society as a whole. Our model is unlike Smelser's in that it is grounded in empirical data and does not rely on the premises of structural functionalism, nor do we see disorder as the result of strains and readjustments at the level of the social system as a whole.

One solution to the problems posed by models which are either too diffuse or too specific is to narrow the focus of study to the patterns of interaction within the event itself.

> The basic questions that framed my field observations and analysis aimed at determining, 'what collective interactions are actually taking place here and now, and unfolding over time?' and 'how do these interactions operate or function?' Theoretical and ideological considerations as to, 'why these behaviors took place', 'what were the conditions that gave rise to them' or, 'how do publics, press, police, politicians or organisations define the behaviors?' go beyond the intent of this study. (Wright, 1978: 9)

While this might initially seem an appropriate approach to the study of flashpoints, in Wright's (1978: 54) case it leads to a purely formal analysis of spatial patterns of crowd behaviour: characterizing 'looting' for example as 'the spatial movement of goods by people out of premises' adds nothing to our understanding of why people loot. We could not justify such a self-imposed limitation, which has the effect of taking the events out of their political, cultural and social context.

A model of disorder
It seemed to us that what was needed was a model of explanation which was flexible enough to encompass a variety of types of disorder while at the same time allowing for the uniqueness of each situation. It should be able to incorporate different levels of analysis, from the most general societal context to the most specific pattern of interaction. The model we developed involved analysing any individual example or type of disorder in terms of six levels: structural, political/ ideological, cultural, contextual, situational and interactional.

Structural. The structural level of relations between groups refers to the relative distribution of power and resources. Examples are class, gender and ethnic relations. Conflict may arise if disadvantaged groups are unable to improve their position and thus have little stake in the institutions of the existing political and social order. In contemporary Britain, economic recession and political policies have marginalized certain groups and communities and differences of interest between such groups and the state have become sharper. Underlying confrontations such as those between employers and workers or between police and black people are real differences in their stake in the order of things, which are inherently conflictual. Such conflict will not necessarily result in disorder unless additional factors are present at other levels.

Political/ideological. The activities of political institutions — government, pressure groups — and ideological agencies such as the mass media help to create a context in which disorder may occur. This may take the form of either policy decisions such as public order legislation, or a climate of opinion, created by the ideological stance of the mass media, which claims to identify the instigators of disorder and hence creates 'scapegoats'.

The emergence of law and order as a central political issue in Britain over the last fifteen years has produced many such examples. The general election of 1979 was fought partly on a law and order platform. The police have since been encouraged to widen their discretion in dealing with public order situations — in ways recently formalized in the Police and Criminal Evidence Act 1985 and the Public Order Act 1986 — and they themselves have become increasingly vocal on a range of political issues (Reiner, 1985). Marginal groups have become targets of 'moral panics' (Cohen, 1973): in the early 1970s these included squatters and black youth (Hall et al., 1978) and more recently the 'hippy convoy' (Vincent-Jones, 1986).

Such was the case with the coal dispute. Extraordinary police powers were underwritten by a government and press campaign to portray striking miners as, in the words of the Prime Minister, 'the enemy within'. This definition of the political situation was unlikely to encourage either miners or police to adhere to the letter of the law.

Cultural. By 'cultural' we refer to the ways in which groups of people understand the social world and their place within it, their definitions of the rules which do or should govern behaviour and how they define themselves and other social groups. It includes what Gramsci (1971) refers to as 'common sense' and what Moscovici (1985) would term 'collective representations'. The diverse cultures of ethnic groups, youth sub-cultures, particular occupations and localities give rise to specific ways of defining situations and provide a cultural repertoire of norms of action relevant to that situation. As such they provide a basis for collective mobilization and action.

They also carry with them beliefs about the rights which are held to accrue to them as members of that group, or as individuals in general. They foster certain characterizations of other social groups and expectations of how they are likely to behave in a given situation (Holdaway, 1983). If the groups involved have differing or incompatible definitions of the situation or of what their rights are, the potential for conflict is increased. One group's harmless fun may be another's hooliganism.

However, while discrepant perceptions of a situation may increase the likelihood of disorder, this is by no means inevitable, provided that participants in a potentially conflictual situation are prepared to compromise and accommodate each other's objectives, as when both police and pickets evolve a set of agreed norms as to what is acceptable on the picket line — a 'good clean shove' being permissible, whereas throwing bricks is not. Whether such accommodation is reached will depend on factors at other levels.

Contextual. This level refers specifically to the dynamic temporal setting in which disorder occurs. Typically, disorderly events do not come 'out of the blue'; they have a specific history before they erupt into public consciousness. This is one of the levels at which communication processes are salient, since a history of conflict or of bad inter-group relations provides a context in which any incident can become highly charged. Specific communication processes include rumour (Shiboutani, 1966) whereby information spreads by word of mouth along existing social networks — the 'grapevine'. The speed at which information travels through such channels may mean that large numbers of people appear as if from nowhere — fuelling understandable but usually unfounded suspicions that the events were pre-planned.

Additionally, media sensitization may occur. Widespread publicity given to incidents of disorder in other areas may predispose people — particularly law-enforcement agencies — to interpret a minor incident as the precursor of major disorder, as in Cohen's study of the 'Mods and Rockers' (Cohen, 1973).

To the extent that spectacular manifestations of disorder do take members of the local community, the police and the public by surprise, this is an indication that relevant warning signs have been ignored. Some forms of disorder, such as inner city riots, may be *relatively* unpredictable, while others, such as picketing and demonstrations, are less so. As our case studies show, an anticipation of trouble can itself contribute to disorder. It may also stimulate efforts to defuse the situation and prevent it from getting out of hand. Much depends on the nature of the specific situation (see Chapter 7 below).

Situational. Here we include the spatial context, the setting, of the event. Clearly this has a bearing on the form taken by activities within it, making some forms of behaviour more likely and others more difficult (Wright, 1978). This will be seen in police crowd control tactics at the demonstrations studied. However we would emphasize that this spatial context is always mediated by social and cultural factors. For example, certain locations have a symbolic significance in that they constitute the territory or 'turf' of a particular social group. In both the Haymarket fracas and the community disorders at Maltby and Grimethorpe, one of the points at issue was the right of members of the public to be on the streets as opposed to the police right to move people on. Hence the importance of analysing the spatial and social location of the particular situation.

Interactional. This is the level of analysis where 'flashpoints' occur. We define these as actions seen by the participants as breaking the unwritten rules governing behaviour between groups. A particular action is seen as an index of unwillingness to accommodate to, or a wilful infringement of, previously established norms of behaviour. Such actions may heighten the emotions of the participants, particularly if they include intensifying factors, such as locations or individuals of symbolic importance to the participants. For example, the arrest of a well-known individual such as a high-ranking trade union official or an MP, or rough treatment of a senior politician by a crowd of demonstrators, will be perceived as more significant than that of a less prominent individual. Similarly, the arrest or harsh treatment of someone from a 'vulnerable' social category — a woman, a child or an elderly or infirm person — will intensify the moral indignation of participants.

The way in which actions are carried out will also influence the outcome; a particularly brutal arrest, or degrading treatment of an individual by police or by a member of a crowd will also inflame the situation. Examples of such intensifiers from our case studies include the public handcuffing of an arrested youth to railings, and an attack on a young policewoman.

However, the course of interaction even at this late stage is *not irreversible*, and serious escalation may yet be prevented by actions designed to restore the ruptured status quo, for example apologizing for any excesses, or immediately releasing an arrested person.

We are arguing that incidents of public disorder can best be understood as resulting from a combination of factors operating at different levels, as outlined above. This does not mean that the probability of disorder can be mathematically calculated on the basis of the number of relevant variables which are present. In fact we are sceptical about the claim that such an analysis is possible. Our argument is that where factors conducive to disorder are present at all these levels, disorder will be more probable, and in some cases inevitable. Conversely, working backwards from the event itself, if a specific instance of disorder is investigated, it will be found that predisposing factors of the kind we have outlined were present.

Case study I: the 'Thatcher unwelcoming' demonstration

The first case study deals with events on the evening of 28 April 1983, when a crowd of between 3,000 and 5,000 demonstrators greeted the Prime Minister, Margaret Thatcher's, arrival in Sheffield for the city's most prestigious social event — the annual Cutlers' Feast. The crowd was noisy and boisterous, and their reception clearly conveyed the depth of local resentment towards the Prime Minister, but in spite of earlier anxieties there was little sign of disorder and the demonstration remained peaceful throughout.

The background to the demonstration

The annual Cutlers' Feast is an important Sheffield tradition dating back to the fifteenth century when it took the form of a dinner held at the Annual General Meeting of major figures in the trade. Since 1624, the Feast has also been associated with the election of officers and the passing of accounts; the Master Cutler's principal guest is normally invited on the basis of gratitude for past or anticipation of future favours to the cutlery industry.

At various points in its history the Feast has been the focus for political protest. There were thus historical precedents for the reception given to Conservative Prime Minister, Edward Heath, when he attended the Feast on 18 March 1971. His arrival in Sheffield coincided with growing controversy over the government's Industrial Relations Bill. As the Prime Minister stepped from his car, one of the 300 demonstrators gathered outside the Cutlers' Hall threw an apple at him. Police moved in to arrest the culprit, fighting broke out and eleven arrests were made.

Eight years later a Labour Prime Minister, James Callaghan, received an unfriendly reception on his visit to Sheffield in February 1979 — not as a guest of the Master Cutler, but to receive the freedom of the city. His visit took place during the so-called 'Winter of Discontent' when the government's counter-inflationary policy had incurred the anger of the trade union movement, and Mr Callaghan was met outside the City Hall by 200 demonstrators campaigning against low pay. Though there was no public disorder, a handful of demonstrators gained access to the building and heckled Callaghan during his acceptance speech.

The decision to invite Mrs Thatcher to the Feast in 1983 seemed likely to provoke a hostile reception. During her years in office the Prime Minister had become a regular target for angry protesters, especially trade unionists and students. Given the strong local political culture of Sheffield — a centre of radicalism for over 200 years and now referred to only half jokingly as 'The Socialist Republic of South Yorkshire' — protest seemed inevitable.

The initiative for a demonstration came at a steelworkers' rally in Sheffield on 29 January 1983. The day before, a local newspaper published the news of the invitation to the Prime Minister. Several speakers at the rally called for an organized demonstration of feeling towards the policies of her government. A political activist approached two of the main speakers and expressed a willingness to organize and publicize a demonstration on condition that the speakers act as 'figureheads', which they agreed to do.

A 'Thatcher Reception Committee' was formed around this nucleus, soon joined by other groups and organizations. When the Reception Committee approached members of the Labour group on Sheffield City council, they discovered that the local Trades Council and the District Labour Party were already considering forming an 'Unwelcoming Committee' of their own, so the two groups joined forces.

This proved an uncomfortable alliance, with the Reception Committee suspicious of the motives of the Labour Party dominated Unwelcoming Committee who were thought to be seeking publicity in the run-up to the local elections. There were differences at the level of strategy and tactics, with the Reception Committee advocating 'bringing the city to a standstill', while the Unwelcoming Committee favoured an orderly demonstration free from any controversy which might divert attention from the important political issues involved. These differences were not resolved, and relations between the two groups worsened, culminating in an acrimonious meeting early in March when the two groups split permanently.

However this split did not prove detrimental to the organization and promotion of the event. All parties worked together in a desire to mobilize as much support as possible. The Unwelcoming Committee's greater formal links with local political and trade union organizations, their status as the publicly acknowledged organizers of the demonstration and their better access to the media enabled them to place their emphasis on an orderly expression of views at the head of the agenda.

Observation of the demonstration
The nature and timing of the demonstration allowed us to analyse it

in detail. We followed the planning process by attending meetings and holding discussions with the organizers. We undertook a survey of the crowd, interviewed the police and monitored media coverage of the demonstration, which we attended as participant observers.

Our crowd survey — which was random in the literal rather than the statistical sense — provided a rough profile of those present: 83 per cent under thirty-five; 10 per cent under eighteen; 52 per cent males. Two thirds of those interviewed belonged to organized political groups, most commonly the Labour Party and CND, or to trade unions, although smaller political organizations including women's and ethnic groups and tenants' and pensioners' associations were also present. Almost half were students, a fifth unemployed, a third worked in non-manual and a tenth in manual occupations.

It was a mainly young, middle-class crowd of political activists with a range of issues for their dissent. 'All Tory policies', nuclear disarmament and unemployment were the most frequently cited, though racism, public spending cuts, steel closures and public transport policy were also mentioned.

The Thatcher Unwelcoming demonstration was overwhelmingly peaceful. Some minor hostility was in evidence; fruit, bags of flour and raw eggs were thrown at the coaches transporting the Master Cutler's guests to the feast, resulting in thirteen arrests.

The only dramatic incident of the evening occurred when a police horse panicked and fell, banging its head on a car and shattering the windscreen. The animal bolted and was temporarily out of control, having thrown its rider, but was soon recaptured before further damage was done. Neither horse nor rider was hurt.

This incident coincided with the arrival of the Prime Minister who was thus able to walk swiftly and unceremoniously into the Cutlers' Hall apparently oblivious to what had happened and almost unnoticed by the demonstrators.

Our observers stressed the carnival atmosphere, with music and street entertainers keeping the crowd amused and occupied and dampening any expectation of disorder — just as the organizers had intended. A succession of speeches from the platform which had been set up outside the Cathedral also kept the attention of the crowd.

The climax of the event was a one-minute's silence in honour of the 94,000 unemployed of South Yorkshire. This was followed by a mass rendition of 'Give Peace A Chance', after which the demonstrators drifted away, many of them to Sheffield City Hall for a well-publicized 'Alternative Feast of Fun', which, it was stressed, had been arranged for the benefit of the *ordinary* people of Sheffield.

Explaining the absence of disorder

After the demonstration, representatives of both the police and the organizers provided similar accounts of why the protest remained peaceful. The organizers cited such factors as the preliminary organization of the event, the 'responsible' attitude of the crowd, and the rapport which had been built up with senior police officers. For their part, police acknowledged the responsiveness of both the organizers and the crowd as a whole, and considered that their own sensitive handling of the situation had been a major factor.

The organizers maintained that the small number of arrests had occurred because, as one of them said in a local radio interview,

> . . . one or two policemen acted out of the spirit of how the whole thing has gone and one or two of the crowd have acted out of the spirit of how the whole thing has gone. One thing's for sure, I've been speaking with the senior police officers. They're very satisfied with the whole tone and spirit of the demonstration. I'm *more* than satisfied with how the vast majority of police have handled themselves. I regret that some people — on *both* sides — did allow it to get into a situation where there have been some people carted off. (BBC Radio Sheffield, 29.4.83 — our emphasis)

This coincided with the police view, expressed in an interview with the Deputy Chief Constable, that a few of the demonstrators 'allowed the situation to go to their heads a bit'.

This however is not a sufficient explanation for the virtual absence of public disorder, so it is essential to take into account the levels of analysis outlined above.

Structural. Any demonstration involves an issue which is contentious and which people feel strongly about. It may also be an index of underlying social conflict. However, some conflicts are more deep-rooted than others. In this case, although the reason for the demonstration was dissatisfaction with current political policies, this did not betoken a rejection of existing political forms per se. It thus lacked potential for conflict.

Political/ideological. The prevailing political/ideological climate was also conducive to an orderly demonstration. This was a routine political protest organized by and on behalf of democratically elected local politicians and members of other local organizations who could not be regarded as 'subversive' or threatening to the existing social order, and whose relationships with the local police were by and large good. This created the preconditions for the development of an *accommodation* between police and demonstrators, which could be activated by liaison, as seen below.

Cultural. There was a shared cultural tendency for the demonstrators to eschew violence. Nearly all the demonstrators — 91 per cent — came from the Sheffield area with its long tradition of peaceful political protest and civic pride. The policing of the demonstration was carried out by members of South Yorkshire Constabulary, who shared the sense of local solidarity. The large middle-class component of the crowd, as well as the high membership of organized political and other groups, suggests a prevailing commitment to conventional political processes in which political violence is seen as counter-productive.

When asked to describe who they thought *might welcome* trouble at the demonstration, our sample cited 'Mrs Thatcher', 'the police', 'the media' and 'a small minority of the crowd', while they thought that this violence would not be welcomed by the organizers or the majority of the crowd. For the demonstrators, disorder was seen as potentially harmful to their cause, especially as many were demonstrating in favour of peace.

The crowd were seasoned demonstrators who knew the rules of the game. The presence of women and children is also likely to have reduced displays of 'machismo' and aggression characteristic of all-male crowds. Even the most determined troublemakers might well have been deterred by the presence of babies in slings and toddlers in baby buggies.

Contextual. The context for the event was defined by media coverage, and the plans made by the organizers and the police. Local press treatment varied. The business-oriented *Morning Telegraph* was condemnatory of the demonstration; its leader writer in the 28 April edition considered it 'shameful' that a guest of the city should be treated to such a reception. The leader forecast 'the whole squalid shabby business' would be entirely predictable; 'the converted yelling shoulder to shoulder with the converted'. References to 'rent-a-mob' were used to denigrate the protesters, and it was asserted that such 'exhibitionism' would serve only to damage Sheffield's reputation.

In contrast, the pre-demonstration editorial appearing in the city's more widely read evening paper, the *Sheffield Star*, saw the demonstration as 'a welcome chance for Sheffield to state its case and express its feelings — and it should not be wasted'. The following evening's edition carried 'an open letter to Mrs Thatcher', appealing to her to recognize the protest as 'a human cry of distress from a community that is suffering and full of fear for the future'.

The organizers of the demonstration regularly appeared in the local media to urge that the demonstration be kept peaceful, warning against providing Mrs Thatcher with an occasion to dismiss the demonstrators as a 'mob' or 'rabble' and emphasizing that the demonstration was about policies not personalities. They further reinforced the message of non-violence with printed leaflets handed out to participants at the beginning of the demonstration, which called on them to 'remain peaceful and disciplined, for it had never been the aim of the organizers to try and physically prevent the Prime Minister from attending our local dignitaries' Beanfeast'.

From the beginning the organizers liaised with the police, who were sensitive to the demand for a communal expression of dissent by the people of Sheffield and raised no objections to the demonstration. Their implicit granting of legitimacy to the demonstration was reciprocated by the organizers, who appreciated the need for the security of the Prime Minister to be safeguarded. Hence a close liaison developed. Accommodation was manifested in arrangements such as the agreement to allow self-stewarding of the early stages of the demonstration by volunteers from the Amalgamated Union of Engineering Workers.

Situational. Considerable thought was given by the police and the organizers to the physical setting of the demonstration. For example, the organizers complied with the police request for the demonstration to take place on the forecourt of the Cathedral opposite the Cutlers' Hall rather than in the street directly outside. The advantages of this were that, firstly, it allowed normal bus and ambulance routes to be kept open, and removed the need for constant police attempts to clear the road which might have involved arrests for obstruction. Secondly, it facilitated police observation and monitoring, from the high buildings surrounding the space, enabling troublemakers to be accurately pinpointed, thus making random or mistaken arrests less likely. Finally it created a natural square around which the police were able to erect simple crash barriers to contain the crowd. As the Deputy Chief Constable of South Yorkshire explained, this was an important consideration in crowd management:

> The important thing with crowd control is to get there *before* the crowd. If the crowd are there before you, you've got to use force, normally, to get them back, so immediately you're on the wrong footing. The crowd, by and large, will fall in behind whatever you erect. (Interview)

Another crucial factor was police permission for the erection of a platform in the Cathedral forecourt from which speakers could address the crowd and entertainers hold their attention. As the Chair of the Unwelcoming Committee stated in a radio interview, 'the decision was *absolutely key* in making sure that the demonstration was orderly' (Radio Sheffield, 29.4.83).

Other police tactics aimed at regulating the spatial context included the decision to transport the guests to the Feast in coaches to discourage contact with demonstrators, and the refusal of permission for a rival demonstration of loyalty by Conservative trade unionists.

Interactional. The site of the demonstration had been designed to maximize orderly interaction within the crowd and between the crowd and the police. The speeches, while primarily aimed for political effect, helped to keep the crowd's attention. The distribution of balloons and the presence of musicians and other entertainers helped to create a festive atmosphere, and reduce boredom and the likelihood of disorder. An important factor in regulating the behaviour of the crowd was the 'one minute's silence'. Apart from its obvious symbolic value, this helped to ensure that the participants did not resort to other, more idiosyncratic forms of protest which might have been more difficult for the police. It also acted as a 'punctuation mark', concluding the evening's activities, and giving the signal for the crowd to disperse, thus avoiding the aimless 'milling around' often found at the end of demonstrations, a danger time for potential disorder.

Self-policing by stewards minimized contact between police and the crowd. The gradual build-up of the police presence was carefully planned to coincide with the steady arrival of the demonstrators. Reinforcements had been brought in from outside South Yorkshire, but only as a precautionary measure. As one officer explained:

> We're bringing in policemen from West Yorkshire. Whether we use them or not depends, of course, on how the demonstration goes. But I do stress that it has been the organizers' intention — and we have had an awful lot of cooperation from them — that it will be a peaceful, dignified, demonstration and I would hope not to use many policemen. But of course, you've got to cater for those people who've come down there purely to cause trouble. (Interview)

The predominance of local police officers may have been crucial. Members of the research team and observers at the front of the demonstration stressed that individual police officers took every opportunity to chat good-naturedly to the crowd. This was based perhaps on an official commitment to maintaining good long-term relationships with the community, and was in line with a specific instruction from senior officers to 'jolly' the proceedings along.

Hence the police were careful to remove any person or group whose actions might have been construed as provocative by the demonstrators. One of the Master Cutler's guests, a local Conservative councillor, was threatened with arrest for waving a blue handkerchief and making v-signs from one of the front windows of the Cutlers' Hall. Although a potential 'intensifier' was present in the person of the Prime Minister herself, her arrival did not provoke major disorder, aided perhaps by the incident with the police horse which distracted attention.

The arrests did not provoke retaliation by the crowd or draw in other participants. This was partly because miscreants were able to be pinpointed exactly by rooftop surveillance, and their position conveyed to officers on the ground. They were able to deal with incidents promptly, and did not have to chase through the crowd with the danger of arresting the wrong person and provoking a violent reaction.

Interestingly, in at least two of the arrests we observed, demonstrators actually assisted the police in pointing out the offenders. This is an index of the strength of the cultural and situational norm of non-violence shared by the demonstrators, and the legitimacy accorded to the police role. (See Chapter 6 below.)

The political effectiveness of the demonstration
The peaceful nature of the demonstration was welcomed by organizers, participants and police. Paradoxically, its peacefulness rendered it so un-newsworthy that the media accounts were driven to highlight the minor incidents of flour-throwing which did occur, and the drama of the police horse. This was the only part of the proceedings to appear on the national TV news.

Our survey carried out after the demonstration to discover the extent of public knowledge of it, and attitudes towards it, confirmed the suspicion that the public was largely ignorant of who the demonstrators were, and what issues they had been protesting about, although the majority of respondents had heard of it.

In terms of its effectiveness in changing the attitudes of government, the demonstration was a pointless exercise, of purely symbolic value — a view shared by the survey respondents. Interestingly, this belief was shared by many of the participants interviewed during the demonstration. This suggests perhaps the existence of a disillusionment with the conventions of peaceful protest. While this does not necessarily imply the existence of a readiness to engage in more violent forms of action, it seems likely that frustration with existing channels of protest *could* lead to more violent manifestations of disaffection, if *other* factors conducive to such an outcome are also present. This was the case in the following example, that of the NUM rallies which took place in Sheffield the following year.

Case study II: the NUM rallies in Sheffield, April 1984
The second of our two case studies concerns the public disorder surrounding two rallies by members of the National Union of Mine-workers (NUM) in Sheffield city centre in April 1984. The first rally saw sporadic violence between miners and police outside NUM headquarters, whereas the subsequent rally was an entirely peaceful affair with no arrests. However on both occasions there were major episodes of disorder involving confrontations between miners and police officers as the miners made their way back to their coaches after the rally. An explanation of these incidents requires detailed analysis of both the events themselves and their wider context.

The background to the rallies
The setting for the 1984–5 coal dispute has been extensively documented elsewhere (Beynon (ed.), 1985). The National Coal Board (NCB) announced on 6 March 1984 that there was to be a cut of four million tonnes in national coal production. Furthermore, as part of its drive against 'uneconomic' pits, the Yorkshire area gave notice that it intended to close Cortonwood colliery, in the South Yorkshire coalfield. The NUM announced its opposition to the closure, and brought its members out on strike on an area by area basis, beginning with Yorkshire.

When the membership in more 'moderate' areas such as Nottinghamshire refused to join the strike, the Yorkshire miners crossed into Nottinghamshire in an attempt to bring them out by picketing. When this failed a delegate conference was called to bring the recalcitrant areas in line with national policy by constitutional means. The first rally, which accompanied this delegate conference on 12 April, was an attempt by striking miners to persuade their national executive to reject a motion by the Leicester area of the union calling for a strike ballot of the full NUM membership. The second rally, a week later, was a lobby of NUM delegates to a specially convened meeting, again in order to forestall attempts to hold a ballot.

We observed both rallies and the incidents occurring after the first rally at first hand. Our reconstruction of incidents after the second rally is based on eye-witness and media accounts.

The first rally — 12 April

Observation of the first rally
The rally of 12 April took place outside the NUM's national head-quarters in St James' Square, Sheffield. Seven thousand miners from throughout Britain were present, as were 2,000 police officers drawn from ten separate forces (South Yorkshire Police Report, 1985).

The arrival of representatives of pro-ballot areas, such as Ray Chadburn and Henry Richardson of Nottinghamshire area, was greeted by extensive pushing and shoving as the demonstrators surged forwards, jeering to indicate their derision at the attitude of the pro-ballot 'moderate' areas. Similar surges, this time signalling support, greeted the arrival of executive members *opposed* to the ballot, such as Peter Heathfield and Mick McGahey. In both cases police prevented the demonstrators from reaching their targets.

On numerous occasions, the miners linked arms and surged violently into the police ranks. Punching, kicking and hair-pulling took place as miners and police clashed and miners were wrenched away from their colleagues by police. A wall of police standing ten deep in places held off a succession of charges and kept the miners to some thirty yards from the NUM building. Then, with a chant of 'one, two! one, two!' the police would push the demonstrators back to the rear of the courtyard. Missiles, including empty drink cans and placards on stakes were thrown in retaliation, particularly by those suffering the worst effects of the crush. Finally, having succeeded in temporarily overpowering the demonstrators, the police would ease the pressure and reorganize their ranks in preparation for the next charge. This sequence was repeated a number of times.

Shortly before the meeting of the executive, the NUM president, Arthur Scargill, appeared at an upper-floor window of the multi-storey building to address his members. Referring to recent events, he said:

> This is yet another example of a police state. We will do anything in our power to stop the closure of our pits, the butchery of our industry, and the sacking of our members. (Yorkshire Post, 13.4.84)

This again led to a surge of crowd activity, apparently expressing appreciation at his remarks and resentment against the police.

At the end of the meeting, Scargill emerged from the NUM offices to inform his members of the outcome. Two decisions were conveyed. Firstly, the motion calling for a national strike ballot had been ruled 'out of order' and would be referred to a Special Delegates' Conference on 19 April, when there was a strong likelihood that it would be rejected. Secondly, the Delegates' Conference would also consider amending the union rules so that a simple majority of ballot votes, rather than the 55 per cent stipulated by current rules, would be a sufficient basis on which to call a national strike.

Plainly euphoric at this outcome, the demonstrators engaged in their final and most concerted push against the police ranks. It seemed to our observer that this was intended as a final gesture of defiance and show of solidarity.

After the rally
At the end of the rally, a small number of demonstrators remained behind to wait for the Nottinghamshire delegates, Ray Chadburn and Henry Richardson, to emerge. They were set upon and jostled as they tried to reach the car park, as was a TV crew filming the event. Later, when asked by reporters what they thought of their reception, the two men responded not by condemning their assailants but by publicly criticizing their own Nottinghamshire members, whom they urged to 'Get up off their knees and stop being scabs'.

Later in the day, police were summoned to several public houses in response to complaints about miners' behaviour. During one incident, two miners were ejected by the landlord of the New Inn, opposite the Sheffield Trades and Labour Club in Duke Street. This was significant in shaping the context of the rally the following week, as were the treatment of the Nottinghamshire delegates and the incidents occurring as the miners returned to their coaches.

After the rally, a long procession of miners marched five-abreast through Sheffield city centre towards the Wicker, one of the main roads out of the city, where many of their coaches were parked. Their large numbers caused a certain amount of disruption to pedestrians and road traffic. At first the accompanying police tolerated the situation, but as the procession meandered unpredictably through the streets, bringing traffic to a standstill, the officers became visibly more frustrated by their inability to control the situation.

The marchers eventually reached Lady Bridge, which leads to the Wicker. At this point a senior police officer arrived on the scene, accompanied by a unit of reinforcements, and gave orders to clear the road. Almost at once, in the words of one witness,

> The hitherto tolerant behaviour of the police escort changed to one not only of complete intolerance, but to one of positive aggression. Police began to push and thump the miners in their backs. The unfortunate individuals then proceeded to turn around ... they were grabbed by one lot of policemen and thumped in the abdomen by others ... Other miners were being pinned to the ground and assaulted. At no time did I see a single blow struck by a miner at the police. (Sheffield Policewatch Report, no 1)

Field notes made at the time corroborate this account. Some miners were pushed on to the kerb, others were kicked on the body and legs by police officers who herded them towards their coaches. Anyone who protested was immediately arrested — sometimes by six officers at a time.

Explaining the disorder
Such incidents contributed to an image of the rally as essentially disorderly and as a direct result of the activities of the union executive

and especially its president, Arthur Scargill. This was the view taken
by the press. We analysed twelve local and national newspapers for
their version of the causes of disorder. The common account, ignoring stylistic differences, ran as follows.

> The miners who were gathered round the NUM headquarters were all
> well-behaved and in good humour. The miners were incited to disorder by
> a speech by Scargill but the police maintained order. Some police officers
> were injured. At the end of the meeting, the police presence was relaxed
> as the majority of pickets/demonstrators dispersed. However, there was
> further violence as the leader of the moderates, Ray Chadburn, was jostled
> by a handful of miners as he left the building. The violence was set in the
> context of the deepening conflict between the moderate and militant
> wings of the NUM.

The photographs and captions used to illustrate these newspaper
stories reinforced this explanation of events. Most of them used
photographs of an injured policeman. A typical cartoon was that of
the *Daily Star*: 'One of Ten Police Officers Injured during Clashes
with Demonstrators'.

In this they were apparently following the official police view, as
put forward by the Deputy Chief Constable of South Yorkshire:

> Mr Scargill's announcements clearly led to a surge in crowd activity. I
> think they excited the crowd. I think anybody doing this sort of thing should
> do it responsibly, with the intention of calming people, not, as seemed in
> this case, to have a counter-result, which happened when the crowd
> surged forward. It resulted in a number of policemen being injured and a
> number of arrests being made. (Yorkshire Post, 13.4.84)

This must be seen as an over-simplified version of events. It fails to
take into account that there had already been a number of clashes
prior to Scargill's appearance. It also ignores the symbolic nature of
the surges which accompanied the appearance of the delegates from
Nottinghamshire. As for the violence after the demonstration, while
it is an easy matter to identify the 'flashpoint' on this occasion as the
sudden police initiative in moving into clear the road and make
arrests, neither this incident, nor the violence at the demonstration
which preceded it, can be understood without other levels of analysis
going beyond the immediate situation.

Structural. The potential for conflict, and thus the precondition for
disorder, was increased by the fact that the event was not only a
demonstration, but also a manifestation of industrial conflict, since
the demonstrators were all members of the same striking trade union.
The underlying economic situation of industrial decline, lack of

profitability and worsening unemployment since the early 1970s provides the structural preconditions for increased levels of industrial
conflict (Gamble, 1981). The crisis has been particularly acute in the
coal industry which also, for historical reasons, has an exceptionally
powerful regionally based union organization among the workforce.
Thus there existed both the scope for conflict over strategies aimed at
improving profitability by rationalizing the industry and closing pits,
and the means of organizing resistance to such strategies.

However, the structural preconditions for conflict are not sufficient to explain its actual occurrence, or to predict whether the
conflict will remain within the accepted norms of public behaviour or
flare into violence.

Political/ideological. The political climate was highly charged.
There was a great deal at stake for the government. At the simplest
level it was necessary for the strike to be defeated in order to ensure
the success of their economic strategy, which involved among other
things the dismantling of the nationalized industries and a move away
from dependence on coal as a major energy source. These tactics had
been outlined by a Conservative Party policy group headed by Nicho-
las Ridley MP in 1976, and became known as the Ridley Report
(*Economist*, 27 May 1978). In addition, however, the miners, and in
particular their leadership, were identified with the Saltley debacle of
1972 (see Chapter 2 above), when a mass picket of miners and other
trade unionists forced the closure of a crucial coke depot, blamed by
some for the 'bringing down' of the Conservative government in
1974. The Prime Minister had been forced to climb down in the face
of the threat of a miners' strike as recently as 1981. There was hence a
desire on the part of the government to avoid a repetition of past
events — and possibly to avenge them.

The Ridley report was as much a manual of political tactics as of
economic strategy, advocating not only the building up of coal stocks
and conversion of power stations from coal to oil in preparation for a
strike, but also covered a range of contingencies including the recruitment of non-union lorry drivers to transport coal across picket lines
to power stations, cutting social security payments to strikers and the
mobilization of large mobile squads of police to counteract flying
pickets. Thus the political terrain for confrontation, and the political
means to deal with its possible consequences, were well prepared.

The ideological terrain was also well prepared. Once the strike was
underway, the miners were subjected to a concerted ideological
campaign of vilification in which some politicians and sections of the
press lost no opportunity to denigrate the strikers and their leadership. The strike's legitimacy was challenged by the miners' refusal

to hold a ballot as required by the government's trade union legislation. The dispute was further undermined by being presented as a politically motivated action, resulting from the deliberate machinations of the union's left-wing leadership. This culminated in June 1984, when striking miners were linked in public discourse with terrorists and subversives by the Prime Minister's famous reference to 'the enemy within'.

The ideological themes given particular prominence were those of 'the right to work' of individuals opposed to the strike, the dangerous consequences of a surrender to 'mob rule' for the preservation of 'law and order', and the flouting of 'democracy' represented by the miners refusal to hold a ballot as required by the government's industrial relations legislation. This constituted an attempt to persuade public opinion that the miners and their leadership were attacking the very basis of society by undermining individual freedom and the rule of law. This was in sharp contrast to the public image of the miner at periods of less acute ideological struggle, when the hard and dangerous nature of the miner's work and the close-knit nature of mining communities receive more sympathetic, if somewhat patronizing ('salt of the earth'), coverage. Particular prominence was given to the issue of violence in picketing, and the intimidation of working miners by strikers and flying pickets.

One of the consequences of this type of representation of the strike and of strikers was to reduce the amount of discretion available to the police in how they dealt with picketing, thus encouraging a rigid enforcement of the letter of the law. They relied on charging miners with offences which depended on police perceptions, such as 'conduct likely to cause a breach of the peace' and 'obstruction'. Though the Employment Act of 1980 gives employers the right in civil law to sue trade unionists involved in secondary picketing, these provisions were not used by the NCB.

Instead, reliance was placed on police enforcement of the criminal law. Thus the police had discretion to define and regulate what happened on the picket line, especially the acceptable size of a picket, and whether or not a breach of the peace was likely to occur. This had serious consequences for police–picket interaction. The way the issue had been framed in political, ideological and legal terms affected relationships between police and miners in all the areas in which they came into contact, not only on the picket line but at rallies and demonstrations and within mining communities.

Cultural. Studies of both miners (Dennis et al., 1956) and police (Cain, 1973; Holdaway, 1983) suggest that both share an occupational culture in which group solidarity is paramount. Both groups will close ranks in the face of a perceived enemy, and loyalty to fellow group members under attack is an automatic response. This meant that miners would retaliate against police attempts to arrest their mates, and police would go to the rescue of colleagues under attack.

This solidarity is combined with a macho orientation typical of all-male groups involving an emphasis on physical toughness. Violence and the threat of it are occasionally used by both groups. Confrontations between police and pickets thus became in part tests of male dominance of a kind more commonly found on the football terraces, where indeed many of the pickets derived their chants and songs.

Police culture is further characterized by strong orientations to 'action', 'excitement' and 'control' (Manning, 1979; Smith and Grey, 1985). These were evident in police frustration at their inability to prevent the miners from blocking the roadway, and the vigour of their response once they had been given the go-ahead to move in and clear the way. This is graphically illustrated by the words of one police inspector who was unable to be present at the rally:

Yesterday it was purgatory in here because there was an incident in which a couple of thousand bobbies were *fighting* and I wasn't even there. I had other things to do. But it was what I joined the police force for. So it was *purgatory*. (Interview)

The possible cohesive effects of a shared local culture were missing on this occasion, since the miners came from all over Britain, and the police present were drawn from several outside forces, so there was no shared commitment to the maintenance of good long-term community relationships as there had been at the Thatcher demonstration.

Contextual. The context for the rally was the six-week-old strike. Miners and police had already been brought into confrontation on picket lines and on roadblocks, creating a communication context in which expectations of conflict were high. Indeed, some of the demonstrators had arrived in Sheffield with very recent experience of the new police tactics.

An incident arose on a bus journey to Sheffield to lobby an NUM Executive meeting. The bus was stopped by the police approximately five times on the way, all in Staffordshire. The police refused to accept our destination, and said that we were going to picket at a pit. In order to ensure that we went to Sheffield, a police car led the bus on the 'correct' journey in order to make sure that we went to Sheffield and nowhere else. (East and Thomas, 1985: 139)

In addition, there had been no preliminary communication or liaison between the police and the organizers about ensuring an orderly return to the coaches after the demonstration — or indeed about any other arrangements. This was an index of the lack of accommodation between the two groups, which helped to set the scene for the disorder.

A wider communication context for the meeting had already been created, not only by the media in general but also through the NUM's own publicity network, including national and regional union newsletters and newspapers, as well as discussion at union meetings. This had emphasized the splits within the union, and the significance of the motion calling for a ballot. A symbolic importance for the event was created, casting the representatives of the pro-ballot areas as personifications of the 'moderate' tendency, and thus as heroes or villains, depending on the stance adopted towards the strike.

The police perception of this context was summed up by the Deputy Chief Constable in charge of the operation:

> What you got at that meeting was a large number of people who did not like certain members of the NUM Executive. To quote a few names, there was Bell from the white-collar section, and Chadburn and Richardson from Notts. Now, the attitude of the Nottinghamshire miners was that they should continue to work and the vast majority of people there believed that those lads who were on the moderate wing of the Executive would be voting against their wishes. So, one of our principal objectives was to ensure that everyone — whether a Scargillite, a McGaheyite, a Bellite or whoever he might be — those who had business in that building were able to get in and out without being physically assaulted. (Interview)

The context thus shaped police perception of the kind of event it was likely to be, and the kind of tactics which would be needed.

Situational. The spatial context was of some significance. The setting for the demonstration was an enclosed space in front of the NUM headquarters, surrounded by buildings, mainly office blocks and other business properties. The NUM headquarters had symbolic significance since it was the seat of the executive and belonged to the union whose members felt they had a right of access to it. Additionally, the layout of the venue meant that the demonstrators were crushed together and hemmed in by the encircling police, with obvious potential for pushing and shoving.

The Deputy Chief Constable in charge of the operation revealed police concern about the site of the rally:

> The potential was particularly obvious, especially considering that most picket line confrontations do not take place in the middle of a major city. All those people had moved into a confined space in the middle of some of the most expensive business properties in the middle of a major city that

did not particularly want them there. They were within a hundred yards of the Cutlers' Hall, very close to the City Hall and very close to the offices that run down the High Street. There were six or seven thousand people, all from out of town, all wandering around aimlessly, trying to eat, drink, and urinate (*sic*). You had all the ingredients. (Interview)

A key space in front of the building had been colonized by a group of miners: whether to ensure a good vantage point or to stake out a symbolic space we have no way of telling. The Deputy Chief Constable gave this action a sinister interpretation:

... the ground was taken in the middle by miners, I think from South Wales, who took over a kiosk type of place from midnight onwards. Now, one must ask why they had taken it over from midnight onwards for something which wasn't going to start until 11 o'clock in the morning, I think. (Interview)

His definition of the situation appeared to be informed by experience of policing mass pickets and football crowds rather than political demonstrations.

... the potential for disorder, particularly as a large number of people had drunk quite a lot, and had travelled quite a long way to do it, was *a bit like caging up a lot of football supporters who had travelled a long way only to be kept hanging around for anything up to twelve hours or more.* (Interview; emphasis added)

Thus the location of the rally and the definition of its potential held by those involved were already highly conducive to the outbreak of disorder.

Interactional. From the beginning of the rally, the lack of political or physical room for manoeuvre between police and miners was obvious. Even initially humorous exchanges were barbed. Thus what might have been merely ritualized bouts of pushing and shoving in a more routine industrial conflict soon escalated into fighting; each charge by the miners became a flashpoint for renewed bouts of violence. The appearance of members of the executive heightened tension and caused the crowd to surge forward.

Somewhat ironically, the relatively enclosed site of this confrontation was a limit on the violence. Once away from the rally, a flashpoint had more room to explode. It did so on the streets of the city centre. The immediate cause of the disorder at the Wicker was the police decision to clear the roadway. The miners saw the police move as sudden, arbitrary and ruthless. The arrival of police reinforcements new to the situation who perceived it as more threatening than it was only exacerbated matters. As so often happens in such situations, a pattern of expectation became a self-fulfilling prophesy.

The second rally — 19 April

Observation of the rally

The atmosphere of the second rally was in marked contrast to that of the previous week. Although the underlying structural, political and cultural factors remained the same, processes at the contextual and situational levels were very different, and this ensured that the rally remained orderly.

Media coverage of the violence at the previous week's rally dismayed local opinion, and created a context more favourable to accommodation. Both the police and the NUM were anxious to avoid a repetition of the disorder and the attendant bad publicity, and were responsive to conciliatory ideas put forward by members of the local police authority and Sheffield City Council.

According to *Labour Weekly*, senior South Yorkshire police officers had been 'deeply distressed' by reports of the Wicker violence. The Deputy Chief Constable hoped that a repetition of the previous incidents could be avoided. Liaison was carried out through intermediaries:

> There was direct liaison between ourselves and the leader of Sheffield City Council — that, and the direct involvement of the South Yorkshire Police Committee. It was our intention to obtain the cooperation of the NUM, which we hadn't had, to provide a carnival-type atmosphere. There was very bad publicity for the NUM for what happened at the first week ... The hopeful intention was that they would be able to police themselves, so that any suggestion of police provocation could be debunked. (Interview)

The deliberate shift towards greater accommodation was reflected in communications within the police senior command structure, and the decision to treat the operation as a 'normal' demonstration rather than to prepare for violence. As the Chief Constable explained:

> I was ringing up from Majorca, where I was having the first holiday I had had for sixteen months, and I said, 'Well, I think I'll come back'. And I was told by my Deputy that 'Well, if *you* come back, that's not giving it the low profile — you are "flying back in", and that's not giving it the low profile that we are trying to achieve, and I would ask you not to bother'. This was an indication of the attitude generally that we were trying to adopt. (Interview)

The potential for disorder was further reduced by the Nottinghamshire delegates' public dissociation from the views of their rank-and-file, making it unlikely that they would be subjected to the derision of the previous week.

NUM leaders adopted crowd management strategies, on the advice of Sheffield Trades Council, who had organized the 'Thatcher

Unwelcoming' demonstration. A platform was erected opposite the City Hall, where the conference was taking place, enabling the demonstrators to be kept occupied listening to speeches and entertainers. The larger space available outside the City Hall helped to reduce the crush.

The rally passed off peacefully. Malcolm Pitt, the respected President of the Kent area of the NUM, acted as master of ceremonies, and repeatedly urged the miners to ignore the police, warning them that any violence would be duly exploited by the media.

Contact between police and demonstrators was reduced by the use of NUM marshals — the 'self-policing' hoped for by the police. The behaviour of the police at the rally also reduced the likelihood of violence being triggered. Two reports from Vincent Hanna of BBC 2's *Newsnight* programme bear this out:

> 7.45, and a police decision is made to have breakfast. There are 200 officers on duty with 400 more on standby. A week ago in Sheffield there was violence after the Miners' Executive meeting, and today police appear to want to restore some strained relationships with the union. So, they walk in two's instead of groups, and, it is rumoured, even offered the police band to entertain the crowds. It was declined. Today their operation is deliberately low-key. (*Newsnight*, BBC 2, 27.4.84)

Any incident which looked likely to upset the fragile 'contract' between police and crowd was immediately defused:

> It's 9.30, with 7,000 miners now in the square, and the delegates begin to arrive, pushing through a noisy, if good-tempered, line of NUM marshalls. The police are spotted approaching and there is instant chanting. *An inspector rushes to send them away.* It's still a low-key day. (Emphasis added)

Chadburn, reviled by demonstrators the previous week, was accompanied into the City Hall by Scargill. This symbolically emphasized Chadburn's support for the majority position on the executive, and helped to discourage repetition of the previous week's violence.

Thus both police and organizers took steps to ensure that any propensity for disorder was averted or discouraged, and the rally was entirely peaceful. The account in the *Sheffield Star* that evening was headlined: 'Miners Make It a Gala', 'Police Presence Low-Key' and 'Singing and Dancing — Just Like Blackpool on a Bank Holiday'.

Explaining relative order
In terms of our six levels, there had been some significant changes from the previous rally. Some factors remained: the structural causes of the conflict had not been removed; the political and ideological onslaught on the miners had if anything intensified. The cultural

values of miners and policemen had not altered in the space of a week, and the broader context of police–miner relations had deteriorated daily on the picket line.

However the immediate context had been changed by the experience of the previous rally which neither side wanted to see repeated. This led to responses at the situational and interactional level. Both sides adopted strategies for controlling their own members, whereas there had been improvization the week before. The site of the rally was less claustrophobic, and the attentions of the crowd were focused. Importantly, the police adopted a low-key approach.

What this shows is that even the most conflict-ridden situation can be kept orderly, given accommodation between the two parties involved. However much depends on the presence and the abilities of their leaders. In their absence, a contract cannot always be maintained. The collapse of such a contract was evident in events after the rally.

After the rally

Two incidents of disorder occurred after the rally, one relatively minor and one more serious with sixty-eight arrests and many injuries.

The cake van incident. Our only reports of this incident came from police accounts. In the words of the Deputy Chief Constable, South Yorkshire Police:

> What sparked that incident was the unfortunate arrival too soon of contractors who were delivering food and refreshments to the City Hall for an evening function. A certain number of demonstrators who hadn't eaten all day raided that vehicle and helped themselves to the cakes and sandwiches. The owners of the refreshments called upon police to stop them. A number of my officers moved in to do so, and had the worst of the encounter. I think the miners were from Durham. The police were outnumbered very strongly and had to retreat. I turned up at the scene, and found that it was largely controlled, but that there was an extreme bitterness because a number of miners had been arrested and a number of policemen had been injured. (Interview)

Although the police involved were from South Yorkshire, and desirous of maintaining the existing accommodation, the nature of the 'flashpoint' incident made a breakdown likely apart from frayed tempers on the part of hungry miners. The initial event was a criminal act, so the police had no choice but to intervene, and felt no compunction about using force:

> The attacks upon the police officers were so violent that the officers were required to draw their truncheons to protect themselves. Several police

officers were surrounded by drunken, violent demonstrators and beaten severely, their colleagues being forced to mount rescues, and having to use their truncheons in order to do so.

More police officers attended the scene, and riot shields were despatched, but in the event not deployed even though police officers came under a barrage of missiles comprising house bricks and bottles. The situation eventually calmed, with demonstrators being coaxed onto their waiting coaches and escorted out of the city. (South Yorkshire Police, 1985)

Whatever the other side of the story, there seems to have been little scope for police discretion. A crime had been committed and the disorder arose primarily over attempts to make an arrest.

The Trades and Labour Club incident. The initial impetus for this disturbance was a complaint from the licensee of the New Inn, opposite the Trades and Labour Club, that miners were kicking on the door, demanding to be let in. The establishment had deliberately closed down over lunch time because of the incident after the previous week's rally when two miners had been ejected. In response to the complaint, a group of police approached a larger group of miners. According to the Deputy Chief Constable:

Initially, the police were heavily outnumbered and two officers who were trapped in a doorway drew their truncheons to protect themselves. According to the licensee of the public house, the miners had come from the Trades and Labour Club after a long drinking session, and many of them were drunk. (Interview)

Subsequent police accounts emphasize that when vanloads of reinforcements came to the assistance of their colleagues, they were immediately confronted by a 'drunken mob' emerging from the Trades and Labour Club:

They were staggering about and shouting, from which I could only draw the conclusion that most, if not all, were under the influence of drink. (Police officer's court evidence, *Sheffield Morning Telegraph*, 17.10.84)

Police also claimed that a group of miners charged them, shouting 'Here we go! Here we go! Here we go!'

A different version of events was presented by several eyewitnesses, including Richard Caborn, the MP for Sheffield Central and Bill Michie, MP for Sheffield Heeley. At about 3 p.m. Caborn, a trustee of the Trades and Labour Club, was outside the Club giving directions to some of the Durham miners on how to get back to their coaches. It was his view that the miners were leaving the Club in an orderly fashion when the police arrived. In his words:

> Two police vans arrived and parked at the traffic lights in Duke Street . . .
> on the city centre side of the lights. The vans unloaded and I think about
> twenty police constables got out, and started to walk diagonally across the
> road towards the Club. I walked towards the police constables in front of
> the miners looking for the person in charge, an inspector or sergeant, I
> could only see police constables. I put my arms up and addressed the
> police generally, saying, '*There's no trouble in this Club. I am a trustee of
> the Club and a Member of Parliament for this area*'. I said this as I was
> walking towards the police constables and they were walking towards me.
> I said the words in a loud voice sufficient for them to hear me. I heard a
> police constable say to me '*fuck off*'. (Caborn's statement to police;
> original emphasis).

The situation then began to deteriorate: according to Caborn,
police began to arrest miners indiscriminately. Two police officers
chased a miner into the crowded club entrance and drew their truncheons. As Caborn appealed to the officers to put them away, he was
knocked to the ground. On rising to his feet, he saw a police officer
hitting the club sign with his truncheon and heard him shout 'Get
back you bastards!' to the miners. He then located a Police Inspector
at the edge of the crowd, and asked him who was in charge, but the
officer was unable to tell him.

Media accounts emphasize that police reinforcements were
constantly arriving on the scene. A procession of police vans said to
have contained mostly West Yorkshire police was observed stretching back for a quarter of a mile (*Sheffield Morning Telegraph*,
24.4.84). Several eye witnesses described the aggression taking place
as largely one-sided:

> I was really shocked to see it in Sheffield. The police were very forceful.
> We saw them grabbing miners and pulling them about. One policeman
> pushed a miner down a grass bank and another knelt on top of him. I
> found it quite upsetting. The miners did not seem to be doing anything.
> (*Sheffield Morning Telegraph*, 19.10.84)

Meanwhile Michie, the second MP, was trying to calm the situation, but when Caborn looked across, he saw Michie being arrested
by two police constables. Caborn ran across to explain that Michie
was trying to calm the situation, and was an MP. One of the officers
responded with 'What's an MP?' according to Caborn. However,
they did release Michie.

The two MPs instructed the miners' coaches to be sent for, but
according to Michie, attempts by NUM stewards to marshal their
members away were hampered by the growing police presence and
by the build-up of angry miners who refused to leave the area until
they could establish where their arrested colleagues were being detained. Some miners engaged in a sit-down protest, but NUM lodge

officials persuaded them that this tactic would prove ineffectual and might easily lead to further arrests.

At this point, the Durham Area representative on the Executive arrived. He had been on his way to the railway station when he had been alerted that a confrontation was taking place, and had gone to the scene to help restore order.

According to his signed statement, which he related to Caborn, the behaviour of police officers was extremely provocative. His own efforts to liaise with the police and calm the situation were first ignored and then undermined by police, culminating in an inspector snatching away the loudhailer he was trying to use to address the miners. Peremptory police orders to the miners to board the buses only produced an exodus of those already on. In the ensuing mêlée, the executive member was knocked out, had two ribs fractured and spent two days in hospital.

The *North Eastern Journal* estimated that this Durham miners' official was not the only casualty on that day: eighty-two miners and ten police officers received injuries during the incident.

Media and legal accounts were critical of the police behaviour. Even the *Sheffield Morning Telegraph* (21.4.84), a newspaper generally supportive of the police during the coal dispute, made the point:

> The police authorities have been unable or unwilling to answer his [Richard Caborn's] claims that a force of young constables — without even a sergeant to control them — launched into a public, and by all accounts, ugly brawl in a Sheffield street. These were not police officers aware of this city's tolerance of peaceful demonstrations, but officers from an outside force, presumably with no knowledge of the average miner other than a fear that any miner is a political bobby basher.

At the subsequent trial in Sheffield of eight Durham miners accused of various public order offences, the defence counsel referred to the event as one in which 'the normal constraints on police behaviour got thrown overboard'. He accused the police of behaving indiscriminately, and said that the situation could easily have been defused had they shown greater cooperation. The presiding magistrate dismissed the charges against four of the defendants, but found the remainder guilty as charged. He nevertheless criticized the police evidence as 'unconvincing and unsatisfactory' and added, 'I am not satisfied that the police were as tactful as they might have been' (*Sheffield Morning Telegraph*, 20.10.84).

Explaining disorder
This incident reveals the tenuous nature of the accommodation between miners and police which had governed behaviour at the main rally. The location of the incident, a Trades and Labour Club, invited

interpretations in terms of the invasion or defence of territory. Definitions of the encounter as potentially conflictual had been encouraged by the wider context of police–miner hostility and the experience of the previous week's rally. The non-local police forces involved had not had their expectations of violence reduced by specific instructions from senior officers to adopt a low-key and non-aggressive approach. But even among the local police, lack of leadership meant that these instructions were ignored. In the case of the miners, those who would have provided leadership were denigrated. All attempts to defuse tension were rejected, producing a 'ratchet effect' of increasing violence and mounting retaliation.

Thus the kinds of changes at the contextual, situational and interactional levels which had ensured order at the second rally as compared to the first were reversed. This allowed previous patterns of behaviour to reassert themselves.

The nature of the initial complaint of drunkenness was important in determining the police response. It is difficult to avoid the conclusion that the conduct of the police was inexcusable. Different tactics could well have had a quite different outcome. In that sense, the incident was avoidable. The flashpoint need never have occurred. But the circumstances surrounding it are those which our model would have led us to expect.

Conclusion: diagnosing disorder

In the conclusion we review our substantive findings as to why disorder did or did not occur in the particular incidents studied; we then discuss the theoretical adequacy of our model of levels of causality, and finally we raise some policy considerations.

The case studies compared

To recapitulate: we studied three demonstrations, two peaceful and one disorderly, and the violent incidents occurring after the NUM rallies. We have outlined the specific factors responsible for disorder or the lack of it in each case, in terms of the theoretical framework. We shall now make some explicit comparisons between the events.

The most striking contrast is between the peaceful anti-Thatcher demonstration and the disorder at the first NUM rally. There were basic differences in the composition and motivation of the crowd. In the first case there was a largely middle-class gathering, half of whom were women and children, making a moral protest against the policies of the Conservative government. In the second instance, the crowd consisted exclusively of working-class male trade unionists engaged in what they saw as a struggle to defend their jobs and their communities. It does not need a social scientist to predict that the first crowd is likely to be more orderly than the second.

However it would be simplistic to conclude that some crowds are inherently more prone to disorder than others. Trade union rallies can be orderly even in the middle of long-running disputes, as was shown in our other picketing case study, the 1980 steel strike (Waddington and Jones, 1985) as does the second NUM rally. Conversely, middle-class crowds can become disorderly, as in recent campus incidents (Manchester City Council Report, 1985). Nor is the presence of women and children necessarily a deterrent to disorder, as many incidents at the Greenham Common peace camp have demonstrated.

How the crowd is handled by the police is at least as important as the nature of the crowd. It may be that if demonstrators are bent on creating disorder, the police will feel bound to react accordingly. But the police do not play a merely reactive role: they also play a part in creating the conditions which make disorder more or less likely. It seems clear that on occasion police action can produce more disorder than it prevents.

Police decisions are one of a set of factors which in our view can be isolated as critical for the maintenance or disruption of order. In our analysis of the 'Thatcher Unwelcoming' demonstration we identified four elements which seemed to promote order:

— The demonstration was centrally and systematically planned by a group committed to the avoidance of violence.

— There was as a consequence formal consultation with the local police from an early stage in the planning.

— Concerted efforts were made to channel the responses of the crowd through the provision of marshals, speeches and entertainments, the one minute's silence and the 'alternative feast'.

— The police for their part acknowledged the right to demonstrate, gave advice on the layout of the demonstration and avoided heavy-handed tactics.

These four elements were precisely what was lacking in the first NUM rally. The miners' leadership had more pressing concerns than the avoidance of disorder; far from managing the crowd, there seems to have been a desire to let them have their head. There was no communication between organizers and police either before or during the rally. Hence the police reacted in kind to the miners' surges.

The attempt to maintain order at the second rally involved reversing all these elements of the situation so that they corresponded more to those present at the anti-Thatcher demonstration. Communication between organizers and police was set up through third parties. Serious attention was given to the physical location of the rally, and the crowd was given focal points for speeches and entertainment. The police even offered the use of the police band to entertain the crowd, though the offer was declined. Speakers continually emphasized the desirability of keeping order and avoiding unfavourable publicity. Hence the police felt able to adopt less interventionist tactics.

The violence which occurred after the rally did so when the implicit bargain which had been struck between the miners and the police could no longer be sustained. It was breached initially by the cake van incident, a simple case of theft. In the more serious Trades and Labour Club incident, the police actions showed that they had abandoned the conciliatory style established at the main rally. The place, the time and the leadership were different: the bargain struck elsewhere was no longer seen as relevant.

These case studies illustrate that even in the most conflict-ridden situation, strategies with the potential to forestall disorder can be adopted. But the contract with the crowd is a fragile one which can easily be breached. In addition, our general model suggests that there are other factors which affect the situation.

Explaining disorder: the model

The way in which our comparison of these demonstrations relates to our proposed model can be represented in a table.

The table provides a checklist of factors which may predispose a situation towards disorder. The list could be extended, and other factors would be relevant if types of public disorder other than static demonstrations were to be included. However it does seem possible to make some generalizations about the contexts in which flashpoints may erupt and the responses which cause them to escalate. In terms of our model, disorder is most likely to occur in the following conditions:

The demonstrating group has or feels itself to have grievances whose remedy requires some change in the nature of the social order (structural level).

The demonstrating group's claim has not been generally recognized as valid and/or its campaign has been defined as a threat to law and order (political/ideological level).

The demonstrating group and the police share no cultural definitions of the situation, except a mutual acceptance of violence as a legitimate response (cultural level).

There is a recent history of conflict between the demonstrating group and the police, giving rise to expectations of violence, and liaison has been poor or non-existent (contextual level).

The venue for the demonstration is one where crowd and police are brought face to face with nothing to channel and occupy the crowd (situation level).

The leaders of the demonstration do not recognize or cannot

TABLE 1
Factors predisposing to disorder

Levels of analysis	Case study		
	Thatcher Demo	NUM rally 1	NUM rally 2
Structural			
Conflict between groups	−	−	−
Marginal group involved	−	−	−
Conflictual situation	+	+	+
Political/ideological			
Alienated/disenfranchized group	−	+	+
Politically dissenting group	−	+	+
Group(s) politically delegitimated	−	+	+
Group(s) ideologically vilified	?	+	+
Cultural			
Strong group solidarity based on			
Territory	+	−	−
Occupation	−	+	+
'Machismo'	−	+	+
Cultural meanings discrepant	−	+	+
Negative stereotypes of other group(s)	−	+	+
Contextual			
Local history of conflict	−	−	+
Media sensitization	−	+	+
Lack of liaison between groups	−	+	−
Situational			
Lack of organization	−	+	−
Symbolic setting	−	+	−
Symbolic targets present	+	+	?
Claustrophobic setting	−	+	−
No focal point for crowd	−	+	−
Interactional			
Specific incident involving			
Threat to prominent person	−	−	−
Threat to vulnerable person	−	−	−
Arbitrary treatment	−	+	−
Brutal treatment	−	+	−
Arbitration rejected	−	−	−
No concessionary gestures	−	+	−
Aggressive demeanor of police	−	+	−
Aggressive demeanor of crowd	−	+	−

Notes
+ = Factor present.
− = Factor absent.
? = Factor ambiguous.

persuade demonstrators of the need to avoid violence and/or the police react harshly to trivial infringements of the letter of the law (interactional level).

There were fewer of the factors conducive to disorder in the 'Thatcher' demonstration compared to the two NUM rallies. In the second rally, virtually all of these conditions were met, as they were in many picket line confrontations, especially that at Orgreave. Similar conditions obtain in relations between residents and police in many inner city areas.

However in spite of the similar weight of factors at the structural, political/ideological and cultural levels, the second rally differed from the first in the lack of predisposing factors at situational and interactional levels. This made for a very different outcome.

This suggests that deep-rooted underlying conflicts are a necessary but not a sufficient condition for the outbreak of public disorder (see Chapter 7 below). They form the antecedent conditions for flashpoints to occur. In this respect our analysis, if not our proposed remedies, is similar to that of the Metropolitan Police whose Public Order Branch (A 8) has drawn up a list of twenty high-risk estates on the basis of indicators of potential disorder which refer to the context of disorder rather than to the incidents themselves. They identify factors such as 'high visibility', environmental factors including estate design and a history of gang fights and hostility to the police (reported in *The Guardian*, 12.7.86). That these indicators have several times alerted police to the possibility of trouble without it materializing does not mean that flashpoints are illusions, only that there is unrealized potential for one. A flashpoint incident does have to occur. Anything can become a flashpoint in these conditions, particularly if it can be seen as symbolizing the grievances of an entire group or community. But more immediate factors are decisive in determining whether the flashpoint escalates into violent public disorder. This conclusion has both theoretical and policy implications.

Theoretical implications
Our explanation so far takes the form of a set of empirically grounded generalizations concerning factors conducive to the genesis of disorder. This does not constitute a fully fledged theory of public disorder. Such a theory would need to explain why these particular factors are significant, whether some are more important than others and whether and how they are interrelated. These questions will be pursued in more detail in a forthcoming book (Waddington et al., 1987); the following is an attempt to sketch why our analysis differentiates these particular levels of explanation and what are the relationships between the levels.

At the most general level, *structural* relations of domination, exploitation and exclusion exist between social collectivities, based on class, race and other factors, which make relationships between them inherently conflictual. Thus dominated or marginal social groups are likely to come into conflict with the police as representatives of the state, which represents the dominant social forces.

However, structural conflict and inequality may not be perceived as such, and marginalized groups may not be politically visible. Overt conflict may not appear at the political level, but be repressed, muted, diverted to other targets, mitigated by various forms of social provision or expressed in socially sanctioned forms. Ideological campaigns may focus on marginal or powerless groups and minimize more real conflicts of interest. It has now become commonplace to observe that class or other objective structural features do not necessarily translate themselves into political forces; but if underlying structural conflicts do give rise to political movements and ideological campaigns, the potential for major conflict is increased.

The cultural level of analysis refers to the ways of life and thought which develop on the basis of shared material conditions and a common position within the social structure. A group's culture gives it a common way of perceiving the world, and a basis for mobilization and solidarity if threatened which may have profound psychological roots. Cultural differences between groups may exacerbate conflict, particularly if these include negative stereotypes of other groups or are based on differences of interest.

The *communication context* of events will depend partly on processes at the political and ideological level, and partly on previous events, in that a flashpoint will provide a context affecting the likelihood of further flashpoints, particularly if the event receives widespread publicity. This context is dynamic, unfolding over time and specific to a particular area. It cannot be assumed that wider social conflicts will be manifested in the absence of such a communication context. The time dimension is an important one often neglected in sociological accounts which concentrate on structural factors.

The spatial level is often overlooked, although it can significantly influence the kinds of behaviour. However, the significance attached to the location depends also on factors at the contextual level — what has already happened there — and the cultural level — what the location means to a particular group.

Finally, there is the interactional level of analysis where the flashpoint occurs. Although influenced by the setting, the context and the cultural traits of the participants, as well as political/ideological influences and wider structural determinations, the unfolding of events is not inevitable. Much depends on the individuals involved and how they react to each other; psychological factors enter into play. Expressions of conflict can be minimized and possible flashpoints defused by appropriate communication. Yet an aggressive reaction may raise the temperature. Once a cycle of aggression and counter-aggression has been entered, only dramatic gestures of expiation will break it and prevent the flashpoint from igniting.

This conception of 'flashpoint' is where we started. It is in itself a model or an implicit theory of disorder which combines the two ideas of antecedent conditions and precipitating incident. However, we found this model unsatisfactory, since it draws attention to only structural and interactional levels. It has to be further elaborated in terms of the other levels of analysis. These are necessary in order to explain the processes which mediate between the structural and the interactional levels.

We refer to 'levels of analysis' because we are arguing that these processes exist at different levels of generality, and although in a sense each level can be seen as a precondition for the ones below, they do not fit neatly inside each other like Chinese boxes. They operate also on different time scales: some refer to extremely deep-rooted and stable social relationships and processes, while others refer to more dynamic and fleeting interactions. Some refer to social, others to psychological while others to physical/temporal phenomena, so they are different in kind and need to be analysed separately.

Although it is possible to summarize the model in the form of a checklist of factors conducive to disorder, as we have done, it must be recognized that since these are not all of the same type, they cannot be treated as separate variables, or simply added together to produce a 'disorder quotient' for a given situation. Nor does the model constitute a predictive theory of disorder. Its theoretical value is as an analytical aid; its practical value is as a sensitizing device which draws attention to the kind of situations where disorder is likely to occur, and suggests why this is the case.

To summarize our detailed analysis of cases of actual or potential public disorder suggests that disorder is rarely planned or premeditated by the participants, but that it is explicable and at least partially predictable.

Policy implications
Our policy recommendations are based on the assumption that both citizens and the police wish to avoid disorder. This may not always be the case. We have encountered situations where members of the public believed that the situation justified recourse to violence, and

where the police exacerbated disorder when other options were open to them. There is little point in mutual recrimination as to who instigated disorder in particular cases. The ultimate causes of public disorder lie in the wider social context. We therefore offer analyses and recommendations which address this context.

As far as structural causes are concerned, a social structure which systematically generates inequality and deprivation will simultaneously generate the potential for conflict and hence disorder. Unemployment may not 'cause' riots in any simple or straightforward sense but it certainly does not make them less likely. Resentment at racial disadvantage may find other expressions than direct confrontation with the police, but it is idle to pretend that ethnic minorities do not have real grounds for believing that they are being excluded from society. These are the problems which urgently need to be addressed if violent conflict is not to become endemic.

The way in which such grievances are handled in the political arena is crucial. We take it to be a basic principle of a democratic society that individuals and groups have a right to be heard, even — or especially — if theirs is a minority voice. If formal political institutions do not articulate their grievances, if political leaders seek to make political capital out of branding them as the opponents of democracy, and the mass media wilfully misunderstand and misrepresent their case, then we should not be surprised if they turn to violence against the symbols and agents of the state, historically, the last resort of the excluded. It lies within the power of politicians and the media to eschew defamatory rhetoric which heightens frustration and may indirectly perpetuate the disorder they deplore.

At the cultural level, society shows an increasing diversity of cultures, values and life-styles unmatched by a corresponding growth in tolerance. It seems likely that the police force as a whole has insufficient sensitivity to the problems of policing such a society: cultural conflict between groups becomes crucial when one of those groups is the police. No doubt they have projected on to them resentments which are not of their making, and which should more properly be focused on those who make rather than enforce the law. None the less, the strategy of solving public order and other policing problems by force is one increasingly favoured by those in power and promoted by the police.

It is a characteristically male cultural trait to respond to difficult situations, whether at home, at work, in leisure or in public life, with brute force. It is not generally emphasized that violent disorder is with few exceptions a male activity. If society should attempt to systematically eradicate aggression as a male trait, rather than promote or at least condone it, this would progressively remove one source of violence. There is little indication that this is happening on a large scale in contemporary Britain.

At these levels, all the indications are that society is likely to continue to produce situations of potential disorder. This poses acute problems for policing strategies which have now become the focus for heated political debate. Hence no discussion of the policy implications of public disorder can ignore questions of police organization and practices.

Institutional police response to the problem of public order has concentrated on the need for specific equipment and training for riot control, backed up by demands for an extension of existing police powers to define acts as criminal. This is an admission of defeat in ways that the police appear not to realize. It assumes that order can only be enforced by the threat or the use of violence.

There are, however, alternatives to reliance on technology and the criminal law. They may not have the apparent simplicity of such solutions or offer a quick pay-off. The ultimate objective has to be the restoration of a trust between the police and the whole community which can serve as the basis for negotiation in volatile situations. Although the present chapter has concentrated on demonstrations, other types of public disorder such as industrial picketing and community disorder raise similar issues in relation to policing strategy and tactics. At least five major issues are involved: self-policing, liaison, minimum force, training and accountability.

Self-policing. Firstly, it would seem that the most orderly crowds are those which are allowed to regulate themselves, since this cuts down contact between police and demonstrators and helps to prevent the emergence of a police–crowd confrontation (see Chapter 6 below). This is not always feasible, particularly when the demonstration is one which attracts support from heterogeneous groups, or when the demonstration has been organized at short notice. Where there are marshals or stewards, or representatives/leaders of the groups involved, it seems that police cooperation with them is preferable to an attempt by the police to assert their own authority through coercive measures.

Liaison. Issues such as stewarding, the venue for a demonstration or protest, or the route to be taken by a march, can best be resolved by effective liaison between police and organizers. The new Public Order Act specifies that the police must be notified in advance of marches and demonstrations and have the right to impose certain conditions. Such conditions are best negotiated with the organizers rather than imposed unilaterally by the police, thus creating the suspicion that such conditions are aimed at reducing the visibility and effectiveness of the demonstration.

However, liaison presupposes a certain *accommodation* between the police and the community which may not exist if the political climate or the history of police–community relations are fraught with tension. Successful liaison requires communication skills on the part of both police and organizers, and perhaps more importantly, a recognition by both sides that the role of the other party is legitimate. It also raises questions of police accountability.

Minimum force. It is not only ethically desirable but also pragmatically preferable that police tactics should involve the exercise of minimum force. Preparation and 'tooling up' for trouble produce a psychological predisposition to interpret situations in terms of threat. For example, there is some evidence from our field notes and interviews that the appearance of police officers in full riot gear at Orgreave *before* any disorder had in fact occurred suggested to some of the pickets that confrontation was inevitable and expected, and led them to be more aggressive than they would have been. Violent police tactics may have the effect of creating the very disorder they are ostensibly designed to pre-empt. In a volatile situation, a violent arrest, particularly for a minor or technical offence, or of an innocent person, will almost inevitably set off a violent reaction among the crowd. There are cases when 'law' and 'order' are incompatible, and a trade-off has to be made between the costs and the benefits of a rigid enforcement of the law in tense situations. Calculations of this kind are notoriously difficult, and unpopular with the police, whose training and professional orientation stress a more legalistic approach, but are none the less essential.

Training. The training period undertaken by police officers is at present too short to adequately cover all aspects of the complex and demanding role of the modern police. There is some evidence that training in for example racism awareness does not produce a long-term change in attitudes, and its effects do not long survive the impact of experience and the influence of the police occupational sub-culture (Smith and Grey, 1985: 517). This is not an argument against such training; rather, an argument for improving, extending and reinforcing it by effective supervision of newly trained officers during their early years (see Chapter 4 above).

Particular attention needs to be focused on communication — not only at an interpersonal level but at the level of the community. This need is recognized to some extent by community liaison officers, but not necessarily transferred to other areas of police work. Recognition of the differing cultural values of different social groups will not necessarily improve understanding between them and the police unless it is backed up by specific training in appropriate communication skills and translated into concrete forms of liaison. A greater commitment to improving the negotiating and interpersonal skills of police officers might well obviate the need for training in riot control, which appears to be the current priority of certain police forces.

Accountability. This is currently the most vexed issue in policing. It was raised in an acute form by the riots of 1981, with the accusations of heavy and racially discriminatory policing in inner city areas (Scarman, 1981; Kettle and Hodges, 1982). The miners' strike further raised a number of questions about the policing of picket lines and the legality of police tactics to prevent secondary picketing (Fine and Millar, 1985; NCCL, 1984; Baldwin and Kinsey, 1982; Jefferson and Grimshaw, 1984). However, one of the lessons which could be drawn from our research is that the relationship between the police and the community cannot be left to goodwill, or to the preferences and priorities of Chief Constables, but must have some statutory force.

Effective policing requires the knowledge and consent of the community and a recognition by the police that the community has a right to be consulted. The mechanisms for accomplishing this effectively remain to be worked out. We tend to agree with Reiner (1985) that 'police accountability' is not a panacea but an arena for political debate and calculation. However, the acceptance of the principle, realized through whatever mechanisms, would enable the competing definitions of 'rights' which so often underlie social conflict and public disorder to be discussed and negotiated by the police and representatives of the communities they serve.

This discussion should not be taken as endorsing the view that the problem of public disorder can be solved by better communication. This would be to neglect the deeply entrenched divisions which generate conflict and which our theoretical model emphasizes. But the effects of social divisions can be either reinforced or moderated; we would argue that political and legal initiatives which seek to restrict the expression of dissent are in the long term counter productive. For example, the recent Public Order Act, in extending police control over the route or conduct of marches and demonstrations, and introducing new categories of offence such as 'disorderly conduct', increases police powers while doing nothing to define and protect the rights of demonstrators and pickets. Existing laws already give the police considerable powers to define acceptable behaviour, and whether or not the law is being infringed (McBarnet, 1978). The problem is not one of lack of powers, but of the way in which existing powers are exercised.

We have emphasized the importance of the police role and of police tactics because our case studies suggest that it is at the level of interaction between the police and the crowd that 'flashpoints' occur, and *it is how these initial incidents are handled by the police which decides whether or not the incident escalates*.

The police have the power to help construct a 'definition of the situation' which is shared by demonstrators, both organizers and crowd, provided that the latter want and are able to control their behaviour. The ability to create and maintain a bargain or 'contract' with the crowd is in our view the central factor in preserving order at demonstrations. The alternative currently favoured of restricting the right to demonstrate seems inimical to the exercise of democratic rights, and may exacerbate existing grievances. Public disorder cannot be permanently prevented by force: this Chapter has suggested alternative strategies.

References

Ardrey, R. (1970) *The Social Contract*. London: Collins.

Beynon, H. (ed.) (1985) *Digging Deeper: Issues in the Miner's Strike*. London: Verso.

Bowen, D. R. and Masotti, L. H. (1968) 'Civil Violence: A Theoretical Overview', in Masotti and Bowen (eds), *Civil Violence in the Urban Community*. Beverly Hills and London: Sage.

Brunt, R., Critcher, C., Jones, K. and Jordin, M. (1987) *Representing the People: Case Studies in Media and Politics* (forthcoming). London: Comedia.

Cain, M. (1973) *Society and the Policeman's Role*. London: Routledge and Kegan Paul.

Cohen, S. (1973) *Folk Devils and Moral Panics*. London: Paladin.

Dennis, N., Henriques, F. and Slaughter, C. (1956) *Coal is Our Life*. London: Eyre and Spottiswoode.

Downes, B. (1970) 'A Critical Re-examination of the Social and Political Characteristics of Riot Cities', *Social Science Quarterly*, 51, 219: 349–60.

East, R. and Thomas, P. (1985) 'Road-Blocks: The Experience in Wales', in Fine and Millar (eds), *Policing the Miners' Strike*. London: Lawrence and Wishart.

Field, S. and Southgate, P. (1982) *Public Disorder: A Review of Research and a Study in One Inner-city Area*. London: HMSO.

Fine, B. and Millar, R. (eds) (1975) *Policing the Miners' Strike*. London: Lawrence and Wishart.

Gamble, A. (1981) *Britain in Decline*. London: Macmillan.

Geen, R. G. and Gange, J. J. (1977) 'Drive Theory of Social Facilitation', *Psychological Bulletin*, 84: 1257–88.

Gramsci, A. (1971) *Selections from the Prison Notebooks*, ed. Q. Hoare and G. Nowell-Smith. London: Lawrence and Wishart.

Hall, S., Critcher, C., Jefferson, T., Clarke, J. and Roberts, B. (1978) *Policing the Crisis: Mugging, the State and Law and Order*. London: Macmillan.

Halloran, J. D., Elliott, P. and Murdock, G. (1970) *Demonstrations and Communication: A Case Study*. Harmondsworth: Penguin.

Holdaway, S. (ed.) (1979) *The British Police*. London: Edward Arnold.

Holdaway, S. (1983) *Inside the British Police: A Force at Work*. Oxford: Blackwell.

Jefferson, T. and Grimshaw, R. (1984) *Controlling the Constable*. London: Frederick Muller.

Kelly, J. E. and Nicholson, N. (1980) 'The Causation of Strikes: A Review of the Literature', *Human Relations*, 33: 853–83.

Kettle, M. and Hodges, L. (1982) *Uprising: The Police, the People and the Riots in Britain's Cities*. London: Pan.

LeBon, G. (1952) *The Crowd*. London: Ernest Benn.

Littlejohn, G., Smart, B. and Yuval-Davis, N. (1978) *Power and the State*. London: Croom Helm.

Manchester City Council (1985) *Report of the Independent Enquiry Panel*. (Leon Brittan's visit to Manchester University's Students' Union, 1 March 1985).

Manning, P. K. (1979) 'The Social Control of Police Work', in Holdaway (ed.), *Inside the British Police: A Force at Work*. Oxford: Blackwell.

Marsh, P., Rosser, E. and Harré, R. (1976) *The Rules of Disorder*. London: Routledge and Kegan Paul.

Masotti, L. H. and Bowen, D. R. (1968) *Civil Violence in the Urban Community*. Beverly Hills and London: Sage.

McBarnet, D. (1978) 'The Police and the State: Arrest, Legality and the Law', in G. Littlejohn et al. (eds), *Power and the State*. London: Croom Helm.

Moscovici, S. (1985) *The Age of the Crowd*. Cambridge: Cambridge University Press.

NCCL (1984) *Civil Liberties and the Miners' Dispute*. London: NCCL.

New Society (1982) *Race and Riots '81: A New Society Social Studies Reader*. London: *New Society*.

Olson, M. (1965) *The Logic of Collective Action*. Cambridge, Mass.: Harvard University Press.

Potter, J. and Litton, I. (1985) 'Some Problems Underlying the Theory of Social Representation', *British Journal of Social Psychology*, 24: 81–90.

Reicher, S. S. (1984) 'The St Paul's Riot: An Explanation of the Limits of Crowd Action in Terms of a Social Identity Model', *European Journal of Social Psychology*, 14: 1–21.

Reiner, R. (1985) *The Politics of the Police*. Brighton: Wheatsheaf.

Scarman, Lord (1981) *The Brixton Disorders 10–12 April 1981*. London: HMSO, Cmnd 8427.

Shiboutani, T. (1966) *Improvised News*. Indiana: Bobbs-Merril.

Smelser, N. (1962) *Theory of Collective Behavior*. New York: Free Press.

Smith, D. J. and Grey, J. (1985) *Police and People in London: The PSI Report*. Aldershot: Gower.

Southgate, P. (1982) *Police Probationer Trainer in Race Relations* (Home Office Research & Planning Unit, Paper no. 8). London: HMSO.

South Yorkshire Police (1985) *Policing the Coal Industry Dispute in South Yorkshire*. Sheffield: South Yorkshire Police.

Tarde, G. (1901) *L'opinion et la foule*. Paris: Alcan.

Tiger, L. and Fox, R. (1974) *The Imperial Animal*. London: Paladin.

Tuck, M. and Southgate, P. (1981) 'Ethnic Minorities, Crime and Policing', *Home Office Research Study No. 70*. London: HMSO.

Vincent-Jones, P. (1986) 'Private Property and Public Order: The Hippy Convoy and Criminal Trespass', *Journal of Law and Society*, 13, 3: 343–70.

Waddington, D. and Jones, K. (1985) 'Flashpoints of Public Disorder: Some Empirical Findings and Theoretical Considerations with Particular Reference to the Steel

Strike of 1980 and the Coal Dispute of 1984–5'. Paper presented at the British Sociological Association Conference, Hull, April 1985.

Waddington, D., Jones, K. and Critcher, C. (1987) *Flashpoints of Public Disorder* (forthcoming). London: Methuen.

Wright, S. (1978) *Crowds and Riots*. Beverly Hills and London: Sage.

6

The peaceful crowd: crowd solidarity and the Pope's visit to Britain

Robert Benewick and Robert Holton

Crowd solidarity: the Pope in Britain

The Pope's visit to Britain in 1982 provided an excellent opportunity to investigate a neglected but important dimension of the study of crowds. This initiative represents an attempt to apply social analysis to peaceful crowds in the tradition of Durkheim's seminal but under-developed work on the collective conscience and patterns of social solidarity (for a discussion see Lukes, 1975; Holton, 1978). Unlike the other chapters in this volume, our research is very much a pilot study. The focus is on a very limited set of events, and their social significance. Our data base is composed of a range of materials including open-ended questionnaires, interviews with a sample of participants at key events during the Pope's visit, participant observation reports from the researchers, and media accounts of these events. This chapter makes use of the questionnaires and interviews (prospective and retrospective) with participants, and the media reports of the Wembley Mass. While we draw some substantive conclusions we are equally concerned with the difficult methodological problems involved in the study of crowds.

Theoretical framework and research design

The overwhelming rationale for studies of crowd behaviour has been an interest in social disorder, protest or pathology (see LeBon, 1896; Milgram and Toch, 1968; Rudé, 1964). From this viewpoint crowd behaviour provides both an index of breakdown in existing social relationships and institutions, and a challenge to society to restore or create suitable conditions for social order. In recent years racial riots, industrial disputes, football disturbances and conflicts between police and young people have been situated in this context. The main policy implication of this research has been the identification of structural and environmental problems that are seen as lying behind collective behaviour — the setting of an agenda for change that policy-makers must address. At a more immediate level too, research into the processes of crowd mobilization, especially the flashpoints that transform anger and frustration into overt disorder and violence, can also offer police authorities insights into the equally urgent operational problems of keeping the streets safe and orderly.

There is, nonetheless, another way of looking at crowd behaviour — one that informs our own study of the Pope's visit. This builds upon the observation that most occasions of mass assembly (or crowding) are not violent, pathological or disorderly. Most crowds are peaceful in the sense that they neither pose challenges to the preservation of public order nor threats to prevailing conceptions of social order within the community. Most crowds like those during the Pope's visit, even where elaborate planning and management are involved, are peaceable, indicating that there is nothing inherent in crowding together as such that produces aggression or psychopathology.

The peaceful crowd might not seem, at first sight, to be a particularly important object of enquiry. It poses no immediate or urgent problems for either social analysis, policy-makers or police. Phenomena such as a crowd of shoppers in a retail complex, people gathering to watch street theatre or of sunbathers on a beach may be of little sociological or political interest. On the other hand, peaceful crowds of a less involuntary kind, e.g. families and friends greeting the troops returning from the Falklands or pop fans, old and young, at the Live Aid concert may be of far more interest and importance. Following the work of Emile Durkheim, there is the strong possibility that peaceful crowds mobilized for some mass public ritual may function to express and strengthen processes of social solidarity and social cohesion. On deeper reflection, research into such crowds may offer vital insights to both social analysts and policy-makers, in the sense that they help to explain why protest and disorder are not endemic. A better understanding of the conditions under which crowds remain peaceful and orderly has great interest both as an index of the basis and extent of social solidarity and consensus, and as an encouragement to policy-makers to protect and nurture the legitimate expression of free speech and political opinion, thereby avoiding costly processes of mass policing and litigation.

In his 1978 paper on crowd study, one of the present authors, Holton (1978: 223–7) pointed out how little research exists on peaceful crowds within modern Western societies. In Britain, the study by Shils and Young (1953) on the Coronation of 1953 is a relatively isolated example of the application and extension of Durkheim's framework. The theme of law-and-order crowds has been discussed by social historians, but mainly as an instance of social protest whereby loyalty is expressed to an existing social order (see Hobsbawn, 1959; Rudé, 1964: 134–48; Cunningham, 1971). Such data has not been used as an index of social consensus and integration. This lack of interest in the peaceful crowd may of course represent the reality of social conditions in a wide variety of historical settings where social breakdown and conflicts seem pervasive. While there are those who interpret the spate of crowd conflicts in Britain in the past decade in this way, it is difficult to accept this breakdown model in its entirety, without some attempt at direct assessment of the extent of social consensus. To be sure, there are strong prima facie reasons to suppose that social consensus is in a very real state of crisis in certain milieux, such as the policing of the inner city (Hall et al., 1978).

At the same time there is comparatively little systematic evidence to show how generalized these particular patterns of breakdown may be. Within this context we argue that the peaceful crowd offers one potential index of the nature, extent and limitations of contemporary social cohesion — an index to put against the burgeoning literature on crisis and breakdown.

The highly undeveloped nature of peaceful crowd studies is reflected in the lack of existing operational and methodological experience and guidelines. Compared with the richly elaborated procedures of protest crowd research best exemplified by the social historians, Rudé (1964) and Thompson (1971), we have faced extreme difficulties in studying this topic. There is very little received wisdom as to the importance of participation in crowd behaviour as the locus of political and cultural socialization and mobilization. Since Durkheim wrote at a time prior to the development of modern mass communications it is as well to be sceptical about the centrality of crowd participation to the re-affirmation and re-modelling of social solidarity. The importance of being there, rather than watching it on television, has to be proven rather than assumed as a given. This scepticism is reinforced by the more general point that mass political and cultural expression may have become increasingly institutionalized and orchestrated in modern Western societies. In this sense crowd assemblies have increasingly become 'media events', manufactured by public relations machines, rather than simple unmediated expressions of authentic popular behaviour. This argument has been put very confidently in much neo-Marxist media criticism, but its empirical plausibility as it applies to crowd phenomena has not been widely researched.

Our research design addressed this problem in two ways. In the first place we compared the testimony of our sample of crowd participants with media reports. We wanted to establish whether there was any deviation between the projection of the visit as a media event, and the picture that participants gave us. Secondly, we invited our sample to keep a record before and during as well as to participate in a series of discussions after the event. This was designed to reveal prospective expectations and their sources, as well as to establish the importance, if any, given to attending the event rather than watching on television or reading about it in the press.

A second set of problems we faced involved the lack of operational sophistication in existing measures of social consensus within a crowd context. Most studies of consensus focus on individual value attitudes established through social surveys, rather than the inference of values from patterns of collective behaviour. This problem is magnified by the spontaneous expressive and sometimes emotional character of crowd assemblies. We could not poll or survey crowd participants in the midst of collective ritual or 'effervescence'. Nor is it clear that rational modes of cognition are sufficient to capture the emotive and cathectic elements involved.

We did not solve these problems, for they are in large measure irreducible difficulties faced in the study of crowds. While the social psychology of crowds has been somewhat discredited by Le Bon's pejorative psycho-pathological approach — an approach which has many resonances in contemporary public opinion about riots — we did feel it necessary to attempt to fathom, however impressionistically, the contours of the mood of the crowd. This was done by a combination of participant observation and reportage by our informants about their emotions.

A third set of problems concerns the difficulty of detecting and measuring the scale and intensity of expressions of social consensus within a crowd context. The wish to uphold 'law-and-order' is an inadequate measure here because it has no necessary connection with peaceability. Peaceability on the other hand is too vague a label to indicate much about values and expectations.

The means of coping with this problem was pragmatic rather than theoretical. We did not seek to operationalize Durkheim's belief that the typical collective expression of social solidarity in modern society would be connected with public rituals affirming the universalism of democracy and individualism. Instead we examined participation in the public ritual of the Pope's visit for solidaristic themes, conscious of the possible atypicality of this ritual as a modern form of crowd behaviour.

We were aware, for example, that many aspects of this ritual would have particular salience for adherents of the Catholic Church not least because the visit represented the first visit by a reigning Pope to Britain. We were also aware of the possibility that the 'religious' and charismatic forms of crowd behaviour involved, may represent the latter-day manifestations of a traditional solidarity outmoded in a secular age, rather than Durkheim's modern pattern of social solidarity. Set against this we expected that there might be interesting divergencies between the universal transnational character of the Church, and the particularity of the English nation-state, that might be represented in some way at a symbolic level.

In the event this element was largely subdued by the outbreak of war in the Falklands, and the consequent attempt by the British government and the Papal managers of the visit to avoid any direct reference to questions of national politics and national interests. On the other hand, this pre-empting of national issues served in some way to magnify the universalistic elements in the Pope's outreach. In particular, the universalistic value of peace projected on a number of occasions — including the ritualistic peace blessing in the Wembley Mass — was of considerable interest as an affirmation of solidarity and consensus amongst those involved. It should none the less be emphasized that our comments on crowd participation centre on members of the Catholic Church. Inferences cannot be drawn from their attitudes and behaviour to the wider British population.

The Wembley Mass reported

A number of considerations influenced the media's coverage and treatment of the Mass at Wembley stadium. In regard to the time-table, it was the second day of the Pope's visit and the event up to then likely to attract the largest crowd. It was also to be the largest gathering in London and because it was taking place on a Saturday it was natural copy for the Sunday papers. It was not the only event for the Pope that day, however, and indeed he attended the service in Canterbury Cathedral in the morning. That historically significant occasion did not receive as wide or as full coverage as the Wembley Mass nor did it attract the expected crowds.[1]

The Wembley setting, not surprisingly, featured prominently, as will be shown, for not only is the stadium identified with football, but a Cup Final replay had taken place there only two days previously. Indeed, Cardinal Hume in greeting the Pope referred to the setting having a place in one aspect of English history, 'both its high points and low points'. On the other hand, the particularist nature of the visit and the Mass as a celebratory and sacred event is perhaps apparent in the absence of comparison with a royal occasion by the media and by our respondents until well after the event.

In addition to recording the television coverage we examined fifty newspapers which provided forty-one different reports. The media approach was one of human interest rather than hard news which was in accord with its being a sacred and celebratory occasion and a peaceful crowd. The reporting of the occasion concentrated on the pre-Mass festivities, the arrival of the Pope and the conduct of the Mass and can be analysed in terms of its informal, managed and formal aspects. The reporting of the crowd emphasized themes of football and the family, as well as recording general crowd responses. The celebratory importance was probably best expressed by *The Times*, 'This surely was the day, if ever, when the Roman Catholics of England stepped out of the shadow into the sun'. A certain fascination was displayed for the pre-Mass ceremonies as if the media was caught off guard by the modern face of English Catholicism. This was where, according to the *Cambridge Evening News*, 'Religion met showbiz . . .'. The pop and folk songs were commented upon as was the informality of the crowd, but there was no comparison or more significantly contrast with a pop festival.

The most important moment of the day as prepared by the Church and perceived by the media was the arrival of the Pope. He was greeted with cheers, flags and the song, 'He's got the whole world in his hands'. *The Kensington Post* caught the moment. 'As his transport entered the stadium, it erupted in a maelstrom of cheering, clapping, shouting and waving flags and banners'. The report is also typical for what it omits — specific mention of the large and prominent anti-abortion banner proclaiming 'Love, Peace and Freedom'. It is as if the media did not want to give any indication of controversy and discord.

The Pope's sermon was quoted sometimes at length rather than reported or analysed so that the social-family themes may not have had their intended impact. The sacred and the trivial competed for space. Several papers estimated the number of Communion wafers in excess of 100,000; there were descriptions of priests wearing knotted handkerchiefs to keep the sun off their heads; and Cardinal Hume's running to catch the Popemobile at the end of the proceedings added the human to the modern face of Catholicism.

For the media then the informal and managed aspects took precedent over the formal proceedings. The football theme dominated the crowd references. *The News of the World* actually assigned its sports editor to the Mass (England was 'away' to Scotland) and he and the *Sunday Telegraph* reporter began their stories with references to the game. *The Sunday Mirror* nearly managed to convert the Pope into a football star: 'He emerged from the player's tunnel to a mighty roar of joy . . . and the great cathedral of soccer resounded to the religious fervour of nearly 75,000 fans'; they sang with football crowd fervour according to the *Kensington Post*; while at the end of the day the *Cambridge Evening News* reported, 'tired but happy, just like a football crowd that had seen its team walk over the opposition'.

The other prominent theme, the family, was intentional in so far that it was a theme underpinning a pastoral visit and was promoted by the warming-up celebratory ceremonies. It was also encouraged by the weather and seating on the pitch. The media identified the crowd as being specifically made up of individual family members, or articulated the concept of a family atmosphere; or portrayed the crowd as representing one big family. The *Sunday Telegraph*: 'Before the Pope arrived, it might have been Blackpool beach on a hot day', *Hendon Times*: '. . . a marvellous experience . . . a family gathering . . . so informal . . . the modern Roman Catholic Church on display'.

Finally, many of the articles, particularly those in the local press, contain comments and statements from members of the crowd. These described their reactions to the occasion rather than their experiences as members of a crowd. Although there are some similarities between these and the responses from those who answered the questionnaire, there are no consistent parallels except perhaps, the generalization that the event can only be summed up in terms of superlatives: 'Wonderful' . . . 'Marvellous' . . . 'Fantastic' . . . 'Great' (*East Anglian Times*). It is now necessary to examine how the crowd experienced the Wembley Mass as distinct from how it was reported.

The Wembley Mass experienced

A questionnaire was distributed through the local parish priests to two people in each of the fifteen parishes in the Diocese of Arundel and Brighton. The people selected were among those who had been successful in a ballot for tickets to the Mass.

The questionnaire was divided into three sections: demographic data; two open-ended questions to be completed prior to Wembley; and seven open-ended questions to be completed following the Mass. The questionnaire was supplemented by two meetings — one large and one small group — following the Mass and follow-up meetings one year later. Twenty-six people returned completed questionnaires. Our respondents were twelve men and fourteen women. They were middle-class, mainly in professional employment and mostly over forty.

Media coverage and the testimony of our respondents agree on the peaceful nature of the crowd. As has been seen, for the media this was newsworthy. For our respondents too the experience of Wembley contrasted with similar crowds encountered at football matches or city shopping. A football fan claimed: 'I go to local matches because the crowds aren't too bad. I've been to an international at Wembley. It frightened the life out of me'. Another respondent expressed her fears even more vividly:

> I had misgivings. As I said, I really am petrified of crowds. I very seldom even go into Brighton on a Saturday and I thought I was undertaking something that could well be beyond what I really could take myself and I thought this could cut out anything that I could gain spiritually from it if I

was so petrified physically. But it wasn't like that at all. I didn't have a simple qualm from the minute I set foot on the coach until the minute I got back.

This indicates that the categories of 'crowd' and 'peaceful crowd' are evident within popular culture as ways of organizing experience of collective life. The respondents also evinced some surprise that crowds could be peaceful and that they themselves felt little fear or sense of threat in the face of such a large assembly. As our respondents said in discussion: 'I never thought I would stand in a crowd and cheer, ever'; 'Even when we come out in our 82,000 odd, I would normally have panicked'. This came across even more vividly one year later when our respondents compared the Wembley Mass with Brighton Hove Albion in the cup final and a visit some had made to Lourdes. Although what was experienced directly and/or indirectly on these occasions was peaceful, the indication was that peaceful crowds are regarded as somewhat untypical of crowds generally. Crowds are to be avoided and are avoided: 'I'm still scared of crowds. I wouldn't go into a crowd if I didn't have to'. This appears to retain Hobbesian overtones of crowds as expressions of imminent violence or threats to the person.

Our respondents, like the media, regarded the Wembley Mass as British Catholicism on display and to which the crowd size contributed. A recurrent theme in our discussions was 'standing up and being counted' in order 'to demonstrate what faith means to the Catholics to the rest of the world'. What the media had viewed as a celebratory occasion was experienced by our respondents, however, as a sacred event in terms of its essentially religious significance. This came across in the group discussions but also in the questionnaires: 'The liturgy followed the normal celebration and in doing so enabled us to join in and feel part of this great unity'; 'Above all what a powerful thing is the united will of so many people all quietly delighted *with* the Pope in his offering of the Mass'. This has to be qualified in at least two respects. A pre-Wembley educational programme had promoted a public relations dimension. This emerged from our questions on expectations and there was a self-fulfilling prophesy, expressed by our respondents, '(I expect) a spectacular example of the strength of the Catholic Church in UK' and 'I anticipate that I will come away with a greater sense of the strength of the Church'. Second, the Mass figures centrally in the responses made to questioning before the event, but less so in retrospective group discussions. It seems likely that this is due in part to subsequent exposure to media coverage which downplayed the religious or sacred character of the Mass. It may also be that a certain dilution of the importance of attendance at the Mass took place over time, as the significance of the

Pope's visit became mediated through discussions with other Catholic friends who had not attended. In this sense the long-term effect of crowd participation may become weakened.

A similar process was at work in regard to our respondents' experience of the Pope. Where the media focused on the Pope's arrival and this was in accord to observed crowd behaviour, it was the Pope's presence rather than arrival that was important to our respondents' experience. Although our respondents described a scene of jubilation, e.g. 'On His Holiness' arrival even the most staid let forth shouts of joy', only two cited the arrival as the most important moment. This suggests a correspondence between crowd management and behaviour and a relative lack of correspondence between behaviour and experience. It is important to note, however, that in our retrospective discussions the arrival of the Pope figures more prominently, which again points to the intervention of the media, non-attenders and, of course, group dynamics.

For a number of respondents the Mass was an intensely personal experience or, as one person described it: 'Although in the presence of thousands it was as though the Holy Father was talking to me personally'. At the same time the descriptive labels used by our respondents, 'atmosphere', 'affirmation', 'belonging' and 'unity' provide ample evidence of a collective experience. Or as expressed more fully, 'I felt rather emotional and yet joyful at the unity of people around me'; 'It was fantastic being a part of that large group of people all praying and singing together'; 'It was total participation wasn't it?' Considerable communications took place between complete strangers such that by the time the Pope arrived relationships had built up between groups around the stadium. Five respondents mentioned the festive or family atmosphere and six referred to the sharing of food, drink and binoculars. Eleven respondents also wrote in a more generalized way about the sharing of thoughts and feelings. As one of them stated: 'Naturally, people were talking to their immediate neighbours and sharing their excitement', while another commented, 'From 1 p.m., which was the time we were in place, until the start of the Mass we made friends with those around us'. It seems possible to suggest that this networking performed a stabilizing function and contributed towards the sense of expressed unity and belonging.

Analytical observations
It is difficult to describe our crowd as a discrete entity in the manner that the media do and can even be seen to be entitled to do. It can none the less be analysed in terms of its integrative characteristics: celebratory, peaceful and sacred.

Celebratory

As a set of formal proceedings, the celebratory aspect may have influenced the media as a display of 'updated' Catholicism. However, this theme had little direct impact on our respondents. What is missed by the media emphasis on celebration is the impact made by the Pope's presence upon the Wembley crowd. The experiences of our respondents suggest none the less that the theme of celebration did provide a backdrop to building up informal non-confrontational relationships among the crowd.

Peaceful

Participants in the Wembley Mass tended to explain its peaceful character in two ways. The first was to stress the Pope's 'charisma' which was felt to reach out to individuals. It was the aura of the Pope's presence, however, rather than the drama of his arrival as highlighted by the media. The second was to emphasize some collective property generated by all participants. One way of describing the latter feeling was to affirm that: 'We were all on one side'. This was the view that was most prominently advanced during our discussions and the characteristic that distinguished the Wembley Mass from other crowds that they had experienced. The contrast with football crowds was again evident. The respondent who attended the international at Wembley noted, 'you've got a loser haven't you. And half the crowd is antagonistic with the rest'. Another respondent picked out the family theme: 'We were predominantly families setting out who normally would never go to football at Wembley'. A third member of our sample observed: 'You didn't have to know them well, you just followed the crowd and everyone was greeting everyone else. I remember a sister chatting up a policeman and he said, 'I wish every crowd that came here was like this. I've never enjoyed being with a crowd so much.'[2] Such explanations appear to rule out the importance of policing measures as the explanation for orderliness, which in turn reflects a view that crowd discipline may arise from intrinsic not extrinsic sources.

The sacred

It is clear from the questionnaires and group discussions that it was the liturgical ritual rather than the celebratory that was important to our respondents. Most of them experienced the day as a re-affirmation of religious faith and devotion. But it is also apparent that the liturgical ceremonial was more important than the theological and it may be that the sense of celebration contributed to this. What took place was a series of moments of collective re-affirmation of religious faith. The main catalyst was the presence of the Pope. His personal impact was expressed in terms of a sense of privilege at being in proximity to a holy man, to his capacity to 'strengthen' the faith of English Catholicism. This testifies to the primarily charismatic character of the Wembley Mass crowd.

Conclusions

Our first conclusion is to stress the distinction between media reports and the direct experience of crowd participants of a major event in the Pope's visit. Being there was an irreducibly significant experience for our sample of Catholic adherents, even though they were not entirely immune from the retrospective influence of media reports and discussions with non-Catholics.

Secondly, we emphasize the point that the crowd was in many respects pre-selected by the institutions of Catholicism. Of particular importance here is the careful selections, preparatory meetings, Masses and educational classes held in Diocese and parish prior to attendance at Wembley. A strong example of this orchestration involves the theme of 'family'. This has both religious connotations (the motif of the seven sacraments for the tour) and social implications (for birth control policy). The salience of these issues was already evident before attendance at the Wembley Mass, as evidenced in the questionnaire responses completed prior to the event. It was then picked up in banners and in liturgical devices at Wembley itself. This example indicates the importance of analysing the contextual background to crowd phenomena and the need to analyse relationships between prior events and subsequent quasi-spontaneous features of crowd behaviour. The Wembley crowd was neither a creature of a public relations campaign, nor yet a spontaneous affirmation of crowd solidarity, but a phenomena both mobilized and orchestrated within a pre-existing set of religious institutions.

Thirdly, we claim prima facia significance for the notion of 'peaceful crowd' in two senses. First the distinction between 'peaceful' and 'violent' or 'pathological' crowds is evident within popular experience. Second, the Wembley Mass is itself indicative of integrative rather than conflictual factions within crowd behaviour. While we do not suggest that the integrative and the conflictual need necessarily be mutually exclusive, we do reiterate the underdeveloped character of crowd research into integrative assemblies, and the need for further work.

Fourth, we counsel caution about generalizing about the 'peaceful crowd' from a single and somewhat atypical case-study. While Durkheim's work on the collective conscience informs much of our theoretical stance, we do not claim that the crowd assemblies of the

Pope's visit are especially representative of any modern pattern of crowd solidarity.

Finally, we emphasize an important policy implication of this research. We would argue that a fuller understanding of various forms of peaceful crowd behaviour has important political implications for the promotion and extension of civil liberties. While very large crowd assemblies can never be entirely self-regulating in a logistical sense, it is clear that normative commitment to peaceability on the part of crowd participants represents an intrinsic support for the preservation of public order and tranquility.

Notes

We wish to acknowledge the ESRC for its financial support for the research upon which this chapter is based. We are also grateful to the Arundel and Brighton Diocesan for its full cooperation. We are particularly indebted to Father Francis McHugh and Carol Pearson for their substantial guidance and contributions to the research. Anne Benewick and George Gaskell participated as observers and provided much needed advice and encouragement throughout the project.

1. *The Observer* 30.5.82 was a notable exception.

2. This is not to overlook the need for security as distinct from public order. A photograph in the *Sunday Mirror*, 30 May 1982 shows an armed policeman.

References

Cunningham, H. (1971) 'Jingoism in 1877–8', *Victorian Studies*, 14(4): 429–53.

Hall, S. and Critcher, C., Jefferson, T., Clarke, J. and Roberts, B. (1978) *Policing the Crisis*. London: Macmillan.

Hobsbawn, E.J. (1959) *Primitive Rebels*. Manchester: Manchester University Press.

Holton, R. (1978) 'The Crowd in History: Some Problems of Theory and Method', *Social History*, 3(2): 219–33.

Le Bon, G. (1896) *The Crowd*. London: T.F. Unwin.

Lukes, S. (1975) 'Political Ritual and Social Integration'. *Sociology* 9(2): 289–308.

Milgram, S. and Toch, H. (1968) 'Collective Behaviour: Crowds and Social Movements', pp. 507–610, in Lindzey, Gardner and Aronson, Elliot (eds), *The Handbook of Social Psychology*, 4. Reading, Massachusetts: Addison-Wesley.

Rudé, G. (1964) *The Crowd in History*. New York: John Wiley.

Shils, E. and Young, M. (1953) 'The Meaning of the Coronation', *Sociological Review*, N.S.I. (2): 63–81.

Thompson, E.P. (1971) 'The Moral Economy of the English Crowd in the Eighteenth Century', *Past and Present*, 50: 76–136.

7

The crowd and the community: context, content and aftermath

Geraint Parry, George Moyser and Margaret Wagstaffe

> Any attempt to resolve the circumstances from which the disorders of this year sprang cannot . . . be limited to recommendations about policing but must embrace the wider social context . . . (Scarman, 1981: 6.1).

Introduction

In 1981 a number of cities in Britain experienced serious upheavals in certain of their inner areas. The 'crowd' appeared. This was not what Canetti (1973) has called the 'closed crowd' which, however turbulent, is confined within an arena with restricted exits and entrances and which follows well-established conventions and rituals. This was the 'open crowd' spontaneously spilling out over the streets, its members destroying property and engaging in personal violence.

Reactions varied from sympathy for the plight of the residents of the areas, through shock to outrage. Newspaper headlines at the time reflect these contrasts: 'Rubber Bullets and Despair' (*Guardian*, 1981a); 'Terror of Toxteth' (*Manchester Evening News*, 1981); 'Brixton Youths Go On Rampage As Riots Spread' (*Guardian*, 1981b); 'Brixton: Black and White United to Fight' (*Socialist Worker*, 1981).

Analysis of the causes encompassed a whole spectrum of precipitating factors. The most common regarded the disturbances as an expression of pent-up grievances over deprivation in the inner city — poor housing, unemployment and environmental decay. This was encapsulated in a diagram in *The Economist* (1985: 33), prompted by an affray in Handsworth, Birmingham in September of that year, showing the extent of deprivation in the locality compared with the national and regional averages and labelled 'Reasons for Riots'.

Other explanations focus on the special problems facing youth, and black youth in particular. Living in a society apparently unable to solve the underlying causes of their predicament, it has been suggested that many have turned their backs on the wider society and retreated into a distinctive life-style which may merely comprise dress or fashion in hair, or street life, but which may also involve behaviour regarded as anti-social or even criminal such as drug-taking, vandalism or petty theft (see Chapter 2 above). Such life-styles may be interpreted as a rejection of the values of the older generation which will be those upheld by the political authorities (Inglehart, 1977). The clash of values and behaviour often bring youth into conflict with the police. The disturbances can then be interpreted as the culmination of this conflict with the police at the centre of the explanation (Benyon, 1984: 99–113).

Another explanation is the so-called 'hooligan' theory. Proponents stress not only the obvious criminality of missile throwing and arson but also the looting and even an element of carnival atmosphere. In a controversial chapter entitled 'Rioting Mainly for Fun and for Profit' Banfield (1974) argues that inner cities are populated by a supposed lower class whose poverty and deprivation stem from a basic psychological orientation. They are concerned only with the present and make no plans for the future. They engage in casual vandalism and criminality. The standard responses of investment in services or in welfare payments are unlikely to change this inner city lower-class culture leaving as the only alternative a policy of containment and control. Meanwhile, the youths are likely to engage in what Banfield calls the 'rampage' — an outburst of uncontrolled high spirits which has the effect of 'stunning' an entire community and mobilizing the authorities against them. He also argues that 'much of the inner city residential population are largely cut off from participation in institutions' that regulate behaviour. The professionalization of politics and of services sets middle-class standards and terms to participation alien to the inner city population.

A characteristic of all these varied explanations is that they are based on national factors and conditions. They suggest that civil unrest is largely a response to national, economic or social conditions which are simply more severe in certain localities. Indeed, it would be foolhardy to dismiss such factors as irrelevant. As we shall see, they may constitute a necessary but not a sufficient condition for crowd disturbances. Explanations of crowd behaviour also have to be couched in more localized terms. Locality may be a crucially important factor in crowd mobilization and in understanding the aftermath of disturbances. National trends in unemployment and economic recession are refracted through the prism of locality into the conditions in which the individual functions. However mobile our society, the local spatial dimension is a necessary and major part of our experience. All aspects of mutual aid, organized or informal, are inevitably spatial. Locality, in short, is the milieu in which citizens live out their lives, accumulate experiences and, in some cases, acquire grievances. Moreover, only the better-off can purchase services privately elsewhere in the city if they are dissatisfied with local provision. It may even take money to travel to seek out the particular form of worship one may desire. The poorer one is the less, to use Hirschman's (1970) terms, one can 'exit' from one's local situation if one has a grievance and the more one is forced to use 'voice' if one's complaints are to be heard.

If, however, one's voice is not heard, what alternatives exist? Is it the case, as one radio commentator said, that 'when words fail, sticks and bottles are thrown'? Are crowd disturbances an expression of frustration against a sense of exclusion from the channels of political action and communication? If such crowds are a form of political action how effective a form is it? Our investigation was prompted by these questions. As such it required an understanding of local political circumstances, of the viability of community institutions and of confidence in processes of representation. For where political institutions are strong one might expect grievances to be channelled into conventional party activity. Where these institutions are weak or are thought to be unheeding of complaints, unrest may conceivably lead to direct action against local targets.

In Britain the idea that central and local government has a major responsibility for creating economic conditions and solving problems is widespread. The perceived quality of community institutions and processes of participation may, therefore, provide a significant clue as to why disturbances occur in some areas but not in others. Possible answers may also lie amongst the local elites. The availability of local activists, the presence or dearth of political and organizational skills, will mean that the nature of the interaction between the governing elite of a conurbation and the citizenry will be qualitatively different where the citizenry is drawn from suburbia and where it is drawn from the inner urban ring. It may also differ from one city to another.

In one of the most influential analyses of crowd behaviour Smelser (1962) argued that the emergence of crowds is dependent upon appropriate social conditions, the requisite degree of structural strain, specific perceptions of such tensions, a precipitating incident and, in the absence of adequate preventive control mechanisms, mobilization by activists. Our study seeks to focus on the local aspects of these conditions, strains and perceptions with an emphasis on their political aspects. To revert to Canetti, the crowd may not be a pure 'open' crowd spilling in any direction, but may also have 'closed' aspects — hidden boundaries affected by locality and community.

The research design
The investigation was centred principally on Moss Side, Manchester, which had experienced a major disturbance in July 1981. In the small

hours of 8 July 1981, after a skirmish between police and youths when local drinking clubs emptied, a few shop windows were broken, three or four properties were set on fire and some looting took place. In the evening of the same day, despite attempts by city and community leaders to contain events, crowds formed in Moss Side. A group of youths besieged the Greenheys police station. Others indulged in widespread vandalism, looting and arson in Moss Side and surrounding districts (for a fuller account, see Hytner, 1981: 38–52). Police presence was minimal. The next day, a much stronger police force dispersed the crowds which had again formed in Moss Side, and after this the disturbances petered out.

However, for comparative purposes we also looked at similar inner city areas in Sheffield and Oldham which had not experienced any serious disruption of the kind manifested in Moss Side. The intent was to try to use these areas as a 'control' in order to highlight distinctive features of Moss Side, perhaps not present in Sheffield and Oldham and which might explain why the scale of crowd incidence was so different.

Within each locality we conducted a series of interviews with members of the citizenry and with political and community leaders. In total this encompassed over 120 semi-structured and lengthy interviews divided roughly equally between elite members and citizens. In pursuing this strategy our aim was, above all, to understand the crowd in its context from the perspective of those most directly affected. It is from this base that we can then begin to evaluate the various suggestions which have been made as to the crowd's significance. We realize, of course, that our interviews do not comprise a representative cross-section of opinion in any strict or quantitative sense. However, in the circumstances in which we worked, we question whether such a goal is attainable. In any event, what is meant by a representative 'sample' of elite persons is problematic. What we have sought to do is to reflect a variety of experiences and vantage points.

Our 'sample' of local leaders was constructed by first selecting the occupants of a number of formal positions in the community and then by asking these, and other persons with local knowledge, to suggest further names of individuals who had influence and standing in the locality. The formal positions we identified were roughly standardized across all three communities and included youth and group leaders, organizers of ethnic minority associations, senior personnel in adult and community education and office holders in local government. The 'reputational' phase in turn produced a great variety of people — reflecting the cultural composition of each of the communities involved. Indeed, we found that we were dealing not so much with 'the community' as with a number of sub-communities, each of which had its own leading lights and many of which were, in some degree, antagonistic to one another. In this, however, our aim was to collect a rough balance of views so that all the sections of the wider community were represented.

Our experiences quickly showed that it was not an easy task as some individuals were far more accessible than others (Wagstaffe and Moyser, 1987). Indeed, entry to Moss Side was more problematic than either Glodwick or Burngreave. As the focus of media and research attention, some of its leaders and citizens had developed very negative attitudes towards the kind of exercise in which we were involved. Many believed that research in the past had distorted and misrepresented their views and those of their communities. They also viewed the relationship between the researcher and the community as 'extractive' which gave little obvious return to the locality. Furthermore, some activists who were personally sympathetic to the research believed that their own standing in the community would be undermined by any public show of cooperation.

There is, of course, a broad distinction to be made between the community elite on the one hand, and the political and administrative elite which governs the city on the other. Whilst there were individuals in both categories who expressed reservations about cooperating with us, these were far more likely to belong to the former groups than the latter. Members of the city elite, in other words, were generally more accessible and informative. The same was also true of individuals in similar positions in the other areas.

Where the mass of the citizenry was concerned, access was in one sense easier and, in another, more problematic. The 'sample' was constructed largely through lines of personal contacts and networks (sometimes developed from introductions provided by elite members) and by word of mouth. As with the elite, there were those who were hostile and did not wish to take part.

The interview format was originally envisaged as an informal discussion on fairly specific topics. However, it quickly became evident that a greater degree of flexibility was required and many respondents were happier simply to converse loosely around relevant topics. This arrangement had the merit of producing a more relaxed and informative interview, sometimes lasting over two hours, even if it meant that subsequent synthesis of our materials in the search for significant patterns was more difficult. The large body of materials amassed from these contacts was then supplemented by information drawn from newspaper articles and periodicals, other media sources (such as broadcasts), government statistics, official documents, local authority publications, academic writings and community reports.

The research team also drew upon census data to provide a more quantitative picture of the three research sites.

The socio-economic and physical context — patterns of deprivation

Definitions and data

To say that context must play an important part in understanding the kind of crowd behaviour we are considering is, perhaps, a truism. No crowd comes into existence in a social vacuum; it is inevitably influenced by, and influences, its own environment. What is not so obvious is the identification of those particular features in the crowd's surroundings that are significant. One major set concerns economic, social and physical deprivation which seem an appropriate point of departure for our own study.

At the most basic level, the question we wish to explore is whether or not Moss Side is distinctive in such terms from our other research areas. Is the incidence of deprivation more pronounced or the pattern significantly different? In order to assess such questions, we have initially turned to census data. These possess three advantages: they allow for rigorous comparisons of small areas — of perhaps no more than two or three streets; equally, for some characteristics at least, they include, in effect, the entire population of each particular area thus eliminating problems of sampling and response rates; thirdly, by chance, the census was conducted in the same year as the crowd events. Hence, the data give an accurate portrait of the socio-economic context as it existed when these events took place.

In our view, deprivation is a multi-faceted matter, albeit one in which economic elements may figure particularly prominently. Hence, we have defined different measures of material deprivation for which census materials are available. They cover unemployment, over-crowding, family structure and lack of amenities. These indicators are employed by the Department of the Environment to measure urban deprivation, and serve as one of the bases for granting central government aid. In following these guidelines we are setting our results within the framework of a widely recognized, if not generally agreed, set of operational definitions (Inner Cities Directorate).

The census pattern

Our exploration of deprivation began at the district level. Generally speaking, all three of our 'target' districts show rates of deprivation significantly above the average for England as a whole — as one would expect given that they are all northern, heavily urbanized areas. Of the three, however, Sheffield seems to be the least deprived on average, especially as regards overcrowding and the incidence of single parents. Equally, Manchester is generally the most deprived, above all in the key sphere of unemployment where its rate, 17 per cent, was roughly double that for England and Wales as a whole. But, apart from this, Manchester does not have a worse record than many other districts including some where there were few, if any, crowd disturbances during the relevant period. Clearly, Manchester constitutes a severe case compared with the bulk of districts in England but, at this level at least, there is obviously no simple correlation between deprivation and crowd incidence.

The specific spatial context for crowd events is, most often, far smaller than a district. Both in the disturbances in the United States in the 1960s and those in Britain in the 1980s, the stage has seldom been more than a few blocks across. Is there something distinctive at this level about Moss Side and which is hidden by district-wide aggregation? To tackle this possibility, we undertook a similar analysis of deprivation and ethnicity focused upon key wards in Manchester, Oldham and Sheffield.

Our results showed that Moss Side is not unusual in its overall experience of deprivation. Across the board, in fact, it is not the most deprived ward in Manchester. That distinction, within the limits of the Inner Cities Directorate definition, falls to Longsight, also in the city's inner ring. Even so, it is interesting to note that Moss Side's level of unemployment, 27.8 per cent, was, at the time of the census, the second highest in Manchester and that it was ranked 'number one' on overcrowding and the incidence of single parents. It has a profile very different indeed from that of Didsbury, the least deprived Manchester ward, with levels of deprivation several times the latter. But so too had other wards like Longsight and Hulme. It is difficult to claim that the extent of deprivation would mark off Moss Side from other wards in its vicinity.

We also examined the way our deprivation measures related to patterns of ethnicity. Moss Side certainly has a large ethnic minority population, 39.8 per cent, probably the highest in Manchester. The area linkage with deprivation is, however, non-existent: the enumeration districts (EDs) with a high 'non-white' population within Moss Side are no more likely to have an extreme level of deprivation than those with a relatively low 'non-white' population. This contrasts sharply with wards like Werneth in Oldham and Sharrow in Sheffield where there is a connection. The only exception is, again, in the employment sphere where the correlation is +0.22. This is noteworthy but does not seem so strong as to represent unambiguously the qualitative contextual differences for which we are searching.

Finally, we examined the five EDs in Moss Side showing the highest concentrations of deprivation and related them to size of ethnic population. This showed that they had ethnic populations no different from the ward as a whole. However, they were all clustered together in one contiguous spatial block. Was this something unusual — a sub-ward area of intense dissatisfaction and protest potential? In one sense the answer is obviously yes. Here was an area in which most of the facets of deprivation were present in unusually intense form. This is a reality against which the crowd disturbances must be set. But, in St Mary's, Oldham, the five extreme cases also formed one totally contiguous entity in Glodwick with experiences of deprivation in some respects even worse than those in Moss Side. In short, without gainsaying, as we shall see, what such census statistics actually mean in terms of the personal experiences of individual residents, there have to be other ingredients, it would seem, that made segments of Moss Side's populace so much more prepared to act on their grievances than those in other parts of Britain's inner cities.

Deprivation: the interview evidence
The picture of deprivation revealed by our interviews with citizens and leaders in Moss Side is one which reinforces the conclusions drawn from the census in a powerful, concrete and vivid way. It is a situation in which the many facets of deprivation reinforce each other to produce, for many of those concerned, a life-style which rarely if ever transcends its debilitating reach; in short, a 'sub-culture of poverty' (Berthoud and Brown, 1981: 9).

In this, there is a common opinion that unemployment and poor housing are the most crucial features. Low income makes effective property repair very difficult even when grants are available; poor and ill-repaired housing can lead to ill-health, physical and mental, and family stress. There are also problems of vandalism, burglary, prostitution, litter, physical dereliction, noise and drunkenness, inadequate local services and amenities and difficulties with educational provision in the context of a declining population. More widely still, our respondents have spoken of a process of stigmatization by outside institutions. As one official remarked:

> People resent the fact, for instance, that it's very difficult to organize credit arrangements if you have an address in . . . Moss Side; and that it's not always possible to ring for a taxi and one arrives; or that the milkman doesn't like delivering . . . and if you're more than a week behind in paying your milk bill he stops. There's milkmen here that demand payment in advance. The Electricity Board wants a deposit before it will connect the supply — and that's to do with the location of the address, it's not to do with anything else. And that's bad news and just adds to your difficulties.

However, our interviews also reveal that some individuals are more hard-hit than others. One such group is the elderly. They are particularly subject to financial pressures, to living in poorly heated and maintained accommodation, to health problems and are easy targets for street crime. But the elderly are also the least prone to ventilate their grievances through conventional channels, let alone through the more strenuous activities entailed in participation in crowds.

Another broad category identified by many of our respondents were those from the ethnic minorities. Here the key issue was felt to be the employment market. One individual described the discrimination felt by black residents in these terms:

> . . . (unemployment) is a big problem for everybody but more for coloured people than white. Because, if two people see a job in the papers, and if both of them go down to see the job, whether the coloured one goes first, he says there is no vacancy. The white one go and he get the job. So the discrimination is there right on, right on. When a black man gets a job, or a black woman, they have to be very, very, very, very, very, very good — not like when we come here first. For, when we come here first, nobody ask us if you experienced or anything because they show you.

Of course, racial discrimination in employment is something experienced by all categories of non-whites (Brown and Gay, 1985). Equally, they share the general stresses associated with being ethnic minorities living predominantly in inner city areas. And yet it is important to recognize, as do many of our interviewees, that blacks and Asians have other experiences, needs and problems unique to each. But how these differences might affect their sense of deprivation and expressions of grievance, if at all, would require more substantial investigation to pin down.

Within all sections of the ethnic minority population, however, there is one group who have clearly felt the impact of deprivation to a particularly severe extent — the youth population. Some indication of the problems young people face in Moss Side can be obtained from the comments of a black parent concerned at the lack of what, for other more fortunate sectors of the population, would be very commonplace opportunities and facilities:

> What we would like to see is a nice cricket field, well supervised, where we could arrange sporting fixtures and where we could bring the family and establish a bit of village life. As it is, there is nothing very much for our youngsters.

To some extent, both white and non-white are felt to be affected. 'It is not only coloured youth: white and blacks are in the same boat', as one interviewee put it. And yet, as with the non-white population at large, there are those who are of the opinion that it is among the black youth that the impact of deprivation is most keenly felt.

Some indication of what is entailed can be gleaned indirectly from the census data from Moss Side. Whereas the overall unemployment figure for the ward was 27.8 per cent, that for sixteen- to nineteen-year-olds was calculated at 39.4 per cent. If we then make due allowance for differences between whites and non-whites (and between males and females), those holding a job, however menial and poorly paid, among young blacks would have been in the minority in Moss Side. Within the core EDs we identified, they may well have been in a rather small minority. There is no doubt that our respondents were very aware of the very special difficulties faced by this particular section of Moss Side's population, difficulties that have probably only been compounded as the unemployment rate has steadily risen since 1981.

Although such evidence seems unequivocal, the question is whether this is at all relevant for understanding the crowd? The answer, from any casual inspection of police arrest records, seems to be yes. Those involved were disproportionately young. But it seems important to distinguish necessary from sufficient causal conditions: deprivation seems to have been something approximating the former without being clearly the latter. In other words, multiple and intense deprivation must have played an important conditioning role. But the evidence, not least from the census data, suggests that it could not have been a conclusive condition, otherwise we would have witnessed similar events in Sheffield, Oldham and elsewhere.

The interview evidence seems to support this interpretation. On the one hand, many spoke of the connection between deprivation and the failings of 'the authorities'. For them, deprivation was not a condition that was divinely ordained, inevitable or unchangeable. It was the result of governmental action or rather inaction and of a failure of understanding by the institutions of the wider society. Unemployment, for example, was clearly seen as a matter for which government should take substantial responsibility. One Moss Sider put it this way:

> They pay lip service to the ideals of society but they don't do anything to bring them about because, deep down, they don't care. It is appalling when you think that a baby born today may never work. Our children are pensioners at sixteen.

That such views are far from unusual can be gleaned from a national survey we conducted in 1984–5. In that study, we asked individuals to identify a problem important to them. Unemployment turned out to be the most important single issue, echoing the findings of opinion polls during the same period. Furthermore, most felt that it was something central government rather than individuals or groups ought to tackle. Yet when we asked who the respondents thought had put most effort into dealing with it, very few mentioned the central government. Clearly, there was a huge 'credibility' gap between responsibility and response so far as the government was concerned.

However, if the residents of Moss Side tend to share the perceptions of the wider society, then this again suggests that deprivation is only part of the story. Such a conclusion is, perhaps, powerfully reinforced if we consider the experiences of Glodwick and Burngreave. As our respondents in those areas noted, they experienced the same sorts of stress, neglect and discrimination as those living in Moss Side. Even allowing for some hyperbole, it seems that the interview evidence, as with that drawn from the census, makes Glodwick and Burngreave quite comparable with Moss Side in terms of perceived deprivation — and yet there was no crowd. In these circumstances, the only conclusion we can draw is that already outlined: that material deprivation is a very pressing and grievance-inducing experience borne acutely by only some sections of even the inner city population. At the same time, it is the case that only in some localities did this situation coincide with crowd behaviour. We must, therefore, presume that any complete explanation must look beyond deprivation. In succeeding sections we will consider a number of additional contextual aspects. We turn first to the whole issue of 'community'.

Patterns of community

The idea of community
Although 'community' does not have an exclusively spatial connotation, nevertheless this is the starting point for almost all community studies (Rossi, 1972). If a locality is to be regarded as a community one would anticipate that residents would have a fairly acute sense of its boundaries. Communities are, virtually by definition, exclusive and it should be possible to discern which areas belong and which do not. By extension, residents, and perhaps others, might be expected to identify those people who are 'insiders' from the 'outsiders'. This may be of considerable importance when designating a form of behaviour by reference to locality. There were from the outset frequent references to the role of 'outsiders' in the disturbances in Moss Side, as there were subsequently in accounts of events in Brixton and Tottenham in 1985. Often there are complex reasons why it should be significant to call attention to the role of 'outsider'. For some it is proof of the existence of a conspiracy against authority. For others there may be some hope that, by stressing outside intervention, the

role of the local population may be diminished, thereby suggesting that local conditions are less severe and repressive.

The notion of community boundaries in the context of an inner city is a complex one (Verba and Nie, 1972: 229–47). 'Boundedness' is nowhere, not even in rural areas, a physical, objective quality. It also turns on the perceptions of both residents and outsiders. As Suttles (1972: 22) argues in his analysis of city communities, as well as the physical structure, there is also 'the cognitive map which residents have for describing, not only what their city is like, but what they think it ought to be like'. This cognitive map may show no obvious relationship to any physical or geographical features.

Images of community

Suttles has also advanced the view that, in discussing 'community', sociologists have indulged in over-romanticization in making sentiments basic to the concept so that community is regarded merely as expressive solidarity without appreciating its instrumental uses (Suttles, 1972: 264). The tradition is to look at community as something growing up organically from below. Suttles suggests that communities, especially in the city, should also be regarded as constructions by 'advocates' such as estate agents or 'adversaries' who define boundaries by a process of exclusion and limitation such as by describing an area as dangerous or risqué (Suttles, 1972: 34–7, 46–54, 240–1; Crenson, 1983). In other words, communities are defined by a process of collective representation which contrasts one with its neighbours.

Moss Siders of all persuasions are aware of something akin to the process of disclaimer described by Suttles. They see Moss Side as stigmatized by outsiders who define it as an area of deprivation and criminality, against the evidence of experience. This process has concrete effects on the lives of those within what others set as cultural boundaries. In housing they are subject to 'red lining' by building societies and insurance companies — the procedure by which a line is drawn around an area within which loans are not readily granted and insurance premiums are sharply increased, even when compared to other inner city areas. The effect of this stigmatization by the wider population — called, after the main thoroughfare, the 'Princess Road syndrome' by one politician — could be to reinforce deprivation and any self-image of powerlessness and exclusion from the advantages of normal citizens. The area, in short, is defined as a problem area. This is accentuated by the situation of Hulme on the borders of Moss Side. Hulme was the centre of one of the largest rebuilding schemes in the country, employing a mixture of deck access and independent blocks. As one resident reminded us, the planner had claimed to be recreating the crescents of Bath in a modern idiom. Hulme has experienced virtually every physical and social problem associated with the new technology of industrial building (Dunleavy, 1981). It was the boundary with Hulme which was most ambiguous — long-standing Moss Siders distinguishing it clearly from their own community while, for some in city government, they were indistinguishable as areas and as problems.

The media especially, but also researchers, are criticized for concentrating on the problems of Moss Side since this reinforces the prejudices. Even, one activist stated, when one sought to give the media an item of news which put Moss Side in a positive light, it was portrayed as an unusual event against a negative background. It is therefore understandable that one community leader should say that all Moss Siders want is to be left alone, as the people of Hale Barns, a wealthy suburb on the Cheshire borders, are left alone.

There was widespread feeling that the image of Moss Side is unjust. The remarks first of a community worker and second of a senior police officer are typical:

> A lot of people read the papers and think 'My God, do I really live in an area like that?'

> But really, you know, there is a big myth about Moss Side — that it is a bad place to live, that crime is high and it isn't safe to walk the streets, that conditions are appalling. But it isn't true, it's an overstatement, an exaggeration.

There are some who rejoice in the 'tough' image of 'the Moss' among their friends outside Manchester. Others, however, strive for their perception of reality to be understood and shared by those neighbours who now disclaim them and mark off the community from others. Some see the disturbances of 1981 in terms of a rejection of the forces which have constructed and enforced this image, and as a spontaneous uprising against mechanisms of class and racial discrimination that perpetuate powerlessness. Others fear that the same disturbances may simply be used to reinforce the false image.

Loss of community

Princess Road, which was the scene of the disturbances in 1981, was, before the redevelopment of the 1970s, a well-known shopping street. It now has shops down one side only, many still protected by shutters at night. The major shops are now situated in the Moss Side Centre on the border of Hulme. The demise of the Princess Road facilities seems to be regarded as symbolic of the 'loss of community' which is continually lamented in our interviews. It is, of course, always wise to be wary concerning this loss of community. Among our interviews there were some sceptical voices concerning the quality of this lost community:

> Communities were only there because of suffering. Most communities are bound together by suffering and poverty, and people sat at the doors outside and conversed because there was nothing else to do.

This Oldham councillor argued that while modern individuals might appear to live isolated, introverted lives they responded to a more universal community, as evidenced by the response to famine in Ethiopia.

Nevertheless, such reactions are exceptional. In Moss Side, in particular, the loss of community was felt and resented by ordinary citizens, activists and representatives alike. This community is recalled for the support it offered and also for its social discipline and protection. The old had ties with youth and were not in a relationship of apprehension and alienation. Everyone knew one another and where they belonged: 'It was like having a map in your head'.

The process by which this community was lost remains vivid in the memory of long-standing residents and is seen by a wide range of people as the starting point of the problems of Moss Side and Hulme. Community was demolished with the housing, and while some believe that a new community is being created, its links with the old are tenuous. One experienced councillor encapsulated the experience in the phrase 'the strength of the community is dependent on the stability of the community'. Another leading figure conveyed what he called the 'totality of the destruction of Hulme' by recollecting a particular evening:

> One night, in 1968, actually it was Bonfire Night, I was on a bus travelling from Chester Road to Stretford Road, and from there I could see all the way across to Chorlton Road and Moss Lane. Hulme was totally flat, so flat that I could see the bonfires in Moss Side. Acres and acres of desolation. Nothing can survive that, no social organization, no community.

The outstanding feature of Moss Side and Hulme is repeatedly stated to be the lack of continuity of the population. The peak occurred with the large-scale relocation during the clearance scheme. Many who moved from Moss Side and Hulme never returned. Others moved in from different parts of the city. The effect, according to a city leader, is that:

> you are breaking up social units which probably had evolved very slowly over the years. And I haven't yet found a way to redevelop social units. You can put in all the infrastructure and it still doesn't damn well happen. And vertical development doesn't lend itself to neighbourliness, whether on deck-access or high rise. Streets in the sky don't work.

The memory of that period, including offers of nominal compensation for demolition of homes, still rankles with the survivors, all of whom fully acknowledge the poor quality of the previous housing. Moreover, the memory has been handed down to those now active who were not Moss Siders at that time. One community activist described the process as 'legalized violence' and said that 'to knock a person's home down is to make some kind of judgement on that person, at least in that person's mind. So I think that legalized violence was a background to the riots'. Another activist asserted that the 'destruction of their community' was something about which people were not consulted but, instead, Moss Siders were 'utterly disregarded'.

Among those who felt this loss of community in a particular way were some of the older blacks who had settled in Moss Side. They had come from their own community with its particular patterns of support and discipline. One long-term resident doubted whether the British knew anything about community:

> ... what I do not understand is this nonsense about British culture, where people are so separated from each other, where people don't know anything about each other, don't care about each other.

Older blacks in particular felt that their culture had its own virtues. They also suggested that, before the redevelopment of the area, blacks had begun to set up small businesses, in much the same way as the Asians. With demolition, the City Council had 'wiped out the economic base of the black people' which 'set us back two or three decades in self-help and economic development' since the compensation was insufficient to allow regeneration. As we saw in the previous section, the implications for black youth employment were clearly drawn by this older generation.

In Burngreave and Glodwick the story is different. The dislocation is less frequently mentioned by Burngreave residents. The loss of community is related, where mentioned at all, more to the greater atomization of modern society as a whole and linked, despite deprivation, to the possession of home entertainment or a family car. In Glodwick, the talk is mainly of a more gradual incremental loss of the traditional white community as the area gradually becomes more Asian.

Community and sub-community

It may, however, be wrong to talk of *the* community. Instead one should consider inner city areas as composed of a number of communities. This could scarcely be better expressed than by one experienced Moss Side political leader:

Community in the city is not like community in a village, where everyone belongs whether they want to or not, where everyone knows everyone else and everything about them, where when you go to the shops you know all the people you meet. In the city, things are vastly different. It is almost as if a series of villages coexisted in the same area, layer upon layer. Yes, layers of villages. A system of different communities working in different ways.

Both blacks and whites in Moss Side spoke of the sub-communities within the black community arising from the different island origins of the immigrants. There is an occasional hint that the divisions in the Afro-Caribbean community of Moss Side are serious enough to cause difficulties in political communication of black opinion. However, lest there be any suggestion of a policy of divide and rule, it was also clear from 'radical' and 'moderate' black leaders that these particular divisions were overcome in the face of what was perceived as a threat to the black community as a whole.

Our interviews unearthed relatively little tension at a purely personal level between ethnic communities and the white population. Accusations of 'institutionalized racism' abounded against many organizations and against the police in particular. It would also be quite wrong to suggest that racism and a sense of racism were absent. But there were many who believed, particularly in Moss Side, that relations were actually better than most other places. There was a wide recognition that blacks were subject to gross disadvantages, a view which extended even to a respondent who acknowledged that he had once given a protest vote to the National Front.

The most striking cleavage, remarked upon again and again especially in Moss Side, was between young and old. This was not merely between older whites and young blacks, although that is prominent, but between the age groups of all races. The young had less direct experience of the earlier dislocation of the community although, as stated earlier, this remained an essential part of the folk-memory of discrimination. Their immediate experience was of recession and unemployment. Older residents, who claimed to mix reasonably well with their contemporaries of different races, spoke of what they saw as the threatening and anti-social conduct of youths with time on their hands. Yet even these residents showed a certain sympathetic understanding. As one put it:

The young ones have got a big chip on their shoulders. They get shit every which way. No jobs, no money, nothing to do, no nice clothes, nowhere to go. No wonder they're sullen . . . It's after they leave school and they try to get jobs and they have to go on the dole and get that treatment that they get down there and they start getting to lump all whites together and call them honkeys. That's insulting us, you now.

For others, the attitude of black youth expressed an ever more deeply entrenched alienation from white society and also from their more moderate, immigrant parents. The chasm, as one experienced white observer of Moss Side said, was not just about age, 'it's about identity and radicalism' and was creating 'a separate community of militant, aggressive, unemployed black youngsters'.

The extent of this alleged alienation remains an open question (Gaskell and Smith, 1981; Field, 1984). Some evidence suggests that, while voting turnout of black youth is low, they take part as much as whites in some other forms of conventional politics (Studlar, 1986; Welch and Studlar, 1985; Fitzgerald, 1983). If we accept the view of some radical black community leaders, however, their own alienation from established politics reflects, at a more articulate level, widespread feelings among many of the young.

The alleged alienation of black youth is connected by some observers to the assumption of a black identity. With no obvious stake in the wider society and economy, it is suggested, they adopt a life-style and dress which is a sign that they have cut themselves off from parents and the conventional patterns of behaviour of the white populations. The danger, seen by a variety of people, including some moderate career-minded black youths, is that their life-style reinforces the division since its values are incompatible in British society with upward mobility and a better quality of life. This might be called the consensualist view: just as white society must recognize the richness of the culture of the black community, so there must be a degree of mutual accommodation to the other side. In the absence of any early return for such accommodation however, the incentive for the black youth to conform can understandably be regarded as fairly minimal.

Although the black youth may be more aggressively proclaiming their black identity, it should not be supposed that their parents are unaware of it. Older blacks do tend to describe themselves as Mancunians or as British. Occasionally, one will still describe himself or herself in island terms. One long-time resident felt that 'we cannot have one foot in the West Indies and the other 5,000 miles across the Atlantic', but another was happy with multiple identities as British but not English, black and West Indian. This last person added that young blacks counted themselves as British and expected to be treated as any others: 'And how else should they feel?' However, as a younger black in Sheffield argued, other British people do not carry a qualifying adjective whereas white people automatically add the label 'black' to those of Afro-Caribbean descent. The whites impose a black identity over the British identity such that the young blacks increasingly realize themselves to be black and Afro-Caribbean, more than British. On this viewpoint, they adopt the prior identity primarily because they are excluded from any other by the very society in which they are born.

The white residents of all our areas showed a high degree of identity with their locality. There were some signs that, in Sheffield, the belief of one of the councillors that there was a generally warm feeling about the city as a whole, was not, as he admitted it could be, the self-deception to which politicians are prone when thinking of their electorate. Sheffield was described as a 'big village', and this was seen as leading to a great sense of pride in the city and a greater psychological involvement which, to one respondent, helped to explain why Sheffield had not experienced serious disturbances along with other cities in 1981.

The political significance of community

'Community' remains as elusive a concept as it ever did, partly because it can be seen in spatial terms or social terms and partly because it is composed of a curious amalgam of 'objective' conditions and 'subjective' evaluations (Plant, 1978). Despite this, or possibly because of this, community is an idea that has strong roots in all three of the localities we studied. The potential significance of community identity is that it provides an additional political resource in the struggle to promote or to defend interests. A sense of community can help to support political activity. Collective action is, traditionally, the effective response of those who lack the skills and resources to achieve goals by personal action. The support of the community can be an important grounding for such action, even if it is sometimes a defensive response. The outstanding example of community mobilization in Moss Side was the campaign to prevent the transformation of Princess Road, the community's 'high street' which also leads to the wealthy Cheshire suburbs, into a road of motorway dimensions dividing Moss Side in half. Protests and consultative processes achieved a partial success in restricting development to a dual carriageway with limited crossing points. Any loss of community identity makes such organized and collective action more difficult. Whether it would affect the conditions for more unorganized or spontaneous activity as the crowd is, however, problematic.

Certainly there are differences between Moss Side and the other two areas, but they typically point in a number of different directions. The physical dislocation of Moss Side and the related mobility of population were repeatedly emphasized. We have already suggested that one factor in areas where crowd disturbances have occurred may be their specially high level of social mobility and the consequent disruption of community linkages. This has left a legacy of bitterness in Moss Side which, in the view of several observers, has occasioned a vicious circle of mutual rejections and non-communication, going beyond what was reported to us from Burngreave or Glodwick. The long-term political consequences of this experience were commented upon in several conversations. A senior Manchester City local government officer drew a contrast between Moss Side and another inner city area where the redevelopment had left intact the old networks of family and kinship. The result, he said, was that the residents were less hostile to the Council and less suspicious of its intentions than in Hulme and Moss Side. There was less of a division between 'them' and 'us'. They lacked the 'resentful feeling of having been deprived of something valuable and left with something inferior'. What remains of community, some would argue, is a defensive reaction against the effects of unjustified stigmatization of a distinct locality and population.

Part of the difficulty is that we know relatively little, in a systematic way, about how community, in all its component elements, does relate to outbursts of grievances such as happened in Moss Side. It is a matter which presents in particularly strong form the most intractable problem in social research of disentangling objectives, even quantifiable factors from essentially evaluative judgements. A more precise causal connection between community and crowd stays beyond our grasp. Nevertheless, that the destruction of internal solidarities and loyalties played their part in creating the conditions for the crowd is a widely held view among people at all levels associated with Moss Side. So is the opinion that a defensive community can be created in reaction to stigmatization and to what is perceived as unjust and discriminatory treatment. In this respect one element in the story of the context of Moss Side crowd recurs more frequently than any other — the role of the police as a local institution.

Policing and the crowd

Police and community — an overview
Since 1981, the policing of Britain's inner cities has become a contentious issue. Lord Scarman's inquiry (1981) and The Hytner Report (1981) saw the relationship between police and community in many areas of high unemployment and social deprivation as one of extreme tension. This may be triggered into open conflict by some incident which acts as a 'flashpoint' (see Chapter 5 above). These are, however, the culmination of an underlying process of interaction between the police and the community. It is, therefore, germane to examine the nature of this interaction.

It is important to establish how the police and the community perceive each other, for these perceptions, or stereotypes, help to structure or condition each encounter. In this respect, our research revealed marked differences between the three localities. In Manchester, the tension between the police and the community seemed to be much more notable than was the case in either Oldham or Sheffield. Sheffield has had its confrontations but, overall, our conversations suggested that a much more amicable atmosphere prevails, while in Oldham the general consensus seems to be that the policing of the town is satisfactory.

Policing in Moss Side
Hostility and friction between the police force and the citizenry of Moss Side have a lengthy history. Well before the Afro-Caribbeans came into the area, when Irish migrant workers were settling, there was said to be antagonism. One man, who had been in the area over twenty years, said:

> There is a long history of police harassment in Moss Side and of dealing with the community in a way which I certainly wouldn't describe as enlightened . . . My own experience of Moss Side, long, long before there were blacks experiencing the particular problems they have, was of one of people being harassed by the police. When I came to Moss Side it had a reputation of being the area to which all the biggest, thickest and most brutal police were allocated, to beat Moss Side into submission.

These impressions are echoed by many elderly blacks. They generally state that they are now, as older people, well treated but that they have not always been so fortunate. Thus, one explained that much of what is currently perceived as undesirable police behaviour is not new. He related that when he came to England he and others had been subjected to the same kinds of harassment. It is, therefore, easy to see where the roots of the negative stereotype of the police are to be found. Members of the police force both reject these imputations and claim that they are scapegoats in that they are expected to contain social problems not of their making. The point is, however, that the majority of people that we interviewed expressed misgivings about policing. Furthermore, some black residents are convinced that they are the subject of a process of criminalization. Yet other groups claim that policing is inadequate and inappropriate.

The net effect is that relations between constabulary and citizenry tend to be poor and communication tense. One policeman expressed the opinion that the bulk of the population in the area were 'respectable and hard-working' but that there was an element of 'about 400 people' who were criminal, who had 'a lot to say' and who created a 'bad atmosphere'. These reflections were in turn mirrored in the community:

There are police officers who have a very good reputation with the community. The community share problems with them and accept them for what they are. But there are other groups that, at times, certain police officers deny the existence of. But, you know, we've seen them in here. We had an incident where somebody made a false telephone call to the police and we ended up with some special detectives arriving, one of whom had removed his false teeth and came in with a short truncheon, ready for a fight.

A senior officer developed this theme further:

We know full well that there are some problems. Not all policemen are perfect, and not all policemen are as professional and as good at the job as you would like them to be.

Professional people who work in the area confirmed the view that mutually hostile categorization had been created. For example, an experienced social worker felt that, while some policemen were positive towards the community, their efforts were undermined by more cynical colleagues. A senior politician agreed:

Some have a sense of public duty and think they are doing some good with respect to the community. Others are disheartened. Yet others have no faith in, or will, to develop methods of community policing which might help to alleviate the problem. They in turn help to strengthen the case argued by those people in Moss Side who just feel that these police are impossible.

However, not all residents see the police in the same light (Tuck and Southgate, 1981). Some are very antagonistic; some older people feel that the young people provoke the police. Yet others feel that more police are needed and that tighter control of the area is essential. The differing views in the community in part reflect the division which probably exists in all communities between the 'silent majority' and the 'activists'. Many of the former feel that the area is becoming increasingly lawless and demand higher levels of manpower and control. Conversely, the latter, typically social, youth and community workers, are in close contact with the casualties of policing methods in Moss Side. It is these casualties they feel primary responsibility for, and hence are particularly critical of policing methods.

Despite these differences, the overall impression in the community of the police attitude to Moss Side is that, while many serving officers behave towards local people just as they would behave to any other citizen, there are some who are at best unnecessarily abrasive and at worst violent and brutal towards specific categories of people, most notably young black males.

There are also allegations that frequently young black lads are subjected to rough body searches and called 'nigger' and 'bastard' in the process. On the evidence of a local doctor, for example,

> ... the words 'nigger', 'bastard' were the usual method of apprehension ... you were spread-eagled against walls and over cars ... even if the police have the right to do it, it didn't *feel* right to you.

Equally, a councillor recalled violent and intimidatory police behaviour and unlawful detentions after the 1981 riots. He remembered being inundated with pleas from distraught parents whose children, he said, had been held in custody without observance of their rights. The latter allegation was repeated by a Moss Side churchman:

> The ordinary parents in church were getting upset, I mean really upset, because their young people were being picked up off the street and were being held in the police station without their being informed.

One resident reflected that methods of policing in the area were actually a disincentive to the law abiding. The police, being preoccupied with 'clear-up' rates, were inclined to make arrests and bring charges in a rather casual fashion giving citizens, in his view, no great incentive to obey the law:

> They [the police] aren't bothered at getting the right one — just someone to hang it on and clear their books ... You'd think that if you went mugging, the police would catch you, and punish you, and that would stop you from doing it again, and if you didn't go mugging the police would leave you alone. But it isn't like that. Because of this attitude they've got, like, 'there's been a mugging, look around, see a lad, do him for it, balance the books', no one knows where they stand.

There is also scepticism within the community about police disciplinary arrangements and the complaints procedure. Hence, few complain, it seems, because they believe it would be a waste of time. One individual said in a public meeting:

> One of the main things that came out of that enquiry [The Hytner Report, 1981] was that there was a great deal of suspicion about the way in which complaints were being dealt with, and of an absolute lack of confidence in the police organization for dealing with complaints against the police, especially from members of the black community, particularly in Moss Side and Hulme.

To the police, however, the relatively low incidence of formal complaints is taken as an indication of community satisfaction. They deny that their complaints procedure is inadequate and cite cases of officers being disciplined. But the point has been made in our interviews that, even if the complaints procedure does work, information on the outcome of its deliberations is never made available to the community, and the absence of any feedback serves to reinforce the belief that nothing is achieved. In consequence, complainants and potential complainants are simply left angry, frustrated and impotent in the face of strongly felt social injustice.

Some of our respondents felt that the deteriorating situation between police officers and residents was partly rooted in the introduction of the patrol car. First, it has reduced the level and frequency of normal day-to-day contacts in non-conflict situations. Second, it is felt that increased reliance on cars has contributed to the development of a 'them' and 'us' mentality which is more conducive to conflict than consensus. An elderly black observed:

> The older policemen retired and the young policemen coming from training school, they were in panda cars. You ceased to see policemen walking the street so you couldn't develop a real community relationship as such. And today he's here, tomorrow he's gone, and there's a new one, and there's no continuity at all.

In an attempt to counter these trends, therefore, the role of the 'local bobby' has been re-emphasized. It is clear that many residents in the area, especially the elderly, like having a police officer they know by sight, and can have a friendly word with. But, even this remedy has its problems: the police claim that some people who say they want community police officers walking the beat will, in the next breath, complain that the time taken to respond to a call is inordinately long.

However, the problems which beset the police and people of Moss Side go beyond those of stereotype and perception. There are, in addition, structural factors which seem to make matters worse for both sides. The nature of both high- and low-rise accommodation in the area lends itself to burglary and crimes against the person, and makes policing harder than it need be. Hulme, and much of Moss Side before redevelopment, were built on a grid pattern: from the broad, well-lit main road ran narrower side roads interlinked by streets and back alleys in a regular geometric manner. This meant that one or two constables patrolling on foot could keep a fairly close watch on a relatively large area, since the openness of the grid did not afford many opportunities of concealment. Furthermore, as houses overlooked each other, neighbours could keep watch on each other's property. Hence, an effective police presence could be achieved with minimal manpower and low-profile policing.

However, new ideas in housing led to the abandonment of the traditional grid pattern in favour of high-rise flats with walkways and underground parking areas. The problems of protecting this housing from vandalism and burglary is now a topic of comment (*Sunday Times*, 1985). Our evidence also suggests similar problems with the more recent, and more immediately attractive, low-rise houses built around inter-connected squares and cul-de-sacs. In the words of one councillor, they 'became a haven for burglars' providing blind corners where the criminal can waylay the unwary. The beat officer no longer can walk along the road, looking to left and right, and see what is happening in his 'patch'

Another aspect, described by a high-ranking police officer, was the sheer density of population which exacerbated the problems of law enforcement:

> Moss Side can be a frightening place because there is so much concentrated in a small place. High-rise flats mean that people who might be very different are living literally on top of each other. They are all too close together. They haven't got enough breathing space.

This, he explained, underlay and precipitated much anti-social behaviour.

Despite these concerns and conflicts there is goodwill in the community and on the police side. So why does the tension continue? One serious obstruction to improved relations concerns public consultation in policing. For the police, public involvement means having a liaison officer, undertaking joint activities with schools and youth clubs and being involved in community work. To community activists, however, it means accountability: the citizenry instructing the force on how the city should be policed, and holding to account those who default.

One involved and informed commentator reflected,

> ... part of the difficulty about this whole area, is, I think, a misunderstanding, by the police hierarchy, about the difference between police involvement in youth and community work, and the public involvement in policing and police decision-making, and bridging gaps and so on.

To try to resolve these matters the police are experimenting with new forms of community policing and liaison, in an attempt to restore public confidence. But what the long-term outcome will be remains to be seen.

Policing in Sheffield and Oldham: comparisons and contrasts
As indicated above, tensions in Sheffield were far less apparent than in Moss Side. It is true that relations between the police and the citizenry of Burngreave have at times been severely strained and there have been accusations of police aggressiveness towards black people. None the less, the impression from our interviews is that there seems to be a qualitatively better relationship than is the case in Moss Side.

Certainly, the police presence in Burngreave was not experienced as oppressive. Those complaints which were made were rather of police absence: failure to respond quickly enough to calls, especially in cases of attacks on Asians. Youth and social workers in the area, whilst not suggesting that the situation was perfect, felt that there was a degree of approachability and openness in the local force which made a good working relationship possible. Indeed, regular meetings were held between youth and community workers and the local commanders and community policemen of Attercliffe Division, which encompassed Burngreave.

The general atmosphere in these meetings was markedly different from those we attended in Moss Side. Whereas in Moss Side recriminations and bitterness were the order of the day, in Burngreave the meetings concentrated in a constructive manner on addressing local issues and jointly solving neighbourhood problems. Nor were there complaints of police brutality or harassment.

An even more interesting comparison, however, can be made between Moss Side and Glodwick in Oldham as both fall within the jurisdiction of the Greater Manchester police force. The difference seemed to be that whereas the atmosphere in Moss Side was acrimonious, in Glodwick it was comparatively peaceful and cooperative. Thus, both residents and political representatives in Glodwick generally spoke well of the police. Complaints, when they were made, were as in Sheffield of the absence, rather than any overbearing presence, of members of the force. Part of the explanation may lie in the approach of local police management which is strongly committed to community policing, regular meetings and consultations with all interested parties. A senior officer explained:

> What it comes down to basically is good communication. The art of good communication has to be developed. As long as people are meeting and communicating, you have a chance of getting somewhere.

The major difficulty is that while relations improved in Burngreave and remained generally positive in Glodwick, it is clear that between the police and a substantial section of the community in Moss Side there are long-standing and intractable problems of communication. Stereotypes impede efforts at reaching an understanding or *modus vivendi*. Our conversations suggested that confidence in police liaison procedures had not yet been fully restored, while the problems of accountability at the level of the city and county remained national news. Furthermore, proposals for the creation of a new offence of disorderly conduct could conceivably create new tensions, thereby making the police once more the prime targets they were in the events of July 1981.

The disturbances of 1981

Characterizations of the crowd

To the residents and participants of Moss Side, the crowd events meant many different things. Some advanced mono-causal interpretations. Others, perhaps more reflectively, offered complex analyses stressing the interconnected nature of the basic social and economic conditions which underlay the protests. But some of the most striking differences related to the strongly differing interpretations of the role of race.

Was it a race riot? What is a race riot? Even to call the disturbances a 'riot' is problematic. Thus, one member of a black community, in response to this term, retorted acidly 'We don't accept the term "riot". It is offensive to us'. What had happened, she explained, was an 'uprising' — people had risen up against their oppressors and both black and white people had been arrested. However, another black rejoined, in response to the term 'crowd events', 'What are you talking about, "crowd events"? These were race riots and you know it. Don't try and take that away from us'. He felt that the riots were predominantly a black response to racist and discriminatory treatment of ethnic minorities by the wider society.

If black people could not agree on the precise nature of the events nor could whites. Immediately following the first outbreak of trouble, the Chief Constable stated, 'These were not race riots'. This refrain was widely taken up in the media and echoed in *The Guardian* and *The Times* the next day. But an academic who was researching in Moss Side questioned that view:

> Now, the definition 'race riot' suggests to the public black versus white, something serious which we ought to act upon. When, however, we were told that they were not race riots we heaved a collective sigh of relief and went back to sleep. So the actions which followed from this definition of the situation were different from the kinds of actions which would have been called for by an alternative scenario. But really, to deny race as a fundamental factor in these riots is just mad.

Local people who witnessed the events, and those involved in them, however, had explanations other than race to offer. It was widely believed that the trouble was rooted in economic deprivation and especially in unemployment and the lack of opportunities and future prospects for young people. Others argued that the problems were generational, resulting from a breakdown in family life and in relations between young and old. Yet others believed that, as one man put it, 'the lads were out for some fun'. A senior employee of the DHSS saw the riots as the protest of the powerless and alienated.

Indeed, for one participant 'it was good, a chance to hit back . . . it was all young people there, with nothing to lose, no jobs, no houses. The atmosphere was electric'. But, more than any other factor, insensitive and racist policing was cited by our interviewees as having been critical in triggering the disturbances. Thus, a churchman in Moss Side said of the 'Sus' Law: 'that was the final thing which fuelled the fire'.

The build-up and the targets

There are conflicting accounts of how the civil disturbances started. According to the police, the events of 7–9 July 1981 were precipitated by an incident outside a drinking club, which escalated over the following days into a full-scale confrontation. The Chief Constable felt that outside political agitators had fomented unrest in Moss Side, a view shared by some of the politicians who governed the city. One councillor recalled 'there was a travelling circus that knew where to sow the seeds, because certainly, some of the organizing talents on that night were not of local origin'.

Moss Siders themselves, however, offered different interpretations — that the troubles had been brewing for a long time and, for several months, there had almost tangibly been 'something in the air'. Whether they spoke with the benefit of hindsight is a moot point. Certainly, all our interviews were conducted after the crowd events. Nevertheless, one unsympathetic resident disregarding the presence of white youths during the affray recalled that there had been 'festering discontent among the blacks' for a long time. He went on to elaborate:

> You could sense it for weeks before it actually happened. You could feel the tension in the air. It was hot, sultry weather. The blacks were standing around in groups. They were sullen. It was obvious that all that was needed was the spark.

Equally, a solicitor felt that 'everyone knew, after St Pauls and Brixton, that sooner or later Moss Side would go up. It was only a question of time'. This observer seemed to imply that the 'copy-cat' element had been a significant factor in triggering the riots, but as one who took part in the disturbances remarked, 'Even if the events *were* "copy-cat" events, they still expressed real feelings of frustration and anger'.

Were these feelings of anger and frustration vented against political targets? City councillors, when asked if they thought the riots were an expression of frustration with the normal avenues of political participation, were quick to point out that 'not one single council property' had been attacked. This refrain was echoed by professionals involved in both statutory and voluntary institutions in the area. For them, the prime objective of the riots was to retaliate against the mode of policing employed by some members of the local constabulary. One senior politician, for example, when asked 'could you discern any specific target or targets?' replied 'The police, and with justification. Their relations with the community have not been good ... quite a few officers in Moss Side abused their position quite seriously...'.

The aftermath

Within a very short time, the disorders had subsided, and the devastated community could take stock of what had happened, and begin to deal with the aftermath.

The most immediate consequence of the riots was a police presence which was perceived as oppressive. Some residents said that they felt intimidated by the nature of police activities. A middle-class man who lived on the edge of the ward said that, while walking his dog at night in the streets of Moss Side after the riots, he witnessed police manoeuvres which made him glad he was not young and black.

In the longer term, however, policing tactics were modified. Street incidents were dealt with in a few minutes, in order to avoid creating the opportunity for a crowd to form. Also reported was some lessening of tension for a period of about three years, although the degree of relaxation was not something our respondents could agree upon. Some believed that the police had, as one explained, 'eased up on their Gestapo tactics'. Others felt that police and community relations in the area were still very bad. Some considered that the appointment of a Police and Community Liaison Officer by the Metropolitan Council had improved matters. Others, however, were sceptical, regarding the creation of this post as a public relations exercise.

As Moss Side slowly recovered, the police presence subsided to levels more closely approximating the area norm. There were, of course, calls for extra policing, for less policing and for different policing. But, so far as the police were concerned, apart from the short-term saturation of the area in the immediate aftermath of the affray, there were constraints — beyond those of policy — on what they could actually do. One person who had served in the area explained:

> Extra resources for Moss Side could only mean less for somewhere else ... We were always stretched to capacity anyway. There is nothing spare. You can't knit money — or extra policemen, for that matter.

Within the community itself, some claimed to have experienced increased feelings of solidarity and togetherness. So far as the black people were concerned, understanding between the old and young improved. For a long time before the riots the complaints of the young were discounted by the older generation. However, many parents said they had seen examples of police behaviour during the riots which convinced them that the complaints could have been justified. In the words of one elderly lady:

> I've always had a lot of respect for the police but during the riots I could understand why a lot of young people reacted as they did because the police officers were just, to people coming from church, saying some awful bad things, and we just couldn't believe that they would behave that way.

Whether or not the disturbances in Moss Side were intended to be a political protest, they had political consequences. The Council responded with a series of measures. At the suggestion of Moss Side's Consultative Committee, the Moss Side Conference was convened to consider ways in which the quality of life in the area could be improved. Consisting of an array of notables described as providing 'a Who's Who of Moss Side', it produced in its short life a number of specific and general proposals for local action on jobs, environment and participation.

The City Council also directed extra resources into the area. Indeed, some councillors felt that their quantity caused, as one explained, 'quite a lot of resentment in other parts of the city'. Furthermore, policies were introduced to increase the representation of minorities in the city's workforce, to improve communications by decentralization and to increase public participation. Since these were central to the policies of the newly dominant group on the Labour Council it is not possible to claim that they were a direct response to the events of 1981. A certain sensitivity to the particular problems of Moss Side is, however, clearly detectable in our conversations with city officials and politicians.

Although oppressive policing was widely seen to have fuelled the conflict, many people in the community believe that what took place was a social protest by the powerless who, feeling impotent, isolated and abandoned, took the law into their own hands. Perhaps the most perceptive insight was that of a local churchman who remarked:

> ... through all the activity of residents, residents' groups, people's associations and all the rest of it, through the 1960s and into the 1970s, despite all of that, the pleas of Moss Side people that they should be listened to about the conditions in which they live and what should be done about them, those pleas fell on deaf ears. I think it is not too harsh to say that. Those pleas fell on deaf ears until the riots. And then, everybody — but everybody — said: 'We must listen to the people of Moss Side'. And that

frightens me. Because if we've got to have riots in order to get anyone to listen to what is reasonable, then I'm worried about the society in which we are living.

Participation and the crowd

The value of participation

The adequacy of participation in our communities received the widest range of assessment. The contrasts were most marked in Moss Side. There was the radical community leader for whom the channels of participation were perfectly adequate. The problem was that 'there is no real point in participation'. At best, participation achieved some tinkering with the system but it could not alter the fundamental fact of oppression. As he saw it, the financial costs of solving the root causes of inner city problems were well beyond what the current government was prepared to pay. It was cheaper to spend money to equip the police to control the community, including any crowd disturbances which might recur. A prominent city leader saw this attitude as self-defeating, an expression of total alienation from the established political processes which could prevent demands being clearly expressed as a basis for dialogue.

If participation is seen as pointless and, even more, if outside observers can say that participation is unlikely to be effective, low levels of citizen involvement take on a quite different perspective. They are to be seen less as a failure of interest and initiative on the part of a population designated as politically unskilled. Rather, low levels of activity can be more appropriately interpreted as a rational assessment of the use of time and energy in the face of severe structural constraints. If one is genuinely powerless to effect changes there is no incentive to participate. Absence of activity is, therefore, not necessarily apathy. If one already has resources in terms of money, organization and time, political participation can, on past evidence (Verba and Nie, 1972: 267–343; Goodin and Dryzeck, 1980; Pizzorno, 1970), bring a return in extra advantages from political authorities for oneself or one's interest group.

It is not, however, clear that participation was worse than any other similar area — which was not to say that it was high. Taking the conventional measure of voting turnout, Moss Side at around 36 per cent is not atypical for local elections. As one community worker pointed out, these figures seem to indicate no greater disillusionment than in any other inner city area. The figures may, however, overstate the degree of participation. There is some reason to think that the figures for the electorate may hide a considerable number of people who have not been placed on the electoral register.

The evidence from Moss Side on group activity is also conflicting. On the one side, there are accusations that the population is inert, that 'there isn't a lot of striving' and that people assume that 'the Council *owe* us a better life' instead of taking responsibility and learning from mistakes. At the same time one cannot help be struck in Moss Side, as in every community one examines, by the bewildering variety of groups which exist. There are groups for those belonging to each of the West Indian islands. Other black groups range from sports and social clubs to a women's cooperative group which, among other activities, organized an oral history project on black culture. Groups not associated with any ethnic minority include youth clubs connected with community centres, housing associations and parents' support groups. Many of the leaders of these groups are undoubtedly well-known in the area and to the city authorities. From the viewpoint of one city planner, the Moss Side groups are very effective in bidding for what resources are available and have helped to ensure that more money has gone to that area than to many others, even though it may not be the most deprived in the city.

Responsiveness to participation

Our conversations confirmed that there was some sense among the residents that the Council was unresponsive and failed to understand local priorities. One refrain is that the councillors only appear at elections seeking votes. In power they dream up facilities for the locality about which Moss Siders have not been consulted and which they do not want. A proposal for a water-sports facility was one instance offered.

Councillors themselves are aware of these attitudes and their reaction is one of puzzlement. They are puzzled because they claim that Moss Side receives exceptionally favourable treatment in the distribution of resources and because they do not understand how messages from the community are lost or misinterpreted, if this is indeed the case. Establishing the amount of expenditure on a ward such as Moss Side is a difficult task. Councillors insist that allocations are not determined on an area basis but on need — 'worst first'. By such a criterion, Moss Side, although near the 'top' of the deprivation scale, is not the worst off. Nevertheless, it is widely held within the Town Hall that, where discretion is able to be exercised or where there are bids for support for voluntary groups, distribution has favoured Moss Side and Hulme. Typical remarks were:

> My gut feeling is that there is more money going into Moss Side than there is into other areas.

Well then you just share out the cake, and what has happened is: there's eighteen inner city wards, seventeen of them have virtually done without to assist Moss Side and Hulme.

The Councillors insist on their role as being representatives for the city rather than delegates of their wards. Most argued that, as representatives and socialists, their duty was to allocate according to need and on a city basis rather than think in terms of their ward backing. 'Community politics' had little support. Naturally, councillors held surgeries which, as in most city authorities, are dominated, by housing matters, and one councillor described moments when he felt overwhelmed by the multiplicity of personal problems faced by some of his constituents. At that individual level they felt that they, or voluntary services, were reasonably in touch.

At the other end of the scale, that of overall resource allocation, some councillors were less confident about the process of communication. The difficulty, as several councillors see it, is of discovering what the community as a whole wants. Speaking of the period before and after the 1981 events, one councillor involved in allocating resources said:

> Prior to the disputes it was very, very difficult to really know what people wanted, and I suppose, speaking as a person, it's as difficult *now* really to know what the people of Moss Side *do* want, as it was prior to and during the disputes.

In explanation of his difficulty he added,

> Because there doesn't really seem to be a large vociferous majority in favour of any one thing, there's a large vociferous minority in favour of a number of things, and it depends on who shouts loudest as to whether you respond.

The Council could, he acknowledged, have been misdirecting its millions but he had no remotely objective means of knowing whether this was so other than 'obviously what we've done doesn't seem to be curing the problem'. Like several councillors, he expressed some scepticism as to whether the criticisms, views and alternative proposals of certain community leaders were representative of the people at large.

Political parties and participation
That the representativeness of some community groups should be challenged raises questions about the participatory process and the linkages between group activity and party politics. Political parties, in our conversations, were rather like Sherlock Holmes's dog that did not bark. Apart from the councillors themselves, very few people questioned mentioned any interest in local party politics without

prompting. Several claimed no longer to be active in the Labour Party because it had become dominated by younger, radical and more middle-class members whose style of conducting politics seemed alien. Councillors were contacted in their social welfare function, as were voluntary groups. However, our discussions do not suggest that the political parties, and in Moss Side this means the Labour Party, exercise a deep hold on the community. One Labour politician felt that the local population had not responded to the efforts of the Labour Council for the area and that the Party had not succeeded in getting its message across:

> People who still associate with the Labour Party, and indeed could never be part of anything else, are still not flocking to take part in its activities. So I suppose that is a kind of failure.

It has been argued that, in the cities, a new political formation is appearing consisting of radical professional persons working as leaders of voluntary groups or in quasi-governmental agencies, who are also active in the Labour Party (Dunleavy, 1980: 151–9). It is, however, less clear how far this fusion has occurred in Moss Side or, at least, how far it has established roots. Several people saw a disjunction between community activists and the parties. The view survived among some Labour politicians that community activity belonged essentially to the non-political sphere and they feared that its occasional and regrettable politicization was the result of the bias of certain activists, which could even be counter-productive. A social worker suggested that there were two sides to participation:

> . . . there's the party political side and the community political side, and I think that often it may be the party political side which has the voice and the power, while the community political side has the ideas which are positive but doesn't have the power to get them up the ladder.

The result, he felt, was frustration. There was an undercurrent of feeling in the community, among people with no party allegiances, which never got out.

Comparisons and contrasts

Do they order these things better in Sheffield or Oldham? In Burngreave there were fewer signs of the estrangement from the Council found in Moss Side. Councillors, as was mentioned before, sensed a pride in the city. Local tenants' associations had, after uncertain beginnings, established good relations with the councillors and access to the Council. A housewife who grew up locally and became one of the association's leaders said that, after her campaigns, 'I felt as at home in library of Town Hall as I did in my kitchen'.

The Council has fostered tenants' groups. More generally, the current city leadership has made participation a central part of its policy although it is pointed out that such a programme could not have made sufficient impact by the time of the crowd disturbances elsewhere in 1981 to explain the relative quiet of Sheffield. Beyond any such policy there remains a detectably greater sense of political confidence.

One possibly significant difference between Burngreave and Moss Side is that the former has been the scene of intense party competition. The Liberals gained the ward in 1971 and 1972, employing the techniques of 'community politics' widely adopted by them in local government. The Liberals fielded candidates who highlighted neighbourhood issues and, in the words of an opponent, 'actually forced the local authority to do things by embarrassing it'. The Labour response was to practise community politics themselves, acknowledging what they had learned from their opponents:

> ... the Labour Party had to get stuck in and get to know every crack in the pavement, every light that'd gone out on the lamp-post, all the old people, luncheon clubs and so on.

As one Labour councillor described it, this was not community politics in the sense of group activity but 'one-to-one' discussions of individual problems and canvassing — 'over the last three years I've done now't else but knock on individual doors'. The effect had been a marked increase in individual activity, in voting and in contacting councillors. The turnout in the 1983 ward election reached 55 per cent in 1983 compared to a city average of 45 per cent. There had not been a noticeable input from pressure groups. As a party, their hope was that they were building up local Labour membership and support since, ultimately, the Liberals went down to defeat because they had failed to capitalize on the efforts of individual councillors by building up a party base and ensuring that the citizens developed a new party identification. On this interpretation, the Liberals had not succeeded in fusing community politics and party politics. That this remains a not fully resolved tension might be gauged by the remark of a Labour councillor:

> It's about community politics, and I mean that in the best sense of the word, in that ... I still find it uncomfortable to be described as a politician because I really don't think I am ...

When we turn to Glodwick we find no sign of 'community politics' of the type found in Burngreave. One councillor considered it was merely another device for a new sectional interest in the Labour Party to get power — 'when I hear the word "community" I reach for my gun; you know, it gets up my nose'. Generally, politicians in

Oldham adopted the more traditional stance of representatives who had been elected to do a job:

> ... at the end of the day ... it's elected representatives who decide and they are the people who stand the brickbats of the public at large if anything goes wrong ... We've got to assume that they trust us to get on with it.

A response to critics within and outside the Party was to challenge them to stand for the Council and get elected rather than indulge in what Schumpeter (1954: 295), the master theorist of this position, called 'back-seat driving'. While public participation, in the form of consultative meetings, including the area committees, was strongly approved there was also an insistence on the need for accumulated knowledge and expertise in local government decisions such as a councillor generally acquired.

There was little sympathy in Oldham for the radical activism which has been a trend among Labour councils. There was, at the same time, very little sign of frustration at lack of political access. One reason offered by councillors, local government officers and citizens was that most representatives live in the ward they represent, or were born and grew up there: they work there, shop there and frequent the local public houses when relaxing.

The differences between Burngreave and Glodwick, on the one side, and Moss Side, on the other, in the citizens' perceptions of political responsiveness may have less to do with political styles and strategies but more, once again, with the continuity of the community. A hypothesis, advanced by a Sheffield councillor, deserves further consideration in the light of evidence from our conversations. He suggested that the continuity of the social fabric in Sheffield (and his own comparisons were with Toxteth and Brixton) helped to sustain political linkages and trust. In Moss Side, the dislocation of the community would, on this theory, have disrupted the political linkages.

A similar link between physical disruption and participation had also been made by a senior local government officer in Manchester. He suggested that, at the time of the clearance, many of the old population chose not to return to Moss Side and Hulme, while others soon departed in the face of environmental problems. Those who remained were often the most vulnerable — the elderly, the single-parent families and those subject to ill-health. These were 'least likely to form action groups and make nuisances of themselves to the Council'. On the more positive side, one Moss Side councillor recognized a more recent tendency for younger, more educated people to move into the renovated property in the district. The residents constituted a very different social group, often involved in community work and providing a fresh activist element. This newer community of incomers and established population will, it is implied, have learned from its past experience, and possess more confidence and ability to articulate grievances and express resistance to threats to community interests.

If there is anything in such a hypothesis about the community base of inner city politics, it is appropriate to ask how far the ethnic minorities form part of the community and whether their participation displays a different pattern. In Glodwick, the Asians are viewed as a distinct culture with a limited degree of integration with the indigenous white community. There is not the 'natural' flow of contacts. Councillors often noted the difference made by the lack of communication with the older Asian women whose status in the ethnic community conflicted with local values. They anticipated a generational change which would cause problems for the Asian community and new issues for the Council, such as compulsory rehousing, which would break up the physical unity of the Asians.

The councillors we interviewed were broadly integrationists and complained that the ethnic groups were never ready to consider this line of development. The case against integration was made by a younger black, active within the ethnic communities:

> What the black community definitely does not want is integration which is assimilation ... A more apt definition of integration will be based on pluralistic ideas, i.e. the existence of both communities, both cultures in parallel, instead of, you know, this whole idea of one melting pot, which is utterly ridiculous; it will not work, it has not worked.

This person was more sceptical of the view expressed by the councillors that participation by the ethnic communities, particularly in local elections, was reasonably healthy. His impression was that black people think 'political parties are racist, they're white institutions' which had done little to reach out to them and to deserve their votes.

A view advanced by many blacks, and mentioned in both Sheffield and Manchester, is that politicians are only interested in acquiring votes and since the blacks are at best a minority and at worst do not vote, the candidates, therefore, have little incentive to show an interest in black problems. The minorities, for their part, displayed not apathy so much as rational non-participation. A Sheffield councillor complained that this merely presented a dilemma. It required somebody from the community to get involved and say: 'Look, you're providing this, but really it's a bit of a waste of time. What we really need and want is this'.

The alternative to listening to the blacks themselves was to listen to community leaders. The representativeness of such leaders was occasionally disputed from a number of sides. As one black in Sheffield put it:

> I haven't elected anyone to be my community leader . . . They're assuming that we're such a tight little community that you can get somebody coming up and they can speak on everybody else's behalf.

In Moss Side, councillors sometimes pointed to divisions between the 'moderate', 'conservative' and older black leaders and the younger radical leaders. The extent to which certain radicals were genuinely representative of substantial black opinion was a subject of some surmise, although our conversations suggested that, among these more radical sections, a few individuals were regarded as speaking for this particular tendency or were seen as the real articulated voice of younger blacks.

Representativeness was, unsurprisingly, a recurring problem for those listening to 'voice'. How could one retain a certain scepticism as to the accuracy of the transmission of opinion without appearing to delegitimize the activists? Perhaps the clearest response came from a senior local government officer who asserted that one should not worry about it. One should accept that most leaders are *not* representative but should not stop the dialogue on that account:

> . . . you can only respond to the people who are talking to you, and hope that the fact that you are talking and you are responding will make other people say 'Oh, can I have something to say on that?' and then it starts to build up . . .

In other words, rather than the time-consuming process of building up machinery for truly representative participation, it may be more effective to continue to respond to existing pressures in the expectation that this will arouse a defensive reaction from groups outside the process.

Such a policy has its attractive side, reflecting liberal ideas of voluntary political activity and of the educative effect of political experience. It does, however, assume a degree of political knowledge as to who is already involved in the political dialogue and of how benefits may be allocated. It supposes that those outside can readily mobilize to get themselves represented. If, in addition, the minority lacks, or believes it lacks, the numerical weight to influence the outcome the expected growth of participation may not take place.

In Moss Side, several of these adverse conditions appear to obtain. While some black groups have achieved modest and useful benefits by putting forward what are seen as 'realistic' demands, other groups have expressed almost total scepticism about the local political process. Although the potential black vote in Moss Side is significant, taking the city as a whole, it is not, some believe, a sufficient bargaining counter to justify intensive electoral mobilization (Crewe, 1983). Some, believe that councillors are only interested in the white vote. Political exclusion, one woman argued, is merely one side of social and economic exclusion:

> Until there are black members of Parliament, black councillors and city officials, bank clerks, librarians and everything else, things will not get better for us.

It could, therefore, be argued that the political parties should not wait for black pressure but reach out more positively to the ethnic community. Unless and until Moss Side becomes, like Burngreave, a competitive party ward it would be the task of the Labour Party to involve the black community. Party activists are, however, ambivalent about their attitudes to this problem — as is evidenced also by the internal debate in the national party concerning the desirability of black sections. Many would hold that, as a class-based party, Labour should campaign for all votes regardless of colour, seeing the condition of the blacks as more extreme than that of the working class, or the unemployed, but not different in kind.

There is an important philosophical issue at stake and also an issue of political style. It is pinpointed in the reply of a councillor to the question whether Labour took the black vote for granted and had not encouraged black participation:

> There's about as much validity in that as saying we take the Catholic vote for granted or the Irish vote for granted and all the other things. If people mean that we've not gone out specifically to woo black voters to join the Party, that's quite right.

He insisted that they campaigned to obtain votes and members from any sector. Such a stance is a reminder that many politicians in Britain would resist the importation of the American pluralist style of politics which consists precisely of building coalitions of interests from the Catholic, the Irish, the black and other voters. For those in the Party who think in the traditional manner, it is simply up to the black community to participate along with other sectors of the working class, to bring forward their views and to try to get selected as candidates. To reject the system is to condemn oneself not to be heard.

There is a sense in which, for the blacks of Moss Side, political deprivation is added to economic deprivation. A widespread belief exists, especially among the young, that the local political process offers no relief to their condition, which in turn discourages participation and appears to reinforce exclusion. On the other side, the established political actors point to the open texture of the liberal-democratic political system and invite involvement. Unless the bridge is crossed, a situation may continue whereby members of the community — black and white — complain that not enough is being done or the wrong things are being done, while the politicians protest that they are doing what they can, or more than other areas think they ought, while living in the political dark.

How far does such a bridge require new techniques of political engineering — new forms of political participation?

Forms of participation: conclusions and prospects
New devices may be envisaged to increase popular involvement in formulating policies, the 'input' side of participation, or in implementing decisions, the 'output' side. On the input side it is sometimes proposed that local elected community or neighbourhood councils might be created (Barber, 1984; Weale, 1983: 178–9). In effect, this would be a revival of the old parish but with much enhanced powers and financial resources. Such councils could have sufficient autonomy and resources to mount neighbourhood improvement schemes which would create jobs for the area. There was little appetite among those we interviewed for any such new area-based representative structure. While its advocates see such neighbourhood councils as islands of consensual decision-making and compromise in the midst of adversarial party politics, the view expressed to us was that they would become rapidly politicized. If controlled by the same party as held the Town Hall they would be superfluous; if by a different party they would generate further conflict.

Considerably more interest was shown in developing institutions for output participation. In Manchester, officers and councillors said that they were looking for ways to develop neighbourhood management of local services with area budgets. Local people would have greater opportunities to comment on how the range of area services are provided. There would also be a local centre for advice, assistance and complaint. Beyond such new structures the Council was, they declared, looking to the development of such semi-formal organizations as tenant groups to exert pressure. Although unelected and probably not strictly 'representative', their local knowledge and concern, it was suggested, meant that they understood the interests of the area on the housing issue better than someone elected on a broader and more political mandate at neighbourhood level.

The great lesson which had been learned from earlier experiences of participation was to avoid arousing excessive expectations. One major cause of cynicism about participation was, it was widely felt, the feeling that the major issues had already been settled and that, at best, the ordinary citizen could only influence the trivial details. Councillors and officers in both Sheffield and Manchester pointed out that this raised central issues of democracy. People are not clear, said one leading Sheffield councillor,

> whether they are being asked to determine the 'map' themselves or whether they are being asked to respond to a set of parameters and boundaries that have already been determined.

A council elected on a particular programme would need to insist that any proposal coming through the participatory process would fit within the council's overall strategy as to the distribution of resources. Decentralization to the community, another councillor pointed out, could put at risk the principles on which the council had been elected. A senior Manchester local government officer argued that one must distinguish between decisions which needed to be taken at the centre, because they were essential to the ruling party's manifesto, and those which were irrelevant to the central strategy and could be made within the local community. There was a danger in looking at policy entirely on a city-wide basis instead of examining the distinctive needs of each locality. City-wide perspectives favoured the professionals over the locals. Local government risked making the same mistake as central government of 'pulling things into the centre', culminating in 'alienation between the community and the local authority'.

Political participation is no panacea for the inner city's ills. While we have suggested that deprivation is not, by itself, an explanation of the disturbances in Moss Side, and perhaps by inference in other areas, it remains the case that unemployment in particular approaches being a necessary, though not a sufficient, condition of mass turmoil. Jobs occupy time and take people off the streets whether or not they grant personal satisfaction and regardless of the spending power they provide. It may be the case that governments will have to accept political rather than economic reasons for job creation.

Over and above economic deprivation it seems, from our conversations, that a sense of 'political deprivation' may compound the problems of some inner city areas. A disturbed community has faced problems in getting the messages of the local population across. The widespread reaction of Moss Side to the experience of redevelopment confirms Lord Scarman's comments on the failure of the 'top down' approach to inner city regeneration which still has its adherents who support such devices as Special Development

Corporations (Scarman, 1981). Our comparisons also point to the importance of building political confidence and, as Scarman (1981) again indicated, of regarding community participation as one component in a concerted and coordinated attack on inner city problems. Such an attack will involve more than local government. Many of the problems of the inner city arise from circumstances which are regional, national or international in scope. Many raise issues concerning the equitable distribution of benefits in the country which are essentially the responsibility of Westminster. One cannot expect local democracy to tackle such matters. Nevertheless, other research has demonstrated that cities do differ in their political and organizational capacity to obtain and manage resources (Hausner and Robson, 1985). The function of local participation is to help determine the allocation of such resources to the benefit of the city as a whole and, at neighbourhood level, in accordance with both the long-term needs and the felt wants of the community.

Crowd actions reflect community discontents in complex ways. The variety of interpretations of the crowd by its members, by local elites, national politicians, media and researchers is itself a proof that it remains an inefficient means of putting a precise message across even about problems, let alone solutions. Community participation increases the reliability of the message and, ideally, stimulates a sense of commitment among participants to peaceful political solutions and procedures. The link was made by a Sheffield political leader:

> The riots we saw in 1981 ... will be, I think, fairly minor examples of reaction compared with what we'd see in the future if, instead of stimulating, supporting, encouraging democracy to work, allowing people to begin to listen and solve their problems, we actually close that valve and suppress differences and opposition by communities. And that's a lesson not simply for the government but it's also a lesson for those of us running major cities that we don't do the same to those who challenge us.

Notes

We should like to thank, first of all, the people of Moss Side, Burngreave and Glodwick and those connected with the areas who spared the time to talk to us about their ideas and experiences. Although we have tried to reflect their views as accurately and fairly as possible the responsibility for selection and interpretation is, of course, our own. In preparing the study we are particularly grateful for the assistance of Neil Day (Melbourne College of Advanced Education).

References

Banfield, E.C. (1974) *The Unheavenly City Revisited*. Boston: Little Brown.
Barber, B. (1984) *Strong Democracy: Participatory Politics for a New Age*. Berkeley and Los Angeles: University of California Press.

Benyon, J. (ed.) (1984) *Scarman and After*. Oxford: Pergamon Press.

Berthoud, R. and Brown, J.C. (1981) *Poverty and the Development of Anti-Poverty Policy in the U.K.* London: Heinemann Educational Books.

Brown, C. and Gay, P. (1985) *Racial Discrimination: 17 Years After the Act*. London: Policy Studies Institute, No. 646.

Canetti, E. (1973) *Crowds and Power*. Harmondsworth: Penguin.

Crenson, M. (1983) *Neighbourhood Politics*. Cambridge, Mass.: Harvard University Press.

Crewe, I. (1983) 'Representation and the Ethnic Minorities in Britain', pp. 258–86, in Nathan Glazer and Ken Young (eds), *Ethnic Pluralism and Public Policy*. London: Heinemann.

Dunleavy, P. (1980) *Urban Political Analysis*. London: Macmillan.

Dunleavy, P. (1981) *The Politics of Mass Housing in Britain, 1945–75: A Study of Corporate Power and Professional Influence in the Welfare State*. Oxford: Oxford University Press.

Economist, The (1985) 'Britain: Poor Handsworth Asians Pay the Price of Prosperity', 14 September: 33.

Field, S. (1984) *The Attitudes of Ethnic Minorities*. Home Office Research Study No. 80. London: HMSO.

Fitzgerald, M. (1983) 'Ethnic Minorities and the 1983 General Election' (Briefing Paper). London: The Runnymede Trust.

Gaskell, G. and Smith, P. (1981) 'Alienated Black Youth: An Investigation of Conventional Wisdom Explanations', *New Community*, 9(2): 182–93.

Goodin, R. and Dryzeck, J. (1980) 'Rational Participation: The Politics of Relative Power', *British Journal of Political Science*, 10(3): 273–92.

Guardian, The (1981a) 'Rubber Bullets and Despair', 8 July.

Guardian, The (1981b) 'Brixton Youths Go on Rampage as Riots Spread', 11 July.

Hausner, V. and Robson, B. (1985) *Changing Cities*. London: Economic and Social Research Council.

Hirschman, A.O. (1970) *Exit, Voice and Loyalty*. Cambridge, Mass.: Harvard University Press.

Hytner, A.B. (1981) *Report of the Moss Side Enquiry Panel to the Leader of the Greater Manchester Council*. Manchester: Manchester City Council.

Inglehart, R. (1977) *The Silent Revolution*. Princeton: Princeton University Press.

Inner Cities Directorate, Department of the Environment (no date), 'Information Note No. 2: Urban Deprivation'.

Manchester Evening News, The (1981) 'Terror of Toxteth', 6 July.

Pizzorno, A. (1970) 'An Introduction to the Theory of Political Participation', *Social Science Information*, 9(1): 29–61.

Plant, R. (1978) 'Community: Concept, Conception and Ideology', *Politics and Society*, 8(1): 79–107.

Rossi, P.H. (1972) 'Community Social Indicators', pp. 87–126, in A. Campbell and Converse, P.E. (eds), *The Human Meaning of Social Change*. New York: Russell Sage Foundation.

Scarman, Lord (1981) *The Brixton Disorders 10–12 April 1981*, Cmnd. 8427. London: HMSO.

Schumpeter, J. (1954) *Capitalism, Socialism and Democracy*. London: George Allen and Unwin (first published 1942).

Smelser, N.J. (1962) *Theory of Collective Behavior*. New York: Free Press.

Socialist Worker, The (1981) 'Brixton: Black and White Unite to Fight', 18 April.

Studlar, D.T. (1986) 'Non-White Policy Preferences, Political Participation, and the

Political Agenda in Britain', pp. 159–86, in Z. Layton-Henry and Rich, P.B. (eds) *Race, Government and Politics.* London: Macmillan.

Sunday Times, The (1985) 'Charles: Making Waves' (Weekly Focus), 27 October.

Suttles, G.D. (1972) *The Social Construction of Communities.* Chicago: University of Chicago Press.

Tuck, M. and Southgate, P. (1981) *Ethnic Minorities, Crime and Policing.* Home Office Research Study No. 70. London: HMSO.

Verba, S. and Nie, N.H. (1972) *Participation in America: Political Democracy and Social Equality.* New York: Harper and Row.

Wagstaffe, M. and Moyser, G. (1987) 'The Threatened Elite: Studying Leaders in an Urban Community', ch. 10, in G. Moyser and Wagstaffe, M. (eds), *Research Methods for Elite Studies.* London: George Allen and Unwin.

Weale, A. (1983) *Political Theory and Social Policy.* London: Routledge and Kegan Paul.

Welch, S. and Studlar, D.T. (1985) 'The Impact of Race on Political Behaviour in Britain', *British Journal of Political Science*, 15(4): 528–39.

APPENDIX

Sources for the study of recent crowd events

John Stevenson

Introduction

Crowd events are some of the most elusive and difficult phenomena to record and analyse. As a social historian who has been involved in studying popular disturbances and crowd events from the eighteenth century to the present day, I have been particularly conscious of the difficulties faced by contemporary historians, social scientists and others in obtaining adequate source materials for the examination of events of this nature. In looking at events in the past, historians have been conscious of the limitations of the materials with which they have to deal, particularly as regards direct 'actuality' records of crowd events, large and small (Stevenson, 1979: 11–16; Rudé, 1964: 3–15). In more recent times, the use of 'oral history' and interview material has greatly extended the range of material relating to the participants in crowd events, while the proliferation of newspapers, official records, and academic research itself have offered a much wider canvas of secondary materials. Moreover, the advent of photography, newsreel, radio, television and video have added new dimensions to our ability to document their nature and development. Amidst this plethora of material, it might be supposed that we are in a good position in regard to the availability of sources useful for studying crowd events, but this is not necessarily the case. Crowd events, even the most static, are frequently very protracted, occurring over several hours or recurring over a number of days. They can also be extremely disparate with, for example, different types of behaviour taking place within a large crowd and over a wide geographical area. The attitudes and behaviour of participants in crowds and of those dealing with them, such as the police, may well, and commonly do, change over time, not necessarily with any uniformity (Turner and Killian, 1957: 103–19; Smelser, 1962: 255–6; Quarantelli and Hudley, 1969: 538–54; Marsh et al., 1978: 58–82).

It is evident then that comprehensive, accurate and representative information about crowd events is always going to be a difficult ideal to attain. Even the availability of a wider range of source materials carries with it the difficulties of the fragmentation of angle and perspective so that what might be considered an 'ideal' record of an event is by no means clear. Someone concerned with the events of fifty years ago, such as anti-fascist demonstrations of the 1930s, might well be grateful for access to newspapers, relevant court records, a handful of surviving oral testimonies, and some newsreel footage, but this pales into insignificance compared with the multi-dimensional coverage which it is theoretically possible to bring to bear on contemporary or near contemporary events. It is, however, very unlikely that the full range of recording and data collection which would satisfy all the kinds of questions which researchers might ask of such an event will be available 'on the day'. Even static events, such as football crowds within stadia, which have provided a 'captive crowd' for video and other forms of recording with a deliberate academic purpose in mind, have usually only been covered in some of the aspects that might concern other researchers. Similarly, 'set-piece' media events such as the anti-Vietnam demonstrations in Grosvenor Square, do not in themselves automatically produce the kind of material which researchers may require. Intrinsically then, virtually no crowd events are recorded in a way which will satisfy all or even most researchers. At least as important, however, is the question of the survivability and preservation of the material that is collected. The street disturbances of 1980–1 and 1985, as well as the long-running miners' strike of 1984–5, have provided important re-cent examples of the difficulties that can arise even for an information-conscious age in obtaining and preserving the sort of information and data which may be of value for different types of analysis and discussion. While a great deal of material of different kinds is available for many of these events, it is often deficient in critical areas, either not having been collected or not preserved for future use.

The purpose of this discussion is twofold. First, it attempts to assess the nature and character of the sources available for the study of recent crowd events in Britain. Although different researchers will have their own views on data collection in relation to the methodolo-gy they wish to employ, none the less, it is important to investigate what kinds of common sources are available for studying recent events of interest in the field of crowd behaviour and those that might be available in the future. I have therefore endeavoured to survey the most pertinent materials, drawing attention to those areas where it appears that major difficulties exist, as well as those where the problems and considerations that apply to their use will already be familiar. Second, it aims to indicate general problems of location and access where these have been identifiable and might be of use to scholars in the field. This forms in part a report upon the Crowd Studies Archive project which was funded in 1983 to help to collate

material and information relating to crowd events, particularly the
street disturbances of 1980–1. The nature of the Crowd Studies
Archive and its scope form the last part of the discussion.

Newspapers
Newspapers form the obvious source for crowd incidents that have
occurred in the past or might occur in the future. Historians and
social scientists will be aware of the difficulties of incomplete coverage and bias which may affect their value as sources. None the less,
they must remain a major element in many analyses of recent or
future disorders, just as they have for those in earlier periods. Indeed, I have had some experience in attempting to collate from a
variety of sources a reconstruction of crowd episodes dating from the
late eighteenth century up to the 1930s. One of the lessons learned, is
that newspapers form a potentially useful bank of information, even
if only at the most basic level of providing a chronological framework
of events. While in some cases, official reports, film and television
coverage, court records, oral history and participant observation may
be of equal or greater importance, it is clear that many incidents are
only recorded in newspapers and newspaper coverage will have
some, if not a major, part to play in the investigation both of the
incidence of crowd events of different types and the detailed examination of particular incidents. The study of violent disorders in
the twentieth century, such as that on Leicester in this volume (see
Chapter 2), have depended primarily on newspapers for a longitudin-
al analysis of the extent of violent disorder. Moreover, it is difficult to
imagine how any survey or analysis of the so-called 'copy-cat' disturbances of 1981 would be able to proceed without major reliance upon
newspaper sources. At a national and local level, they continue to
play a crucial part in the monitoring of incidents, including some
which will not result in arrests or judicial proceedings or be recorded
in other ways.

As a result, it is often to the national or local press that we have to
turn. What exactly are the problems we are likely to confront? First
there is the nature of media coverage. Attention is likely to concentrate upon 'newsworthy' incidents and elements within more complex situations which are likely to achieve 'news' status. At the level
of the national press, this process has been well-documented particularly in regard to political demonstrations, strikes and so-called football 'hooliganism' (Halloran et al., 1970; Cohen, 1972; Marsh et al.,
1978; Macbeath, 1985). In almost every case it suggests that comprehensive coverage of events and their context will tend in both 'quality' and 'popular' press to be dominated by certain news themes and
images, frequently of a stereotyped nature. Even 'in depth' coverage

or analysis will tend to concentrate upon particular 'angles' rather than a minute of account of the events concerned. In other words a simple reconstruction of the sequence of events in a crowd incident may be difficult even in an event well-covered in the national press. Comparisons of the accounts of participants with those in the press have frequently revealed a wide discrepancy in perception and understanding of the events (see Chapter 6 above) with the result that it becomes difficult to place a great deal of reliance upon any single account. If national newspapers have a tendency to intervene at a level which suits their 'news' approach rather than serve the interests of academics, few should be surprised. It is, however, relevant to the concern about sources to recognize that newspaper coverage is only the outcome of a process which begins with individual reporters. As a result it is well to be aware that what is available in the form of newspaper reporters' notes and unedited copy may well prove at least if not more valuable than what appears in print. In this context, quite apart from those studies explicitly concerned with media coverage, interview of reporters, sub-editors and other newspaper staff offer an opportunity to delve further into the nature of particular events.

Many of these considerations concerning national newspapers also apply to local newspapers. It is, perhaps, worth recording that it was not very long ago that almost all medium-sized towns were served by more than one local newspaper. A student say, of the demonstrations by the unemployed of a reasonable sized town in the inter-war years could expect coverage by at least one daily newspaper, plus one or more weeklies. In this situation, at least some comparison of coverage and comment was possible. This is, of course, no longer the case. Even the largest cities in Britain are now often restricted to one daily newspaper, if that, and a restricted number of weeklies. In the case of smaller towns, a single weekly newspaper is now often the rule. As a result, there is far less comprehensive coverage than was the case even a few years ago and there is less opportunity for comparison between the coverage of particular incidents. This affects particularly those which have a tendency to remain invisible, small-scale events which are not immediately newsworthy and which are pushed aside by others. Interview evidence from some of the areas affected by the disturbances in 1981, for example, suggests that there were a number of minor incidents which preceded the main riots which were never reported by the press. One of the consequences then of press amalgamations and mergers, particularly in the provincial press, is a less intense coverage of incidents which might be of interest.

At least, however, the paid-for newspaper is an accessible source, available either through local holdings whether in libraries, museums, archive centres and newspaper offices themselves, or through the British Library newspaper collection at Colindale. More problematic are the increasing number of so-called 'free-sheets' which are distributed to every household in the major conurbations and urban centres in a particular area. Quite inconsiderable a decade ago, there are — at the time of writing — more than 500 of these newspapers in circulation and more promised. While some of these sheets contain little more than advertising copy, an increasing number contain a substantial portion of news and comment. In some cases, they have developed into significant community newspapers, reaching down to a level of 'community' news which has not been available in the past. In other cases, local paid-for newspapers have been turned into 'free sheets' in order to cut costs and have effectively replaced the conventional local newspaper. Whatever their merits or demerits, those 'free-sheets' which have set out to serve a particular community or locality are an important source. Access to them, however, is far more difficult than is the case of 'paid-for' newspapers. 'Runs' of local 'free-sheets' are not systematically collected by libraries and museums nor, crucially, by the British Library. As a result, there is no guarantee that copies of some of these papers are being preserved and it is as well to be aware that there is no automatic or systematic attempt to do so at present.

Also of some importance are the newspapers which are aimed directly at young people. Many of the music papers carried material and comment about the disturbances in 1981. While not necessarily important as recorders of events, they do have a significance as recording comment and attitudes representing or thought to represent the generation involved in many incidents of popular disorder. As 'paid-for' newspapers, the music papers, generally, are available for consultation at Colindale, though there are some ephemeral ones which are not necessarily within the orbit of the normal procedures for storage and copyright. The same is also true of some community newsheets and political handouts, such as the Liberal *Focus* newssheets or those of other political organizations. Whether such ephemeral material is collected depends much upon the initiative of individuals and organizations themselves, though some of it must be of importance to an understanding of the context and reaction to some recent crowd events.

Television
A new dimension has been given to the analysis of contemporary events by the development of broadcasting, particularly television. Anyone concerned in using televised material will already be familiar with debates about 'news' selection and reporting (Glasgow University Media Group, 1976; Hetherington, 1985). At least as

important, anyone who is involved in the analysis of recent or future events will have to consider the question of the availability of this type of material both as a record of events and as comment upon them. In fact, the issue of the preservation, cataloguing and access to this material has proved one of the most interesting, if also most difficult, fields of enquiry, largely because it straddles a wide area of different classes of material and one in which the ground rules for preservation and access are still being established. Starting with television, it is important to recognize that different policies exist between different channels, and between companies. At the moment, the BBC do not have a simple policy towards the question of material relating to contemporary events. Some news and comment material is stored and available, but it is primarily for internal use or for sale or hire on commercial terms. Enquiries about access to any material concerning a particular event have to be made on an individual basis to the BBC and it was stressed, upon investigation, that there were very limited facilities for its use by researchers. As to the type of material available, it was again stressed that what was available was confined to programmes or news items which were, in fact, transmitted. There is, however, no evidence that there is a policy to preserve untransmitted material. On the basis of very cooperative discussions carried out with various members of the BBC archives and library staff, it appears that any untransmitted film shot during, say, the Brixton disturbances or at any other crowd event is unlikely to have been preserved.

Similar difficulties exist as regards to the independent television companies. Again, it was brought home that the television companies are not especially archive conscious. Their main concerns in preserving material are either that it is of some commercial value or that it may be of some internal use, for example, as providing compilation material for a round-up of the year. There was, however, an indication from both Granada and Thames Television that some untransmitted material of relevance to contemporary history might be available, though once again, individual researchers were asked to pursue their own enquiries and obtain the necessary permissions. In broad terms, it was clear that no general policy exists about the preservation of either transmitted or untransmitted material. The latter, which might properly be regarded by researchers as the most important category, is plainly not seen as such by the television companies. Crucial research material in terms of 'actuality' film of incidents is destroyed almost as soon as it is created and it is therefore incumbent upon researchers to make their own arrangements with television companies in order to preserve any 'raw footage' they might be interested in before it is destroyed or erased. As suggested above, the most likely material to survive is transmitted material, whether in newscasts or programmes, although this cannot be guaranteed. ITN, for example, do not have a policy of preserving their news bulletins or the material from which they were compiled. Other than in exceptional circumstances, they claim to preserve nothing. Inevitably, then, the onus is upon those interested in research into contemporary events to make their own arrangements with television companies about preservation and access to material and to obtain the necessary permissions to make their own video recordings of relevant newscasts. It cannot be stressed too highly, that the visual record of crowd events of whatever kind depends in large part upon a completely unsystematic process of selection and preservation. Not only have television companies and organizations different policies concerning the preservation of film which might be of interest, but there are several practical difficulties involved in terms of access and research facilities. Different sections within television companies have different policies: 'news' as opposed to 'features' was one of the commonest dichotomies encountered and this was sharpened by the existence within the commercial networks of ITN as an independent body.

The BBC is a labyrinthine organization which can present serious difficulties for all but the most persistent researcher. It is less the unwillingness of the BBC to assist legitimate research than the establishment of the appropriate section of the organization to approach. The BBC produces a *Guide to Libraries and Information Services* intended as a research guide for their own staff, but which does contain information relevant to an outside user. Broadly speaking, two sections of the organization are of relevance to those interested in the research field. BBC Enterprises, which publishes its own guide is a commercial organization whose main object is the selling of BBC material rather than the provision of research facilities. It is unlikely, but not impossible, that the programmes it is concerned with marketing might be of interest to social scientists and contemporary historians. In general terms they appear most relevant for feature programmes or documentaries concerned with a particular event or issue. A BBC Enterprises guide is produced by the BBC and can be consulted. More significant, perhaps, is the BBC Data Enquiry Service which was formed in 1981 in order to exploit commercially the information gathered by the BBC for use in television, radio and overseas broadcasts. The material collected here is primarily written research material. The press cuttings library contains over 18 million cuttings going back over forty years and updated daily by some 2,000 cuttings. Among the listed categories of material which might be of interest are: 'Political, economic and social events' and 'Political

affairs'. They are, however, a commercial organization, and are
devoted primarily to the provision of research material. Researchers
interested in BBC film or video records of recent events are also
advised to refer to the National Film Archive. It is hard to believe,
however, that other material does not exist. There exists, for example, a BBC news library and it is clear that there are various points
within the BBC organization where material, both broadcast and
unbroadcast, might be stored. As a matter of policy, there is little
doubt that anyone concerned with the televised record of particular
events can only be advised to make speedy and personal contacts with
the companies and individuals responsible. At the time of writing
there are no general rules and no comprehensive central archive of
television material. Moreover, the problem of the proliferation of
sources for material is likely to become more difficult before it
becomes easier. The introduction of cable television, further network channels, and the access to simple television equipment by a
widening circle of freelance companies and individuals requires a
major effort to cover all likely sources of material. A comprehensive
reckoning of all possible television sources of material relating to
crowd events is itself becoming increasingly difficult as the medium
expands.

Video and audio sources
There are some organizations which have taken on the responsibility
to collect material which may be of interest to researchers in the field
of crowd studies. The National Film Archive takes a selection of
broadcast material which may be of relevance, for example, cataloguing and preserving programmes concerning the disturbances in
Brixton and Toxteth and some of the follow-up material. Other
organizations which collect televised material are the North-West
Film Archive, based at Manchester Polytechnic, the Workers' Film
Association, also based in Manchester and the Northern Film and
Television Archive, based in Gateshead. Some video material is also
held by the police, at Scotland Yard and the Bramshill training
college, of crowd scenes which are used for training purposes. It was
notable that one of the most extensive pieces of film dealing with the
Orgreave picketing disturbances was preserved as police training
film. Also notable for the incidents arising from the miners' dispute
of 1984–5 are the materials collected by the various 'Policewatch'
organizations in order to have their own record of potentially controversial events. Although by no means exclusively or even primarily concerned with the visual record of events, these and similar
organizations are possible places where film and video material of
interest to social scientists and contemporary historians on particular

incidents is stored or likely to be preserved. More recently, the introduction of video cameras into football grounds, whether controlled by the police or by football clubs themselves, will also provide a new form of material relating to particular types of crowd event. It is not clear whether much of this material is being preserved, although video of particular incidents has been used to provide the evidence for the prosecution of individuals. Clearly, some material is kept, if only for a short time, but the existence of this technique offers a potentially large archive of footage of this particular type of event. Finally, the film and video material collected by individual researchers or research teams for their own academic purposes should not be ignored in a field where the initiative to record television and radio broadcasts, or to conduct interviews with participants during or shortly after events may well lie only with academic researchers. It ought to be noted, however, that academics are not necessarily the best archivists. Old research data, whether in the form of video footage, other broadcast material, or interview tapes, is often subject to pressures of cost and convenience of keeping them once their immediate use is past. In this respect it is very much incumbent upon people working in the field to preserve as much material as possible that might be of use for future research or, if necessary, deposit it with an appropriate archive, or failing an obvious location, with the Crowd Studies Archive at the Department of History at Sheffield University or the Mass Observation Archive at Sussex University.

Much material exists from the police which may be of use to researchers. Home Office papers, Metropolitan Police records, and other classes of central government records come within the ambit of the Public Records Act. While there are some difficulties in establishing exactly what material exists at least thirty years prior to its release to the public (some documents may well remain closed for much longer), there undoubtedly exists valuable information relating to the Home Office response, operational police procedures in London and longer term policy. Access is a major difficulty here even when the nature of materials relevant to researchers has been established. Within the broad limits of the Public Records Act, however, individual approaches to the Public Records Office and the Home Office can be made about access to material and to express concerns about the preservation of particular classes of material. Historians have been much concerned in recent years about the operation of 'weeding' — the selection of material regarded as unimportant for preservation, and the classification of material as too sensitive for release under the thirty-year rule. It is doubtful whether these will be of much concern to researchers involved in very recent events, but it is as well to bear them in mind in considering what material will eventually come to light concerning particular events.

Local police records also represent a wide category of material which might be of value to researchers into crowd events. They exist at many different levels, including the notes taken by individual constables, the logs of police radio traffic, station incident books, more formal police reports, tapes of police interrogations, the records of disciplinary investigations and proceedings and the minutes of police committees. Of some significance too are two specific recent departures in the police response to crowd incidents, the video recording of street demonstrations, football matches and other incidents and the use by some police forces with previous experience of crowd disturbances in their area of 'tension indicators' to categorize a period of growing tension which might lead to an outbreak of disorder. As the latter indicates, the material which may be of interest to researchers can vary from one constabulary to another. Access is also largely a matter of negotiation with the constabulary concerned and although no systematic survey has been made of the readiness of local constabularies to open their material to research, the clear impression was gained that some were prepared to cooperate helpfully with bona fide researchers. More controversial is the material on individuals and organizations which is known to be a part of both routine police work and that of the Special Branch and parts of the intelligence services. The much-publicized destruction by the Devon and Cornwall Constabulary of some of their files on individuals involved in protest and political groups in 1980 has significant implications both in terms of the fact that such records were kept in the first place and were also being destroyed. It is an interesting historical note that it is upon the reports sent in by the Special Branch to the Metropolitan Police in the 1930s that we have much of our information about clashes between the police and unemployed and anti-fascist demonstrations in this period. Although such material must exist for more recent periods, access to it remains a contentious area.

Criminal statistics are available and, also, a source of considerable research and controversy. In relation to the street disturbances of 1981, the Home Office Statistical Department produced a bulletin on those arrested which was widely reported in the press and is generally available. There remains, however, the problem of the records of court proceedings. In the case of magistrates courts which dealt with approximately 50 per cent of cases arising from the 1981 disturbances, reliance for details of cases heard rests almost entirely upon newspaper reports or the testimony of participants. In the case of Crown Courts there is a more complicated situation. Full transcripts of such cases only exist in certain cases and are generally only available through the official shorthand writers used by the various circuits. In effect, this means that full accounts of even Crown Court proceedings are not necessarily readily available. This is a point that researchers need to be aware of in investigating both the courts' response to events of this kind and the use of court evidence for material relating to crowd behaviour. Equally, it is important not to neglect other areas of the legal process, the depositions given to solicitors or groups such as the NCCL or Justice, may be as useful, if not more so, than formal testimony and submissions in court. Access to solicitors' material would, of course, have to be negotiated on an individual basis, while, clearly, other organizations would need to be consulted as to the availability of their material.

Important material lies in official and unofficial reports and commentary and analysis of events by those engaged in the study of crowd events. The more famous of these, Scarman and the like, may be familiar. We have also to take into account reports of other groups, for example in relation to football disturbances, those of professional bodies, such as the Football Association; for schools, those produced by teaching bodies, such as the NUT; and ad hoc enquiries by those involved in particular types of event, for example, the material produced by the various 'defence' committees in 1981–2 and by other groups who might comment on crowd events, including ethnic groups involved in monitoring racial attacks and harassment. In some well-publicized events, there may be several layers of enquiry, representing differing groups. In the case of the Moss Side disturbances of 1981 (see Chapter 7 above), as well as forming a minor part in Lord Scarman's report on the Brixton Disorders, the events also led to the Hyntner report by the Greater Manchester Council, but also an ad hoc defence committee report entitled 'Hyntner Myths'. In the case of substantial reports such as the Scarman or Hyntner reports, at least as important as the reports are the minutes of evidence from which the reports were compiled. These run to many times the length of the reports and represent the 'raw data' which may be far more useful for research. Finally, as suggested above when discussing video and film evidence, academic research itself generates an enormous amount of material of general interest about crowd events. It is to academic research that we must often look or even belated 'actuality' material whether in the form of interviews, photographs or video. But there is also a growing volume of serious comment, academic and otherwise, which can shed light upon various aspects of crowd events. These were sufficient to provide a substantial bibliography covering the decade from 1973 as the pilot project of the Crowd Studies Archive.

The Archive

The project was set up in 1983 as part of the research programme of the ESRC's Crowd Behaviour Panel to explore the sources available for the study of recent crowd incidents. This set out to identify secondary and other material which would be relevant to the study of crowd events of various types, particularly the street disturbances of 1981. This was followed by a short, three-month project to collate bibliographical and research data relating to recent crowd events. This included bibliographical information, comment and analysis, press reports and such other material as it seemed pertinent to record where there was any possibility of the material not being preserved because of lack of funding. The Crowd Studies Archive was also intended to act as an information exchange between the disparate group of scholar's working in the field. As the funding of the Crowd Studies Archive project was only of limited duration and pre-dated the events of the miners' strike of 1984–5 and the 1985 inner city outbreaks, its sources tend to reflect preoccupation with the inner city riots of 1980–1. The archive holdings are, however, indicative of the variety of data available for the study of crowd events which might not otherwise be preserved and collated in one place.

References

Cohen, S. (1972) *Folk Devils and Moral Panics*. Oxford: Martin Robertson.

Glasgow University Media Group (1976) *Bad News*. London: Routledge and Kegan Paul.

Halloran, J.D., Elliot, P. and Murdock, G. (1970) *Demonstrations and Communication: A Case Study*. Harmondsworth: Penguin.

Hetherington, A. (1985) *News, Newspapers and Television*. London: MacMillan.

MacBeath, I. (1985) 'The 1984–5 Coal Dispute: Newspapers', in Hetherington, A., *News, Newspapers and Television*. London: MacMillan.

Marsh, P., Rosser, E. and Harré, R. (1978) *The Rules of Disorder*. London: Routledge and Kegan Paul.

Quarantelli, E.L. and Hudley, J.R. jnr. (1969) 'A Test of Some Propositions about Crowd Formation and Behaviour', in Evans, R.R. (ed.), *Readings in Collective Behaviour*. Chicago: Rand McNally.

Rudé, G. (1964) *The Crowd in History*. New York: Wiley.

Smelser, N.J. (1962) *Theory of Collective Behaviour*. New York: The Free Press.

Stevenson, J. (1979) *Popular Disturbances in England 1700–1870*. London: Longman.

Turner, R.H. and Killian, L.M. (1957) *Collective Behaviour*. Englewood Cliffs, NJ: Prentice Hall.

Index